CARVING MINIATURE WILDFOWL
with Robert Guge

Carving Miniature Wildfowl

with ROBERT GUGE

How to carve and paint
birds and their habitats

Roger Schroeder and Robert Guge

STACKPOLE BOOKS

Published by
STACKPOLE BOOKS
Cameron and Kelker Streets
P.O. Box 1831
Harrisburg, PA 17105

Printed in the U.S.A.

The quote on pages 69–70 is from *The Audubon Book of Bird Carving,*
by John L. Lacey and Tom Moore McBride (McGraw-Hill Book Company,
1951). Reprinted by permission of McGraw-Hill.

Library of Congress Cataloging-in-Publication Data

Schroeder, Roger, 1945–
    Carving miniature wildfowl: how to carve and paint birds
and their habitats / Roger Schroeder, Robert Guge.
        p. cm.
    ISBN 0-8117-0401-7
    1. Wood-carving—Technique. 2. Miniature craft. 3. Birds in art.
4. Painting—Technique. I. Guge, Robert. II. Title.
NK9704.S36   1988
731.4′62—dc19   87-18133
                                CIP

From Bob to Jody, Seth, Joshua, Caleb, Jordan, Asher, and our unborn baby; to Roy and Vivian Guge; to Woody and Shirly Woods; to Larry Barth; and with thanks to the Lord for all His blessings.

From Roger to the Straubs: Henry, Norman, and Loren.

Contents

Introduction:
With Respect for Birds

There are no fewer than one hundred billion birds in the world, or twenty-five for every human being. In terms of species, there are between eighty-six hundred and eighty-seven hundred. By comparison, there are only forty-five hundred species of mammals in the world today. It is little wonder that many early cultures of man had a reverence for the bird. The ancient Egyptians considered the ibis, a wading bird related to the heron, sacred, calling it a god of magic and wisdom. Two millennia later, the Greeks put the wings of a bird on their god of victory.

Animal gods had no place in the lives of the early Hebrews, but after the Great Flood described in the Bible, Noah wisely sent a dove to look for land while he and his menagerie waited on the ark.

Birds were invested with magic and spirit by the North American Indians. The Indians had vision and saw not the bird's frailty but its power of flight.

The Indians also fed off the birds they revered and cleverly learned to make imitations of them for lures. In some cases these were merely skins stuffed and floated on pieces of wood. But the Piute Indians of the Southwest used more than just feathers. Hunters fashioned their imitations out of tule reeds or bulrushes into the shapes of birds. About the time Jesus rode into Jerusalem to celebrate his last Passover, a Piute stored eleven woven decoys in what is now known as Lovelock Cave in Nevada. The reason he never returned is lost in history, but two thousand years later his decoys were found in almost perfect condition in a reed basket. The duck that the Indian imitated is easily identifiable as a canvasback. White feathers are woven into the reeds. The wedge-shaped head colored with black and reddish-brown native paints is almost perfectly matched to the real bird. Even the pose is realistic. Early settlers and colonists also learned to use decoys to lure birds close enough to kill.

How much the decoy contributed to the killing of birds cannot be estimated, but the number was probably small. However, from the time of William Shakespeare to the present, a span of just three and a half centuries, seventy-eight species of birds became extinct.

While the Elizabethan theater was performing

Shakespeare's plays, an estimated three billion passenger pigeons roamed the North American skies. One flock was believed to have had no fewer than one billion birds in it. But they were easy prey to hunters, and in 1914, the last bird died in a zoo in Cincinnati. Decoys were unnecessary to bring this bird down. During the time of the passenger pigeons' demise, guns were manufactured that could send a cannonload of shot into a flock, killing a hundred or more with one blast. "Market hunters" were a deadly footnote in history for about half a century in the United States as Americans' taste for birds was on the plate and not in the wild.

Yet even market hunters were no match for habitat destruction, oil spills, and a chemical called dichlorodiphenyltrichlorethane. Scientists estimate that DDT saved some forty million people during its pervasive use against mosquitoes. At the same time, the pesticide took its toll on birds, nearly bringing to extinction the peregrine falcon and the bald eagle, among others. Still, it is believed that the number of birds killed annually in North America alone, owing to fatal encounters with buildings, windows, and moving vehicles, runs into the millions.

Despite the failures, there are some remarkably successful and numerous species. One, a tiny waxbill finch, probably numbers ten billion individuals, a population that would make it the most numerous bird in the world, though the domestic chicken, with a population of about four billion, would seem like a runner-up. In the United States, there are some six billion birds at the beginning of the breeding season, and at its end the number may be twenty billion, with 702 species occurring regularly in North America.

Birds differ in remarkable ways. A bee hummingbird measures 2¼ inches long, weighs less than 3 grams, and flaps its wings at the rate of eighty beats per second. By comparison, an ostrich, with almost no wing structure, can weigh as much as 350 pounds. Two seabirds, however, the wandering and the royal albatrosses, have wingspans of 11 to 12 feet.

There are equally amazing facts about other birds. A male Andean condor can live over seventy-five years, and an owl, nearly seventy. An albatross reaches a natural age of forty years in the wild, and Arctic terns, which survive in severe climates, can reach a natural age of thirty years.

Some birds have the ability to fly at great altitudes. Vultures have been spotted at a height of thirty-seven thousand feet. A songbird was sighted at twenty-six thousand feet by an expedition on Mount Everest.

Other species have a remarkable ability to fly long distances at greater sustained speeds than any other organism. Most birds travel between twenty and fifty miles per hour. A red-breasted merganser was clocked at eighty miles per hour; white-throated swifts can reach one hundred. Perhaps more remarkable is that some birds can travel 120 hours without stopping – the equivalent of five days. Even flightless birds do well. An ostrich can run as fast as sixty miles per hour.

Though success would seem to be a byword for this family of creatures, animals with high metabolisms tend to be vulnerable to slight changes in climate or even the introduction of new germs, unlike reptiles and amphibians. For the recent past, this means that more species of birds have been the victims of man than have the other groups of animals.

Intelligence has often mistakenly been equated with the success of a species or group of animals. How intelligent are birds? Apparently, some have a number sense. A raven can be taught to count to seven. This is done by rewarding the bird if it chooses a container with seven spots, regardless of their size, shape, or position. (An elephant will fail the test when the shape of the markings is changed.) Nevertheless, birds cannot invent symbols to be used as tools with which to count, and they definitely cannot associate words with purpose, such as "food" for hunger. And scientists have found no evidence of the presence of consciousness, which can be loosely defined as the awareness of awareness.

Despite the unhuman-like intelligence of birds, a man with a dark vision endowed birds with a hungry eye toward man. Alfred Hitchcock, in his movie *The Birds,* leaves us wondering whether an Armageddon is at hand, or whether birds are exhibiting a temporary pecking disorder. Fortunately, the movie is a hoax. It is a biological impossibility that eighty-six hundred species of birds – or even a handful of those – would stand wing-to-wing against man. Predation between birds and with other animals is more likely.

About the time *The Birds* was first being viewed, there was a movement in this country to portray avian species as something more than decoys, the concept of which had changed little over the two thousand years since the Piute Indian failed to return for his bulrush canvasbacks. Granted, the material had changed from reeds to wood – a plentiful, easily worked commodity found almost anywhere there were huntable birds—but little else had altered. A decoy was still a floating imitation of a duck, though shorebirds such as plovers and curlews were hunted with wooden shapes or silhouettes put on sticks and stuck into the mud or sand. These were called simply stickups. In the early 1970s, men devised means of portraying birds in flight using pieces of habitat such as marsh grasses or limbs of trees, with only wing tips touching the plant or tree. Bird carvings no longer sat on water or sticks, but were given wings with individually inserted feathers. By including a steel feather or two, the carvers were able to attach the bird to carefully disguised steel hidden in the habitat.

In the confines of a glass case on a small college campus in Salisbury, Maryland, a peregrine falcon, alleged to be the fastest of all birds, has picked out a victim. The aerial kill, accomplished with speed, talons, and beak, is swift. The victim is a green-winged teal. Two others of the same waterfowl species are in flight among tall grasses, but they are safe from the selective attack.

This drama is not depicted in an artist's painting. Instead, it is a composition of birds carved life-size, their wings filled with inserted pieces of wood to represent rows of feathers called primaries, secondaries, and coverts. The participants in the drama are held aloft and frozen in the moments of violent death and escape. It was completed in 1973 by a South Carolina bird carver named Gilbert Maggioni. He confounded the public with such pieces at a time when falcons, if indeed they were carved at all, sat on forest-found branches, and ducks merely floated on water. Feathers were not inserts but simple, painted-on lines done with flaired-out brushes. And the notion that birds might interact, fly, or even kill defied a tradition of imitating birds already two thousand years old by the time Maggioni picked up his first carving tool.

Maggioni's peregrine and teal composition might easily be identified as an expression of the agitation of the times during which he was most creative. But he and others had a philosophy in mind. It was to show birds in their natural habitats, get them into the air, and if possible, have them engaged in theatrical displays, sometimes resulting in mawkish scenes of death. Other major pieces of that time portray a pheasant being attacked by a red-tailed hawk, and two hawks killing a copperhead snake—in the air! The art world took little notice of these composi-

tions, sometimes described as museum-like dioramas. Often the birds themselves were overlooked, and interest was instead directed at the engineering of the piece. How are the birds held aloft? the critics asked.

Maggioni's greatest impact was not impressing the public with art; rather, his work stood in sharp contrast to the decoy, which was meant to be utilitarian, with little detail beyond the shape of the species and a paint job that was more abstract than realistic.

But even before Maggioni was born, men from the Midwest, the Atlantic coast from Maine to the Carolinas, and particularly the Chesapeake Bay, were carving ducks that could be displayed on a shelf without ever having to be used to attract waterfowl. Although few duck carvers were extending wings or even inserting the few primaries that project from under the wings of a duck at rest, the bird carving was being emancipated from the stereotypical image of a floating abstract.

The introduction of tools, many from the dental and jewelry industry, and the use of water-based paints helped refine the details of birds after Maggioni mounted his peregrine and ducks. Carved birds soon took on almost mythic proportions, with animate intelligence beaming from glass eyes as well as looks that ranged from fierce hostility to benign understanding.

In the 1980s these wooden birds ceased to soar and strike: only a few took to the air, fewer still hovered over prey. The bird of the 1980s perched on a branch or fed its young or merely rested.

Perhaps Maggioni and his followers held to a Hitchcockian view of birds. But the trend today is strongly in favor of carved birds that keep a quiet and respectful distance from man. The art critics, however, still don't recognize this as art, an attitude that has had strong antecedents even toward bird painters. Bird paintings are rarely found in museums in Europe or in North America. It has been said that copying nature is not necessarily art, but the carefully detailed and painted bird plates of John James Audubon, who recorded the birds of early 19th century North America, are generally accepted as art.

Audubon's birds take on almost bizarre poses. But their lack of sentimentality may make them more acceptable than the incredible number of animal paintings that are refused admission except to the most liberal galleries.

Critics also object that the combination of beauty

Bird artist and folk art carver Robert Guge. Photo by Kurt Butcher.

and biology in a carved bird—though comparable to a sculpture of the human form, and executed with the skill of a Michelangelo—does not make a carving artistic. Craft has usually preceded art, and critics maintain that copies of avian forms, no matter how unique, lack the elements of good composition and good design. They are craft creations. Period. Even the basic material, wood—not a metal, like bronze—may contribute to the notion that these creations are something other than art.

Art critics may also be troubled that nearly all early bird carvers were hunters who went from carving what are called rigs or hunting stool, to carving decorative birds that would attract the attention of people instead of waterfowl. But a few carvers—and then many during the seventies—did not have the hunter's vision of wildlife. Instead, they chose to carve gamebirds, shorebirds (though they were once decoyed), birds of prey, and songbirds.

One interesting exception was a Midwesterner named William Schultz. An avid hunter until his death in 1983, he not only carved hundreds of both decorative and utilitarian ducks, but he also created from wood and paints birds that only the experienced ornithologist could identify: harpy eagles, anhingas, and jancanas were among his numerous accomplishments.

Robert Guge is also from the Midwest, born and still living in a suburb of Chicago called Carpentersville. His father is an active hunter who has been carving ducks for the last two decades. But since Bob started carving realistic birds in 1971, he has shaped only five ducks. The six hundred other highly detailed birds he has created include shorebirds, gamebirds, and songbirds, as well as predatory birds such as hawks and owls. Fifty percent of them are smaller than life-size and can best be described as miniature wildfowl.

Even a casual glance at his work will reveal that he sticks to the natural look of birds. There is little characterization or distortion, as in expressionistic art. On closer examination, it is also obvious that he arranges his birds with exquisite care. Each looks groomed and neat. But in an avian face there might be a suggestion of strength or of survivability. They are birds that look the world in the eye.

Bob's birds have more of a balance of inner mood, although he, unlike Maggioni, deliberately emphasizes the casual, everyday behavior of birds. Even in their simple forms, beauty is apparent, at least on the surface. He has a special aptitude with paints. There is a spontaneity and vivacity of color. It is little wonder that he claims no strict observance of technical formulas when it comes to applying colors.

His carved birds flow from a conviction that birds are special—a source of wonder. A contemporary carver and friend of his, Ernest Muehlmatt, who lives outside Philadelphia, once described birds as flowers that fly. Bob's work might be described as paintings in three dimensions.

He is thoroughly equipped with bird facts, though he rejects blueprints for his birds, often sketching patterns or outlines on the wood without the aid of measuring tools. However, his overall work habits combine a process of interior planning and external layout. There is a predetermined order of work that includes several steps: taking the piece of wood to a band saw; putting details on the wood with tools resembling oversized dental drills and dangerous-looking rotating cutters; sanding the result; burning and scoring the wood to achieve the look of feathers; and, finally, painting the surface. Nevertheless, he may produce a bird so rapidly that one cannot believe the skillfully finished piece was so quickly inspired.

He is so accurate with paints that his birds project life. Yet, he will argue that if he carved a wood duck, noted for its ostentatious colors, and painted it with the colors of a cardinal, there should be little room for doubt about its true identity. The carved wood duck form should still project through its bogusly colored plumage.

Despite the apparent contradictions in his methods and procedures, he does employ a structure in his work that not only allows for seeming inconsistencies, but also permits an outsider to understand him.

Whether he is an artist or only a skilled craftsman who cleverly exploits wood and paint, Bob Guge provides access to understanding the bird-carving phenomenon, which is still limited to North America.

Regardless of the future of bird art, or its place in art history, carvers like Guge will no doubt continue to carve birds, and for the time being what they do will be defined as a synthesis of available wood, high-technology tools, sculpture, and a prodigious use of paints.

Puffins Take 1

Bob Guge writes with clear, precise capital letters **PUFFINS TAKE 1** near the spiraling wire at the top right of a notepad. Two inches below that and in the center of the paper, he then lays a model of a puffin, a member of the auk family that is common to the northern parts of the Atlantic and Pacific coasts. The bird is constructed of clay, not wood, and in its parrotlike beak are three wormy-looking lengths of clay to suggest fish. The bird, though heavy for its species, is not a caricature, for the shape is unmistakable to those who know puffins.

His fingers hold the bird in place with little pressure—the clay is still soft and would compress if he did otherwise. With his free hand, he takes a pencil and slowly draws a line around the puffin's shadow, created by a high-intensity light placed directly over the model. The puffin's head is turned approximately 45 degrees to the rest of the body, so the outline, being only two dimensional, will fail to capture the rotation at the neck. This is not really a problem, though. It is the beginning for Bob Guge, a first step that need not generate perfect patterns or strict formulas of anat-omy. It is just a shape, a "take one" of a project that will require more than two months to complete.

Carpentersville is about forty miles northwest of downtown Chicago, with its twin spires, its stadium, and its waterfront view of Lake Michigan. Carpentersville has sufficient numbers of old trees and buildings to suggest that it is an established community, a quiet town with now-abandoned mills of red brick and large windows. There were great tracts of planting fields until recent sprawling shopping centers paved them over and helped bring more people to the area. There are twenty-three thousand people, a road sign in Carpentersville indicates; Chicago counts 150 times that number.

Four miles north of Carpentersville, where Bob Guge was born, is Elgin, a city known for the Elgin National Watch Company. Between there and Chicago are morainic knolls, covered with grasses, which made excellent farmland. A river runs through both Elgin and Carpentersville. It is the Fox River, and it is less than two tenths of a mile from his home.

Bob lives in a simple Cape Cod, its main entrance

Bob Guge's home in Carpentersville, Illinois.

The deck and rear of the house where Bob does much of his bird-watching.

The kitchen, with its folk art, was featured in the March 1983 issue of Country Living *magazine.*

Seth, the oldest of the Guge children, helps his father with a bird composition done in clay.

under the front peak, which faces South Lord Avenue. Next door, on the left, live his parents, Roy and Vivian, a brother Scott, and a sister named Lori.

Bob's house is a showcase for folk art—mostly anonymously made items that reflect rural and community traditions. Hand-crafted pieces include ones Bob has made, small painted houses and plaques suggesting a rural time unfamiliar to most Americans, and birds shaped in wood and painted to suggest the patina of age. There is even a collection of Amish children's clothes and antique toys. His kitchen was featured in an issue of *Country Living* magazine. In that room, woven baskets hang from beams Bob installed; delicate birds' nests with empty quail eggs rest on ledges; a Hoosier cabinet with a zinc counter and stained glass is against one wall; a doorless corner cabinet holds dairy memorabilia; a potbellied stove acts as a plant stand. The kitchen table is a primitive farm table with a wooden bowl filled with wooden pumpkins, squashes, and corn that Bob carved. Nearby is a highchair passed on from a great-grandfather.

In the living room are a primitive bench that serves as a cocktail table and two Chippendale sofas. In front of the bay window are birds Bob has carved. Prints of painted birds by such artists as Roger Tory Peterson and Robert Bateman are on the walls.

There is a baby in Bob's house. Named Asher, he was born on September 10, 1985. The other children are Seth, eleven, Joshua, eight, Caleb, six, and Jordan, the only girl, age three.

It is Sunday, February 16, 1986, the day he will start to shape puffins in clay. There is little snow on the

Sons Joshua, left, and Caleb in their father's workshop.

Daughter Jordan.

ground, and temperatures will run in the mild forties in Carpentersville. Bob will get up at seven-thirty in the morning, wearing jeans and a sweatshirt with one cartooned puffin on the front, and make breakfast for the family. Jody will help with the dressing in time for Sunday school and church.

There are three cats that keep Bob company in the kitchen, strays that became permanent houseguests. Two of them are silent, old predators with only vague hunting instincts that direct them to the windows to watch birds and squirrels. A fourth cat, named Pig, stays wrapped around the long dowel that supports a white primitive egret that Bob made and stands in front of the house's one bay window. Pig has managed to position himself on the bird's wooden base, made from a cedar log. This is no small feat, for the wood makes up only one half the area of the curled-up cat's body.

Before the children come for breakfast, Bob puts seed out in a tube feeder and on a plywood platform feeder mounted on his deck. He walks out barefooted through the sliding glass doors, unconcerned with the cold that seeps into the kitchen and also keeps the cats in.

He moves quickly in the morning, pouring water for coffee, pushing Lucas, the oldest cat, off the sink. But the cat is used to the rejection and returns within minutes with a springy leap.

Despite the usually low temperatures, a variety of birds appear in Carpentersville in the winter, and during the year, he might observe as many as sixty species of songbirds. What is called the Fox River Valley is attractive to waterfowl as well. He has seen

Bob with his son Asher at a bird carving competition in Ocean City, Maryland.

Bob's wife Jody has her own collection of miniature folk art. Jesse the cat has found a diminutive bed to sleep on.

The picture window in front of the Guge home displays primitive birds Bob has carved.

nearly every species of inland North American waterfowl, even the scoter, more common on New England seacoasts than in Illinois.

If the clay model is a rehearsal for a bird carving, the bird feeder is his research facility, a place to obtain the information that governs the field. In the winter he might easily find goldfinches, nuthatches, cardinals, purple finches, red polls, pine siskins, and tree, chipping, song, and white-throated sparrows. He has carved most of these because, as he puts it simply, he has seem them.

Not all of Bob's bird-watching is done through the glass doors of his kitchen. Twenty minutes from his home is the Crabtree Nature Center, a forest and prairie preserve. In the northwest corner of Cook County, which includes the city of Chicago, there are

more than a thousand acres set aside for educational walks. A variety of trails take the visitor through marshes, woods, tall grass areas, keeping him on foot for a half hour, an hour, or longer.

Before 1830, this land was clothed in forest, prairie, and marsh, but pioneers who stopped in their movement west plowed the fields to plant crops, cut timber for fuel and housing, and drained the marshes. Restoration has been taking place for the past twenty years, however, and a two-mile-long trail will take the visitor through the tall prairie grass that once covered ninety percent of Cook County and more than half of Illinois. It is called the Phantom Trail. The indigenous bison, wolves, curlew, which are marsh birds, and prairie grouse are gone. But the ground is still fertile, and grasses such as little bluestem, switch, and Indian grass flourish, along with swamp milkweed, purple coneflower, prairie dock, and compass plant. Stiff New England asters, goldenrod, and sunflowers add contrasting colors.

Here, Bob can bring his binoculars and see birds that might not come to a feeder. Perhaps he can also store a few facts about habitat that could be used in a future composition.

Sipping his coffee against a backdrop of folk art, Bob describes his passion for observing birds, relating how he usually gets only as close as the magnification of his binoculars. He talks about a bird he was studying. "I'll get to know a bird personally," he begins after pouring another cup of coffee. "I knew this tree sparrow that was feeding on my deck. In fact, we had four of them that one winter. I really enjoyed seeing them all puffed up. But this one crashed into a window of my parents' house one morning. I felt like my best friend had died, I knew that bird so well. But that's what made the final carving so good. And it came quickly because it all came out in the wood so naturally."

The tree sparrow was done in three days—half the time he might otherwise have invested in a similar bird.

He is conscious of time as a factor in getting a carving done. "I'm doing this for a living," he says with a rising pitch in his voice, one that gets reedy and thin with frustration. "I have to sell birds. If I put as much time into a bird as I could, I'd have to ask so much for it, I'd have to start limiting my clientele." He points out that there are more people who can pay $500 for a bird than $5,000, though a contemporary of Bob's, Grainger McKoy of South Carolina, rarely get less

This tree sparrow was one of Bob's most rapidly completed nonprimitive birds; it is both highly textured and meticulously painted.

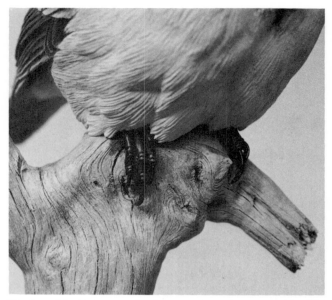

The feet of the bird are made of copper wire and are covered with an epoxy putty.

Bob describes this species of sparrow as a strong bird, built heavier than most birds. Also, it is one that survives well in winter.

Tree sparrows like this one are seed eaters and have heavy beaks.

Bob says that the back is his favorite part of the bird for colors and the way they blend together. He adds that winter birds are well groomed and that feathers line up nicely in rows.

Bob points out that most birds have indented margins on the wing feathers, called primaries. He believes that they help hold the feathers together when the wing is open.

A life-size mantling kestrel Bob completed in the fall of 1985. He wanted to give this small bird of prey a sense of balancing itself by having it stand on one foot. The branch was constructed to reflect the shape of the one wing dropping down. The wavy metal grasses suggest wind. In the collection of Greg and Ellen Baron.

than $10,000 for a single bird. A covey of thirteen quail he carved, nearly all in flight, commanded nearly $100,000.

He tries to explain what are shortcuts but not shortcuts. "I do a lot of birds that are not as done as much as others. But you can't say better or worse. It's just that there's more done on some."

Time is a factor in other ways. He needed to finish a full-size kestrel, which is a small hawk that measures only 10 inches from the bill to the tip of its tail, by last Christmas. It was a young couple's investment in bird sculpture. Time was passing more quickly than he had anticipated. Toward the end of the project (which had the bird mantling, or spreading its wings for balance on a branch, holding a metal and wood grasshopper in its talons) he worked forty-eight hours with just two hours of sleep.

Nevertheless, he feels the piece projects something. "It's a look," he tries to explain, returning to the tree sparrow to support the concept of projection. After a long pause, as if approaching an area of unexplored associations, he says, "I don't know what it is. It just happens sometimes. Everything fits, comes out right. Some bird painters can do this. If I could find out what it is, I could probably make a lot of money."

Bird art has, despite the disclaimers made by the critics, attracted painters. One of them is J. Fenwick Lansdowne of Victoria, British Columbia. His rendering of plumage and feather tracts is meticulous yet so soft, the viewer is hardly distracted by it. Feathers are visible yet delicate. Also, his use of colors brings out the fact that many feathers are somewhat transparent, revealing feathers underneath them. Bob says that Lansdowne's birds "project something that goes beyond a two-dimensional bird. That's exactly right. His birds jump right out at you."

One by one the children come to the kitchen, finding seats at the table, taking small bites of Bob's blueberry pancakes. They have less than an hour to get ready for church. Jody nurses Asher in the bedroom.

Bob, being a creationist, espouses a view that life was created spontaneously on earth and did not undergo epoch-long mutations and changes. The debate over creationism and evolution has passed in and out of history for over a century, from the time Darwin published his observations of species, to the collision of views in a small town in Tennessee where the teaching of evolution was forbidden by law, to the problems of contemporary science texts that are challenged to present both sides of the debate.

A close-up of the bird and its prey, a grasshopper, made from metal and wood.

Bob chose the grasshopper because it is a common meal for a kestrel, which is sometimes called a sparrow hawk. Also, he did not want a mammal or bird as prey, either of which a viewer might find offensive. In addition, he liked the colors of the insect complementing the colors of the bird. Bob often chooses birds of prey to carve and paint because of the power they project with their hooked beaks and heavy brows.

To break up the mass of the tail feathers, Bob split this one tail feather and had it overlap another. Also, he had a specimen, or study skin, that had one feather out of place like this one on the carved bird. He says that it gives more interest to the tail.

Bob gropes for a word to explain his creationist views. "Nonsymmetrical," he says. "That would be better than random. Every bird is the same in a species," he admits. "A robin is a robin. But each has its own personality. People all operate the same way physically. But we're all different.

"There are different ways to portray birds," he says. Lucas has again found his place on the sink, Pig has come in cautiously from his bed under the egret, and nearly a dozen birds have already dined on the seed outside on the deck. "Maybe it comes from having an overall feeling for a particular species. For a bird of prey, you might want an aggressive or strong look. The face is pretty intense on most raptors anyway," he says, as if to suggest that he imposes himself on his birds. "You might want to accentuate the power of the feet, or the shoulders where there are muscles for fast flying. You might want to pull the wings out from the body to show that," which is what he did to the kestrel. "Or you might want to get the feet out where you can see them."

It is time to remove his puffin sweatshirt and ready himself for church. He finishes off the coffee, now cold, and says, "You can exaggerate, even put contempt into a bird carving, as you would into a painting. I can't exactly tell you how that happens. It happens sometimes when I'm working. Maybe I can make a bird smile by changing the angles of the beak or the amount of the brow showing. Make it look more intense or more relaxed. I guess I know these things when I'm starting a piece. The stuff that comes out good, I've visualized ahead of time. I felt real good about my doves. I could see them from the beginning."

The goshawk is Bob's favorite bird of prey.

This miniature was done in 1985.

He says it is an awesome looking bird with its blood-red eyes and a streaked brow.

A full profile of the goshawk.

Bob was amazed at how the colors varied from one goshawk to another, especially on the back and tail. He points out that this species' tail is particularly long, apparently to aid the bird in maneuvering through forests.

Another view of the birds.

A miniature kestrel and goldfinch. A kestrel will occasionally kill other birds. Both were carved from a single piece of wood.

Bob says that there was no particular reason for choosing a goldfinch as the prey, although he had carved goldfinches before this one. He points out that viewers often overlook the goldfinch. In the collection of Jack Wendt.

A pair of award-winning mourning doves, now in the collection of the North American Wildfowl Art Museum, The Ward Foundation, Salisbury, Maryland. Created in 1984, Bob chose them because he could observe mourning doves easily in the wild and get good references. Bob calls this composition a mountain runoff.

The female dove on a rock. Bob says he was doing some sketches of the composition, and the difference in height between the two birds "just happened."

The female has just dipped down to get a drink and, when she looks up, sees the male.

The doves he describes were made as miniatures in 1984. On a round walnut base 12 inches in diameter, a pair of mourning doves, only 5 inches long, look at each other. One sits on a branch, the other on a rock that is actually not a rock, but a shaped and painted piece of wood harvested in jungles ten thousand miles from Chicago. It is called jelutong, and the birds are also carved from it. There are other "rocks" in the water, which Bob imitated with the use of plastic casting resins. He describes the piece simply as two birds, male and female, at a mountain runoff. The birds are now in a museum called the North American Wildfowl Art Museum on the campus of Salisbury State College in Salisbury, Maryland. It is the same museum that owns Maggioni's peregrine falcon and green-winged teal composition.

When Bob returns from church, he will start work on his puffins, first in clay, and the next day, in wood. He would also like these to be in that museum. For that to happen he must first win a competition that is only sixty-seven days away. If he finishes in time, and if he wins, he will be paid $7,500 for his carving.

Work on them will be done in the basement, which is divided into four areas. There is a laundry room with washer and dryer, whose sounds, along with the noise of a television, are an inextricable part of the background noise. There are couches and shelves of decoys, old working birds that once lured live birds within range of hunters with guns. They are part of Bob's collection. On one wall is a sizable swan, a half-round worn by outside elements. This Bob made, one of many primitives that make their way to folk art and collectibles shops.

The male mourning dove.

Upright two-by-fours and paneling separate the family room from a slightly smaller area where Bob gives rough, but not finished, shape to his birds. Styrofoam sheets discolored by wood dust cover two walls to act as insulation; there is a workbench cluttered with a variety of grinding and shaping accessories; a Sears band saw is at one corner; against one outside wall is a lathe, also from Sears. And there is a table saw. The band saw is used to separate an outlined bird from its background. The lathe he uses to make his own bases, round ones with indented and rolled edges. And the table saw reduces the size of many planks of wood, most of which is jelutong.

His stores of wood allow Guge to make very different birds. What he calls his primitives are mostly shorebirds. Their historical counterparts were put on sticks, which held them above sand or water. These

This ruddy turnstone is one of many primitives Bob creates to sell. The painting is impressionistic and done to suggest the look of age.

One of two work areas Bob uses. This one he calls his painting room. It measures 12 by 14 feet.

Bob works in another area to do the rough shaping of his birds.

A black-bellied plover primitive. It has the shot marks and tack eyes often found in antique decoys.

A spotted sandpiper primitive.

have been a large part of Bob's yearly income. He puts bases on them, pieces of driftwood or sections of cedar posts. The largest primitive bird is a great white heron, which stands 3½ feet tall. Great and snowy egrets with S-curved necks are also part of the business he calls "Wings in Wood."

Making primitives is an art in itself. Each is given a suggestion of age, but no more than that. Paint is applied over smooth surfaces and wiped, giving a hint of wear. But he performs no other aging process, such as putting shot marks into the wood or causing the paint to crack, or making the wood split from unequal wetting or excessive drying.

Work is done quickly on primitive birds, almost on a production basis, with quantities of them repetitiously and rapidly shaped with a great spewing of dust. They are then just as quickly painted. But some of the slabs of jelutong from this area get reduced into much finer birds and brought into the fourth area, where their anatomy is meticulously plotted and colors are complemented and harmonized.

In this area, with a modest workbench lit with an impressive battery of fluorescent bulbs overhead and old benches framing three sides, Bob does not do birds like simple "x and y" equations. Here he will mint totally new birds, such as puffins, for clients and contests. It may take a hundred times longer to create a bird half the size of a primitive counterpart.

Unlike the workbenches in the shaping and grinding room, this worktable is kept clean, and when white artist paper is laid on top at the genesis of a new project, it suggests a surgical table.

Sitting at this table on a steel swivel chair, Bob may bring out dormant ideas. He may funnel perceptions

of birds, or forage for information in the many books that are on the level of this table or above it on shelves. Here, he may perceive an attitude of a bird beforehand, percolate or update his thoughts of how birds should be posed. Or, he may kick an idea upstairs and come back to it a year later.

A small heater keeps his feet warm when it is cold, a radio that plays mostly contemporary music and talk shows is within reach, a phone is six feet from his metal chair and almost eye level for someone over five feet tall, and a bathroom is nearby. A small basement window, over and to the right of where he sits, lets in late afternoon light. The area is small, but most of what he needs—small grinding equipment, books, paints—is reachable without his getting up from his seat. This workroom is not off limits to the children. But they usually keep a respectful distance when he works.

A primitive lesser yellowlegs.

A chickadee primitive.

Another spotted sandpiper primitive.

In this same room he will start to perform his alchemy with clay, molding it into puffins. The older boys will stomp through the house in military fashion, Asher will crawl through the rooms of the upstairs. The other children, unaccounted for, will move toys and dolls from one territory to another. But Bob seems oblivious as his mind starts to encode puffin facts. By two the following morning, as the moon shines a pale crescent over the iceless Fox River just west of his home, he will have shaped three birds in clay.

A Robin in the Fox River Valley

Bob thinks, with no great certainty, that it was 1965 when he killed the bird. He does remember that he was supposed to be home from school sick, but wasn't sick. He had a Daisy pellet gun, and the robin sitting in the tree some 20 feet from him seemed ready to be shot. He pumped the gun, because BBs are forced out with compressed air, as much as a twelve-year-old could pump, stood in the backdoor of his home, put the robin in his sights, and pulled the trigger. He remembered seeing feathers fly off the back of the robin, and it sat there, he thinks, for 30 seconds. It was doomed in slow motion, and it seemed to take another 30 seconds for it, claws still clutching the branch, to topple over and fall to the ground. He says he was in tears by the time it was hit, and it was the last bird he ever shot. But it was the beginning of a bird ethic that would later dictate to him that birds are special, and that each individual bird, a robin, for example, has a life and death independent of its species.

This incident notwithstanding, most of Bob's life has passed in a conventional way, though there was a brief period of mild rebellion and long hair. It was mostly unremarkable and lacked anything worthy of other people's attention, except for the fact that by early in 1986, the year he turned thirty-three, he had carved 583 birds, not counting his primitive birds.

Bob's father inspired his interest in birds. One newspaper article has Bob saying simply that his father is a carver. It would be more accurate to say that Roy is an engineer and plant manager who works five days a week at a manufacturing company that makes items for hospitals, hardware such as steel sinks and fire extinguishers. His carving is done after hours and on weekends.

Roy has won a number of blue ribbons, indicating that were there other birds of the same species entered, his was the best of the two, three, or more present. Roy does a respectable job on his ducks. They are not meant to be floated, but displayed on shelves, and he is attentive to the shape, color, and even the attitude a bird assumes that might suggest health, power, or peacefulness. The look, then, is expressive but sensible. His ducks look like ducks and not caricatures.

Bob says Roy has been carving forever, though more accurately it has been twenty years. Still, Roy's carving has mostly been restricted to waterfowl and a few songbirds.

Bob's art is more than just a simple equation of son imitating father, though. Roy's mentor has been a waterfowl carver for about sixty years and is well known in those parts. His name is Harold Haertel. He still lives in the town where he was born, East Dundee, which is near Carpentersville and shares a length of the Fox River.

Haertel was born in 1904. By 1916, when he was twelve, he had the urge to decoy and kill a duck he saw on the Fox River. He decided an orange crate painted with red ink and a spear made of a giant ragweed stalk would suffice. He missed, but he continued to carve decoys. He still carves today, extending his range to include shorebirds and gamebirds.

Harold and Roy have been members of an archery club, and Harold has sponsored a carving group. Roy, a group member for fifteen years, took Bob to some of the meetings.

"Harold had told my dad a long time ago to do songbirds because there would be a market for them," Bob says. But there were few songbird carvers until the 1970s, when a greater interest in bird carving arose. One exception is Arnold Melbye of South Yarmouth, Massachusetts. As early as the 1940s Melbye was creating a variety of masterfully rendered birds. Anatomically, they were quite accurate, and Melbye, still alive and carving, renders plumage with meticulous detail.

"I went to Harold's as a kid and saw his carvings. Maybe some of the seeds were implanted there. I was unaware of Haertel's contribution to the art form then. He was just an older guy who carved birds and worked a regular job. But as more time went by, I started looking at my dad's birds, and I went birdwatching at a nature center near here."

Haertel has also done miniatures during the last several decades. What influence this had on Bob is open to speculation, but Bob's first carving, a green-winged teal, was done as a miniature. He gave the carving to his wife before they were married. The third piece was also a green-winged teal. This had a ten-dollar price tag on its bottom, and that is now owned by Jody's parents, the sticker still affixed.

Bob wasn't satisfied carving ducks. He found he enjoyed carving songbirds more. "I started with ducks because that's what my dad was doing, that's what

Harold was doing, that's what others in the area were doing, so I thought that's what I had to do."

But Bob still had to graduate from high school, spend time working as a commercial painter, and earn part-time money as a drummer before he became a full-time bird carver.

He clusters these experiences together, saying, "I didn't know where I was going after high school. I was working at a paint store, then I was a house painter and a musician. I played in bands nine or ten years, through high school and after. I worked in a recording studio. If someone wanted to do a commercial or a demo record, I would be called. Usually I'd come back from painting and work in the studio four, five, six hours."

He had done his teal during that time and had carved some miniature furniture for his wife's growing collection of folk art. But there needed to be another input before he would leave the drums and the commercial painting. It was a trip to Chincoteague Island, Virginia, and a visit to a man with the unlikely name of Cigar Daisey.

Chincoteague, which measures seven miles in length and a mile and half in width, is located off the Virginia coast of the Delmarva Peninsula. Living there are working-class people, clammers, fishermen, people with a sense of independence. What has made the island famous are its ponies. Originally left on the neighboring island of Assateague, most likely by a Spanish merchant ship foundering off the coast nearby, they were taken to Chincoteague by the volunteer fire department in the 1940s. Ponies are now brought over from Assateague every year during July to be auctioned off. A children's book called *Misty of Chincoteague*, by Marguerite Henry, describes the island. Ultimately, the story made tourism routine. The book also mentions an aging decoy carver named Miles Hancock, one like Harold Haertel who made working gunning stool. Jody's parents had visited Chincoteague and given Bob and their daughter a pair of miniature Hancock ducks, a mallard and a canvasback.

Hancock, who died in 1975 at the age of 86, was a fisherman and a hunter of wildfowl. It was not surprising, then, that he made his own hunting decoys, since relatively few were mass produced, and he probably could not have afforded what was available. He started carving in the 1920s. Of solid construction and somewhat narrow, his decoys have short necks that sit on flattened chests. Sometimes tack eyes were

The second bird Bob ever carved, a green-winged teal miniature 3 inches long. It was done in about 1973.

This pine siskin was also done in 1976.

This mallard is the first full-size duck Bob ever entered in a competition.

A blue-gray gnatcatcher done in 1976.

An egret worked on by both Bob and his brother Scott. It was done around 1975.

This house wren was done around 1979. The leaves are paper.

A miniature gray jay done in 1981.

used on the heads. They have been described as economical and unpretentious.

Why exactly Hancock made miniature ducks is uncertain. What is known is that diminutive birds were, of necessity, meant for decorative purposes. There is, however, a utilitarian story that follows their tradition, one that dates back at least to the beginning of this century. Before relating this story, it would be helpful to discuss the sizes of wooden birds. Oversized decoys have frequently turned up. Geese as big as small Volkswagens were put into expansive waters such as the Atlantic so that flying ducks might be able to spot a familiar species. The visual effect was to fool birds that might not be able to gauge size without other references. The story of miniature decoys is also one of visual deception. On a lake now forgotten, hunters used these undersized decoys because they

were able to carry hundreds of them to the water. The decoys were so effective that guns were not even needed. The ducks would simply fly over, see the miniatures, misgauge the altitude owing to the size of the undersized wooden birds, and die when they crashed into the water.

Miles Hancock's miniatures may have been enough to get Bob to spend a vacation on Chincoteague with Jody and even visit Hancock. This was in 1974. But he had another motive for the trip. Bob had been reading a quarterly publication called *North American Decoy Magazine.* It offered photos of carvings, nearly all ducks, featured carvers who entered contests, and presented a few articles on old decoys. One carver featured had a growing reputation. This was Cigar Daisey.

Bob knew that Daisey resided on Chincoteague Island. However, he did not know his real Christian name, and there was a lengthy list of Daiseys on the island. But he managed to find Cigar's home. Bob remembers the garage well. It had storm windows nailed across its front. As Bob relates it, "Behind the windows there was this guy sitting at a desk with his feet up on it, a big cigar hanging out of his mouth. When I saw Daisey sitting there in the middle of the week, I knew I wanted to carve full time. I told Jody, 'That's for me.'"

He still had to deal with his job as a commercial painter, a job not so easy to leave, he recalls. He had top seniority, though most of the other painters had been laid off, a company truck, and medical and insurance benefits. And the shop was a few minutes from his home. "The boss was good to me. If I wanted to take off for a competition, he didn't mind. Jody and I were both concerned about giving up the benefits. But the economy went down and everyone else was laid off. I was working only a few hours a week."

He is pensive for a few moments. "I just said, 'Hey, I quit' and became a full-time bird carver."

Bob also had to decide whether to continue playing his drums. His time playing could not be spent carving. He quit playing as quickly as he resigned from his job as a painter and has not used them since. (They were taken out of storage a few months before he started his puffins, and Seth has kept them in use.)

Competitions are inevitable for most bird carvers. Harold had attended them, as had Cigar Daisey. Bob's first competition bird was a canvasback duck. The pattern for it was traced from one of the only books available at the time, *Game Bird Carving,* copyrighted in 1972 and written by Californian Bruce Burk.

The standing miniature canvasback, copied from the Burk book, won the amateur division of a competition held in Lincoln, Nebraska. Bob did not attend, but instead mailed the decoy to the show, a practice that prevails even today, despite the fact that some birds arrive damaged. The diminutive decoy also won a best-in-show ribbon.

At one time, carvers were satisfied with a first-place blue ribbon. But good carvers found they could win a blue ribbon if their bird was the only entry in the class. The best-in-show ribbon has a greater appeal for competitors. Were Bob to enter a floating duck such as a canvasback, he would encounter three divisions. One would be for marsh ducks such as mallards and pintails; one for diving ducks such as canvasbacks and mergansers; and one for geese or confidence decoys, called that because their presence would indicate the absence of predators to wary ducks. A blue ribbon would represent the best in a species. Then that carving would be compared to all other diving duck species that won blue ribbons. And finally, the best diving duck, the best marsh duck, and the best goose or confidence decoy would be chosen. From those three entries, the best in show is selected. Strong competition is inevitable.

Bob was still working as a painter when he won his best-in-show award. When the decoy and the ribbon came back to him, he knew how much he wanted to carve full time. It was shortly after that that he traveled to Chincoteague.

In 1923 there was a novel exhibition of waterfowl in a small town on the south shore of Long Island, New York. The *Patchogue Advance* wrote about it in the August 30 edition of that year. In part it read:

> Long Beach and Atlantic City may have their beauty shows in which the fair young chickens smirk before the camera and outdare each other in abbreviation of costume, but Bellport has a beauty show in which nary a chicken appears, but only wild ducks and geese—wooden ones at that—making up an exhibit which is believed to be the first of its kind in history and which will no doubt bring the fame of Bellport before the whole sporting world. . . .
>
> Some months ago some of the leading sportsmen of Bellport got to discussing the fine points of decoy making and management, and there came into being an idea that as men brag some about the superiority of their dummy ducks it would be well to have a competition and award prizes to those whose entries were adjudged by competent authority the best. . . .
>
> Some of the decoys have been finished off in marvelous detail and the grace of their shapes and poise would do credit to a classic style sculptor, while others are rather impressionistic in finish though depicting well the general natural outlines and coloring. . . .
>
> Oddities of the exhibit include decoys which can be taken apart for transportation, ducks whose heads can be turned, ducks with real hair or feather crests, and a set of tiny decoys afloat beside a miniature blind. . . .

It was a historic time for decoy makers. Only five years earlier, a United States congressional act made into law the Migratory Bird Treaty Act, which severely limited the hunting of wildfowl. Decoys were already falling into disuse from the Maine coast to the Chesapeake, westward to the Great Lakes, the Illinois and Mississippi Rivers, and beyond. It was a law to protect waterfowl and birds of all kinds, and it encouraged the outlaw gunner and, later, the decoy collector.

Decoy competition was to remain a curiosity until the 1960s, when real interest arose in having carved birds, primarily duck decoys, "adjudged by competent authority."

That first bird carver's show was nearly three hundred years after the earliest settlers might have combined mud and feathers and a slab of wood to fool the waterfowl they desperately needed for food. It had been forty years since the last Bellport competition and exhibition. This time, it received a title: The National Decoy Contest. Today, as if national were not inclusive enough, it is called the U.S. National Decoy Contest.

Long Island carvers were not the only ones banding together to test the superiority of their birds. Another competition was formed for Iowans. This one became known as the International Decoy Contest, the name perhaps making it clear that it is not held on Long Island and is not just a national show. It was the first show Bob attended in person. He describes it as very exciting. "I saw guys there I read about in magazines. I remember walking in the halls of the hotel and seeing my heroes for the first time. They were real celebrities." In that hotel, before the time of official entry, he was preoccupied with finishing a mallard he had brought for entry, painting those wavy, disruptively patterned lines called vermiculation on the wood. It was finished barely in time for entry. This last minute rush to finish would be something that would continue to plague him for future competitions.

In the spirit of competition, still more carvers organized the Atlantic Flyway Waterfowl & Bird Carving Competition, first held in Salisbury, Maryland, in 1968. As important as the genesis of this competition was the establishment of the Ward Foundation that same year. The charter of this foundation reads, in part, that a memorial would be created to the Ward brothers of Crisfield, Maryland; that wildlife art, carvings, antiques, and hunting paraphernalia would be perpetuated and promoted; and that halls, exhibits, and museums would be erected, established, and equipped, which would preserve those aspects of wildlife art and hunting.

The Ward Foundation is a memorial to Steve and Lem Ward, who made more than decoys. They put small pieces of art out on the marshes and bays. Today, a single Ward bird might sell for $20,000 or more at an auction, though at one time a basket of their decoys sold for $42.

The exhibitions promised in 1968 became competitions in Ocean City, Maryland. That contest is now called the World Championship Wildfowl Carving Competition so that it is not confused with the national and international shows. Between ten thousand and twenty thousand visitors are attracted to the Ocean City Convention Center to see birds of all families and species perch, roost, float, fly, and prey on other birds. Eight hundred carvers bring their work, most consciously hoping for a ribbon.

At "The World," as it is called by most carvers, there are ribbons for ducks of all species. Just as important, there are prizes for songbirds, shorebirds, gamebirds, birds of prey, and seabirds. Three carvers receive special Best-in-World awards. These are presented for a meticulously detailed standing or flying bird or birds; for a pair of floatable ducks that have to be so lifelike that a doubletake is in order; and for a wildfowl carving in miniature.

Until 1980, the Decorative Life-size Carving Class put pelicans, turkeys, falcons, songbirds, and tiny shorebirds on the same table and required that three judges, all carvers, pick out the best carving in the world for that year. The complaints were obvious. How could a songbird, no matter how finely tooled, feathered, painted, and posed, win over an eagle, even if the eagle's feathers were not so well groomed? Birds

of prey, especially large ones, were starting to win over other kinds of birds.

Since 1982, a specific category of birds has been designated each year for the life-size decorative category. In that year, it was waterfowl, and a pair of standing black ducks won. In 1983, the family was shorebirds; a pair of black-crowned night herons took the prize. In 1984, gamebirds were designated. A group of five bobwhite quail in a desert setting won Best-in-World. A pair of doves at a mountain runoff took Best-in-World Miniature. They were made by Bob. In 1985, it was birds of prey. A snowy owl and bonaparte's gull in a lakeshore setting won. A cooper's hawk and dead flicker was the best miniature composition. Bob did not carve it, nor did he submit a World Class entry that year.

Winning a Best-in-World award in even one of these three areas means substantial prize money, even for a miniature carving. In 1985, for life-size work, the award was $20,000; $10,000 for floating waterfowl; $7,500 for the Best-in-World miniature. It also means that the bird or birds are placed in the museum on the campus of Salisbury State College in Salisbury, Maryland. The downstairs part of the museum might have been administrative offices. Now, glass cubes resting on bases house Best-in-World pieces, along with compositions carved before the awards were given. One dramatic composition is a red-tailed hawk clutching the feather of a pheasant in one set of talons. The pheasant itself has yet to be caught and killed.

The family of birds designated for 1986 was seabirds. A seabird is any bird that spends much of its life on or over salt water, including species such as cormorants, frigate birds, pelicans, gulls, loons, and puffins.

Bob had been making what he simply calls his primitives during the week of February 9. Shore and marsh birds were carved and painted, half-round geese and swans were shaped, as were pieces of fruit and vegetables. He explains that he has two markets: one is for primitive pieces, another for his realistic birds. He says there is a good balance between the two types, though making primitives takes up only some twenty percent of his working time. His brother, Scott, helps with cutting out the profiles and does the sanding, while Bob performs the operations of shaping and painting.

Bob has been doing primitives since 1982. He started them because someone had tried to sell him an antique decoy that was not actually an antique. He recalls, "A dealer had told me at a show how these birds were two weeks old. Then a month later, he tried to sell me the same birds as old ones." He remembers the initials MM on their bottoms. Few old decoys were signed, and if they were, it was usually by the owner.

No one knows how many decoys were made before 1918, the year of the Migratory Bird Treaty Act, which greatly reduced decoy making, nor can anyone estimate how many working decoys were made after that time. The figure must be large, however, for one shop in Havre de Grace, Maryland, probably produced one hundred thousand wooden birds between the years 1926 and 1982. But decoys were usually produced one at a time by one person. And some carvers were better at working the wood and painting it than others. As a result, some decoys are more valuable than others. Additional factors, aside from the skill of the maker, are the number of a species he made, when they were made, and their condition. Repairs and repaintings by later generations quickly devalue an antique wooden bird.

The Ward brothers probably made no more than five thousand decoys during their lifetimes. Although they are considered masters of the craft, a single bird of theirs has never been sold for more than $100,000. However, a single bird was auctioned at a price twice that figure in 1985. It had been made early in the century by Joseph Lincoln of Massachusetts. His wood duck fetched $205,000. Later that year, a pintail made by another Massachusetts carver, Elmer Crowell, sold for $319,000. Bob does not own a Ward decoy, nor a Lincoln or a Crowell, though he owns three of Harold Haertel's birds. But Bob has collected a few old, battered ducks, now shelved in the family room.

A few contemporary carvers have mastered the secrets of making a bird look not only distressed, as if long used, but also old. Chemicals that make paint crack and wood that actually is old help with the deception. No one can estimate how many new birds are in collections of old ones. According to one forger, there were probably no more than six thousand shorebird decoys made before the Migratory Bird Treaty Act on New York's Long Island. Today, he says, sixty thousand so-called old decoys have been collected.

Most of Bob's primitives go to galleries or stores that cater to collectors of primitives. One of those stores is in Bar Harbor, Maine. Another is in Carmel, California, and one is in Fort Meyers, Florida.

Making primitives and what he calls "fancy birds" are not entirely separate activities. Bob is aware of a carryover from one type of bird to the other. He says there is a "looseness" when doing an exacting bird representation. "I attribute a lot of this looseness through doing primitives, doing big loose shapes. It's given me the courage to do what I feel because I'm making representations of birds, not copies. I can sketch a bird on a piece of wood without a pattern and put the shape into it that I want."

Bob has even done a few puffin primitives, full-size birds with black and white paint seemingly wearing away from the surface. He has them held upright on sticks fitted into driftwood bases.

One of Bob's first impressions of puffins, ones he saw on a television special, is the way they catch fish. "They'll catch a large number of fish in their parrot-like beaks, alternating them head to tail. It makes it easier to hold the fish that way."

Bob will spend the rest of the evening of February 16 thinking about puffins and their behavior.

A Tapestry of Puffin Activity

"Eastern Egg Rock is a big barren rock, a noisy, smelly place. The puffins there are comical and social. They look like little Charlie Chaplins, the way they jump from rock to rock and seem always to be in a hurry. They'll scurry to look for an insect, turn around, and look at something else.

"The place reminded me of Madison Avenue because of the noise and the way the birds were coming and going all the time."

Floyd Scholz, Vermont bird carver

Eastern Egg Rock, seven acres of peaty soil and wildflowers, is one of six islands off the coast of Maine on which puffins once thrived. But as human colonization increased, poachers destroyed puffins at such a rapid rate, all the way up to Labrador, that John James Aubudon, the father of American bird painting, was impelled to write in 1833 that the puffin seemed doomed. By the 1880s, the puffins were gone from Eastern Egg Rock.

The puffin is returning to the island, thanks to the transplanting of chicks from Newfoundland. Fortunately, puffins are still plentiful in the far North Atlantic, with most of the fifteen million existing birds living near Iceland.

These birds, described as harlequinesque and clownish, belong to the family of alcids, which also includes guillemots and murres. The Atlantic or common puffin is related to two other species: the horned puffin, which breeds from Alaska to northern California, from Siberia to the Kamchatka Peninsula, and the tufted puffin, which ranges from Alaska to Japan.

Though many alcids look like diminutive penguins

Puffin

½ scale

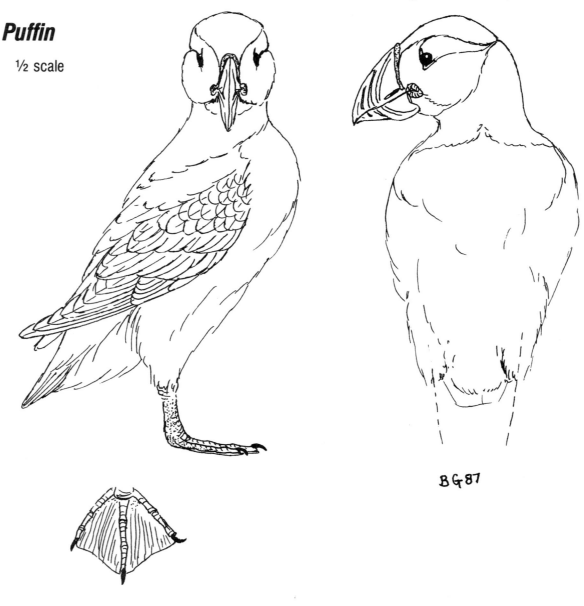

BG87

because of their stance and coloration, alcids are closely related to gulls and terns. A major difference between penguins and alcids is that penguins are flightless, but alcids have a rapid, whirring flight.

The scientific name for the common puffin is *Fratercula arctica. Fratercula* derives from the Latin for "little brother" or "little friar." When rising from the sea, the bird has been observed to clasp its feet together as if in prayer.

Some experts believe that the word *puffin* derives either from the bloated, puffed up appearance of the adult birds or from the powder-puff appearance of the

downy chicks. Other names that have been assigned to the puffin are sea parrot, pope, and bottlenose. It is ironic that inhabitants of several European countries substituted puffin flesh for fish during Lent. In fact, puffins were thought to be fish in earlier centuries.

A puffin of either coast seems well adapted to the water, to the air, and to the land. Its stubby wings can attain four hundred beats per minute, giving it speeds up to sixty miles per hour. Diving from the air or from the water's surface, a puffin uses its wings and feet to move underwater. There, the bird can feed on small fishes, mollusks, and crustaceans, which are swallowed underwater. When feeding its young, however, the puffin can carry up to thirty small fishes at one time, crosswise in the beak. What aids the arrangement are a round tongue and slight serrations on the interior of the upper mandible. As each fish is caught, it is apparently killed by the grip of the sharp pincers at the point of the beak.

This beak, triangular and almost parrot-like, is colorful during breeding season. In the Atlantic puffin, it is reddish-orange at the tip half, with a patch of blue in the rear half. The horny plates of the beak are actually shed at the same time it molts its feathers.

Puffins nest in colonies and burrow in loose soil at the tops of cliffs or on islands. The burrows can be 2 to 4 feet deep. It is usually the male that does the digging, using its beak as a tool. In addition, its webbed feet and sharp claws help dig and throw soil out of the hole. The female usually lays a single, white, vaguely marked egg. Both male and female puffins share the incubation. The birds are usually docile, but a hand put into a breeding hole will be met with an aggressive attack.

Puffin chicks avoid the menace of predators such as gulls by staying deep in these burrows. They even have a toilet chamber that keeps them away from the entrance. When they do finally leave, it is at night, when gulls sleep.

The common puffin weighs only about a pound and measures about 10 inches in length. However, for each degree of latitude one moves north, the linear dimensions of the birds found in the region increase by over one percent. Puffins found in the northernmost part of their range (Spitsbergern, a group of islands four hundred miles north of Norway) are nearly twice the size of those that reside on the coast of Brittany. The biological reason for this increase is larger bodies have a relatively smaller surface and lose heat less rapidly. The process is known as thermoregulation.

Most of Bob's birds have been perched on wood branches or bases. But he wants to try a new idea with this puffin composition. That is, to depict a pair of puffins swimming. They would be spiraling down in the water after fish. To accomplish this with credibility means encasing them in something that will simulate water. To Bob this suggests Lucite.

"I've seen things done with Lucite," he explains. "It doesn't change the light. You look into it and you see exactly what's there, not like glass or water that distorts the image. And it's a hard surface."

For his prize-winning pair of mourning doves, he used an epoxy resin to imitate water. But that was only one-half-inch deep in the base. For the puffins, Bob pictures a cube of Lucite that would measure 10 inches by 20 inches on two sides, and 30 inches in height.

He has in his home a Lucite paperweight with a dandelion encased in it. The flower had gone to seed. The plastic had captured the phenomenon without a fiber out of place. The paperweight cube measures two inches on each side, or eight cubic inches. He weighs it on a scale and finds that it is about one half pound. His ideal block would equal six thousand cubic inches. Bob figures it would weigh, not counting the few additional ounces of miniature wooden puffins and fish, 375 pounds.

Despite the weight, Bob is eager to do the composition. He called several companies in the Chicago area to do the encasement. In the process, he learned that Lucite is poured in levels. At various stages, the puffins and fish could be set into the plastic. He envisions bubbles made from glass beads. Once completely poured, the Lucite would be baked at four hundred degrees or more. The heat concerns him at first, but he remembers that the fragile dandelion

Bob's original idea for a puffin composition was to have two diving birds in Lucite, an acrylic resin or plastic. This paperweight of a dandelion gone to seed convinced him that the composition could be done. The idea had to be abandoned, however, for lack of a company that would encase the seabirds.

A miniature clay model of three burrowing owls made from a material called Sculpey. Having done a composition of three birds will help shape the final design of his puffin piece.

Bob says that a "roundness" to a composition is better achieved with three birds.

Bob has the owls' lines of vision intersect at some central point. Clay models help achieve such designs in three dimensions quickly.

gone to seed was probably baked, and it remained unharmed. He is encouraged to risk a possible thermochemical reaction. By the middle of February, he has found one firm that will attempt the process. The company tells him it will be expensive. Bob confides that he is willing to spend as much as a thousand dollars to have the work done. He feels the price could be absorbed into the piece, or it could win the Best-in-World miniature title. Were that to happen, his profit would be $6,500.

He explains how he found the company he was to deal with. "A friend of mine works for a tool and die place, and he got me a list of companies that deal with encasements and trophies. I had no idea where to start. This one company has an office in Chicago and they said I could oversee the work. I was going to give them a sample to cast that would have the materials that would eventually be encased: copper, filler, acrylic paints."

He asked what effect the firing of the block would have on his combination of wood puffins, paint, and metal feet. He couldn't get a specific answer, and a secretary called a few days later with the advice that Bob should not have the work done.

"I told them I was willing to take my chances, but they said there was a risk of a breakaway, cracks developing. The piece would be destroyed, and I could never salvage the puffins."

He considers doing it himself but realizes that he has no way of firing the block. "That would be a gamble, and I'm not a gambling man, you know what I mean?"

He was upset for days, for he was determined to do underwater puffins. It was to be his entry for the World Championship Wildfowl Carving Competition. He wasn't sure, on February 15, whether he could come up with another idea that would inspire him to do another miniature puffin composition during the next two months.

Three clay models for a trio of life-size burrowing owls had sat on a shelf for a year. Bob pares the clay away from their shapeless wood armatures with a knife. He molds the globs of still-flexible clay into puffin shapes. He loves the feel of clay and its possibilities for preplanning a piece. It is a three-dimensional idea, he says of a clay model. He adds, "I don't refine the stuff enough to keep any of the models." The owls are not permanent displays. They became early rehearsals for the wood that was yet to be shaped.

"Sometimes I'll take blocks of wood and clay and put them on sticks and play with them that way. It's anything that works. I made some rough models for the burrowing owls. It's seeing them in three dimensions."

Clay as a sculptor's medium is not new. In fact, the use of clay predates written history. A pair of skillfully designed bison were found in France's Le Tuc d'Audoubert Cave. They are believed to be at least fifteen thousand years old.

There are also anatomical problems that can be visualized with a clay model. An unfamiliar head both turned to one side and tilted up or down might be difficult to capture in the wood were a reference not available. Bob points out that no mistake is permanent in clay. Skilled fingers can quickly destroy and reshape a body. A head can be severed with a knife, turned and replaced. Wings can be extended or pressed flat against the body with little more than a knife or flat tool.

A Pennsylvania bird carver and close friend of his, Larry Barth, does exacting models of his birds in clay. His reasoning is that he first wants to capture a gesture or basic form in clay with the details being worked out in wood. But after the pattern is made and transferred to a block of wood to be cut on the band saw, the clay is not discarded. As he explains, "If I didn't have the clay model, I'd have to sit there and stare at my wood block and try to visualize whether it's this way or that. But by working out the rough, bold form of the bird in clay, I have that to fall back on, while the details, such as feathers, can be worked out in the wood."

Bob, however, will spend little time with clay. "Some people get hung up on clay and patterns. If I did a realistic clay model, I wouldn't be able to copy it. True, you can't make a mistake in clay. If you take too much off, you can add some. And the opposite, too. But now you've got to put all that into the wood anyway. Clay is fantastic, but," he emphasizes, "you still have to put it into the wood."

"Only a few people can copy from clay and not have stiff-looking birds. Larry is one of them. People who do exacting models don't always do exacting work," he says, lowering his voice confidentially. "Larry is an exception. There aren't many people of his caliber. If I do a realistic clay model, I don't want to do it again in wood.

"But the clay model can help me with a trouble area or get me out of a problem, something I didn't see in

Life-size models of the burrowing owls. These birds have wooden armatures that give support and cut down on the amount of clay needed.

A clay model of an indigo bunting with wings dropped. Metal armatures give support to the wings.

the wood. But if I'm familiar with a species, I won't do it in clay. It's too confining. I like to adjust the wood as I go."

He does admit to wanting to do an indigo bunting with its wings out from the body. For this, he made a clay body, pushed wing-size pieces of aluminum into the sides, and covered the metal with clay.

He thinks he would like to do some birds in a new product he has been using, called Super Sculpey. It is malleable yet hard enough to take meticulous details. When baked at 350 degrees for 15 minutes, it is so hard that it is shatterproof. Bob praises the material, adding that he has growing reservations with the medium of wood. "If we cover the bird up with paint, what difference does it make what we make it out of?" he asks. He identifies what he considers to be the drawbacks of wood. "It's not a medium that's always going to work for what we use it for." He points out that wood, owing to uneven shrinkage and swelling that occurs, will crack. For large birds, it is often necessary for pieces of wood to be glued together. Another problem is that wood will change dimension with seasonal changes in humidity and temperature. "Maybe it's the best medium right now, but it's still not good."

Bob's single clay model of a puffin is very close to half size. He is comfortable with 5-inch-long birds. He has a feeling that these dimensions will lend themselves to a miniature composition. Some birds, when

This composition, called "Two for Approval," has two juvenile burrowing owls interacting with an adult female. Bob had seen live burrowing owls at a zoo in Salisbury, Maryland, and he thinks that may have been the main influence when choosing to carve this species. In the collection of Andy and Sandy Andrews.

reduced to half scale, would be too small, he explains, and would not project well to the judges.

Concrete ideas begin to emerge, even as he continues to shape the clay with a sculptor's model tool. Two designs have begun to form. One would have two puffins standing next to each other. Both would have their necks twisted around to look at each other. He sees the idea in terms of an "in-the-round" composition that could be viewed from a variety of perspectives without losing the message or theme. A single bird, obviously, is difficult to view in the round, even if its head is turned sharply to one side. His burrowing owls were created for in-the-round viewing. To facilitate this, he worked the composition on a simple plastic turntable. The owl sculpture, titled *Two for Approval,* has two baby owls returning to the mother. One has a grasshopper it has caught. Were lines extended from the glass eyes of all three, they would intersect in the middle of the composition. Bob's idea of two puffins would have the birds looking into each other's eyes while both stand on rocks. If a viewer were to walk around them, a front of one bird and back of the other would be visible from any angle. At least some message of interaction would be communicated.

Bob's other idea is to use three birds. He foresees a bigger setting featuring high rocks and grassy terrain, perhaps along the lines of *Two for Approval.*

More concrete ideas are developed. He thinks he might try two puffins on a pedestal-shaped rock, with a third in the water. Perhaps he'll have the third puffin jumping into the water. He revises the idea and decides on no birds in the water. Another revision eliminates the water altogether.

But the rocks keep intruding on the conversation. "Maybe I should stay away from the water and come back to it with the Lucite," he says.

He is uneasy and reluctant to discuss composition, avoiding formal rules that might confine him, though he will use concrete terms, such as a spiral, to describe a shape. A bluebird he did stands on a piece of barbed wire he twisted into an ascending spiral.

He finally admits that a bad composition would offer habitat, be it a tree limb or a pile of rocks, that is too high. His voice sounds grumbly when he says, "I don't like to use those rules. If it looks good, it is good. I don't want to put guidelines to things. A lot of people overdo base and habitat and the bird is gone."

He rephrases his thinking and expands on it. "I've

The composition has each of the juveniles carrying a portion of a grasshopper. Having designed birds with this kind of interaction will help shape his thinking when making a composition with three puffins.

Bob says that the pose for the adult bird is typical of one at rest. One of his puffins will have much the same pose.

always kept the base simple. I'm a bird carver, and I prefer to carve birds. You have to think about time and money. A lot of people want a nice bird carving. Most of the people I sell to aren't interested in habitat. You can have a good composition without a lot of habitat. A lot of it also means twice the time. Can you always sell a piece for twice the money?"

Bob now seems certain that there will be a cluster or pile of rocks, though a new idea intrudes. He might compose a grassy cliff with the three birds standing on that.

He makes a decision. "I like rocks. Period."

His confidence grows as different ideas seem to respond to each other. The idea of a spiral returns. But this time the geometry is turned upward. He has salvaged some of the original theme. Instead of the puffins spiraling down, as he had envisioned them in the Lucite cube, their positions will reflect an upward spiral. The eye should follow up from the lowest to the

highest bird, each on its own level, on an invisible spiral.

He claims that the original idea for the underwater puffins "popped into my head one day." He explains, "I had this idea of a plastic block or a clear block of something with birds in it." He reveals that this vision came after the concept of encasing it in plastic. "I was seeing a spiral of birds in the middle. I saw the block first, not the species of bird. I wasn't sure if it was to be air or water. But something without habitat supporting the birds."

Flying birds such as Gilbert Maggioni's peregrine and teal must be supported by habitat that lightly touches a foot or wing. Steel, strong enough to support the weight of the bird and still act as an inconspicuous attachment to habitat, must be concealed within both bird and habitat to serve as a connection for the point of contact.

Bob saw puffins underwater on a Public Broadcasting System special, an event that completed the association among a Lucite block, water, and puffins. "I decided right away on an underwater piece without the birds touching the bottom or held up by a weed or whatever." This was in 1985, when he learned that the official group of birds to be judged at the World Championship Wildfowl Carving Competition would be seabirds.

"I figured it a good excuse to venture into a project like this. . . . You'd either like it or not like it. And putting the piece into The World would increase my chances of selling it. Ten by twenty by thirty is a lot of plastic, you know?" He thinks that the size will help persuade the judges to award him a Best-in-World title.

The proportions of the Lucite block would suggest ocean depth, with a pair of birds near its bottom and toward one corner. He sees the birds banking as they chase a fish. "You would see them from different angles, four different perspective points," he adds, alluding to the four sides of the block. "I like things to be viewed in the round. It makes sense. It's sculpture, isn't it?"

He reviews the concept in his mind, and calls the four sides "windows." Through each window the view would be different. He is not certain, though, whether the puffins would be chasing a fish. He suggests that it might be a sand eel.

He becomes agitated now that he must find a plausible alternative to his underwater puffins. "It's depressing that I can't do the block." He says that there would have been bubbles in it. "That's typical of them when they're in the water. They have air pockets around them." The puffins, he thinks, would be secondary to the concept of the block. "If I had seen some other bird, it might have been the same composition. Whatever the species, it would be a piece that came right out of me. Well, maybe I got it subconsciously from somewhere." He feels that nothing is new anymore in art.

"Everybody I talked to about this piece thought it was a super idea. The block would be the composition and the habitat. It all fits together."

Bob returns to his present project. He translates the notion of rocks into a hierarchy of geometric mass. He says that a triangular rock would coax the eyes upward to the birds. For this he favors two birds, feeling that a pair offers a better composition with the pyramid shape.

But as he orders his layers of thoughts on puffins and their habitats, the number three begins to dominate his thinking. He makes a crucial decision. "I could have three birds at three levels," he speculates. "I could have a spiral. I'd work the shape of the rock up to reflect that same shape, a three-step rock. Your eyes would follow an imaginary circle created by the three birds. Anywhere you looked, you would see a face."

He pictures three different bird attitudes as well. One would have a bird looking up, another down, the third looking straight ahead. He has come up with a workable spatial illusion. "A lot of threes," he says, following that with a long pause. "That's it. I'll have the rock repeat the same angles as the birds." He laughs. "I see a good-sized piece, about 18 inches high. That's it.

Early sketches suggest that the puffins, perhaps only two birds, will be on some kind of raised level, maybe a grassy knoll.

Another sketch of two puffins turning to look at each other.

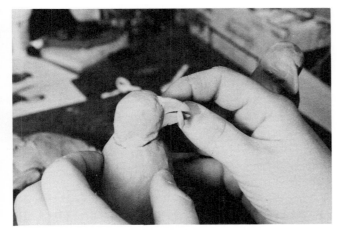

Bob wants one of the puffins, this one a clay model, to have a fish in its mouth.

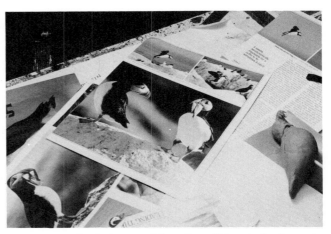

Bob begins to decide that one of the puffins will have its head turned.

One bird would be standing upright, the others looking down at him. I'm happy now, that's what matters. This is going to work."

He starts to shape models of the three birds in clay, still taken from the burrowing owls. He starts to be more specific about the attitudes of the birds, talking empirically about them. One would have its neck stretched out. Another would have its head low but turned. "They may be simple birds, but you could read in their faces that something's happening."

As he manipulates the clay, he says he wants fish in the composition. One bird might have herring or sand eels in its beak. "One guy can say, 'Hey, how about me?' It's an easy way to have two birds look at each other. It's easy because they hold the food in their beaks."

He does some sketches of the composition, neatly penciled into his spiral-bound pad. But now he feels the need for photo references. Barth has given him a folder labeled "Puffins." There are a dozen pages from magazines, mostly *Ranger Rick,* of puffins on rocks, flying, or standing on grassy knolls. These he pins to large sheets of cardboard that he props up on the worktable behind where he sits.

When he has finished with that, his thoughts surge forth with greater flexibility. He has a group of ideas to work with. He wants the bird with fish in its mouth to show that it has just landed. Having the wings slightly extended off the body would accomplish this. "After I get my rock made, I'll see how this works. I could have the other reaching out to grab the fish. It would be nice to show some motion of that bird com-

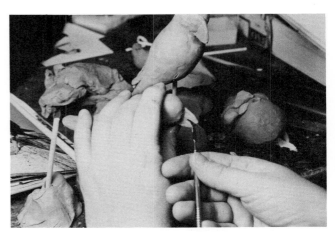

Opening a beak with a dental tool.

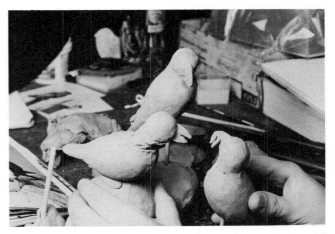

Determined that there will be three puffins in the composition, Bob starts moving the models around to see how they will interact.

An idea that did not work out was to have one of the birds with extended wings.

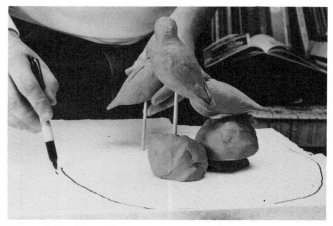

Layers of Styrofoam will make up a temporary base. This piece will be the bottom one.

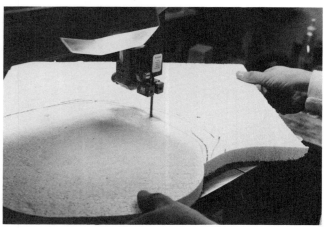

Cutting out inch-thick Styrofoam with a band saw.

ing up to the other one, taking a step, maybe. That would bring the piece together more than the other one just reaching out because of curiosity. I'll cut some cardboard wings. That would add more animation."

But after a while he makes a creative retreat. He doesn't feel comfortable with the wings off the body. He decides he wants to work on the base for a while. Once that is established, he can do more work with the animation of the birds. He will know how they will work together. He is certain, though, that a stretched neck will help create the feeling of looking up. It can also help create the look of a bird lunging forward. Once the base is made, he can adjust the heights of the birds to help with the interaction.

The rock is built from an inch-thick piece of Styrofoam. He cuts out four irregular round pieces on his band saw, each slightly smaller than the previous one, and glues them. Together, they form a stepped-in cone. But four are not enough. He adds a fifth.

He thinks he will make the finished rock mostly from Styrofoam. When covered with a material called Durham's Rock Hard Water Putty, it takes on the surface texture of stone. The Styrofoam would be the armature for the putty, which can be worked with a variety of tools to create different textures ranging from earth to snow to rock. Bob considers this approach because of the lightness of Styrofoam and the ease with which the putty can be worked. Also, he has discovered with other projects that the putty adheres well to Styrofoam. More important, Styrofoam does not absorb the water content of the putty as would wood. Drying is aided by slow evaporation instead of water removal from within, a process which can cause the material to crack and fall off as patches of rock-hard putty.

The putty does not require a great deal of sculpturing, however. The Styrofoam itself can be given a new geometry with a rotary cutter, which will spew away small white granules of the material very quickly.

Bob grinds a pair of grooves in the Styrofoam with a dangerous-looking cutter. He starts at the base of the rock and cuts up and partially around the rock from right to left. Though barely visible when covered with putty, the grooves will still suggest a spiraling ridge along the face of the hard habitat.

Hard-wiring the form of the Styrofoam rock is important now. He must use it to finalize the positions of the three birds. Too great an elevation for one, or too low for another, will destroy the effect he seeks. Yet he realizes that he does not want the rock to be too

By angling the band saw table to cut out the next level, Bob can create a cone effect. By placing the top edge on the next sheet of Styrofoam and outlining it, Bob ensures that the different layers will fit together to form the cone shape.

Bob cuts out a section of the top layer of Styrofoam to lower one bird.

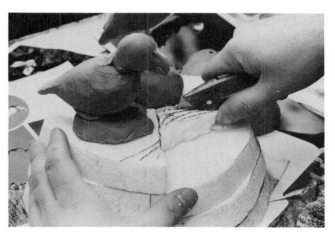

Cutting away more of the Styrofoam.

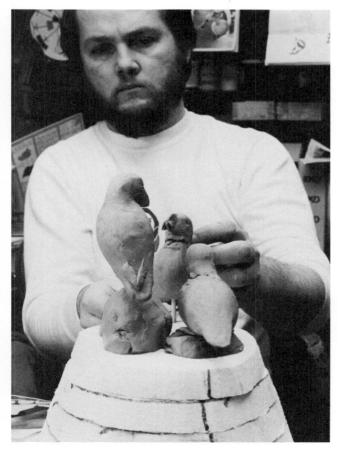

Positioning the puffins on the Styrofoam base. Extra lumps of clay help create height differences.

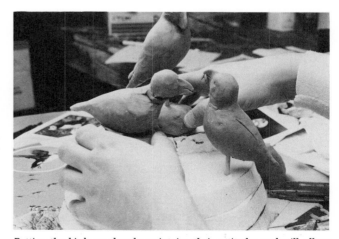

Putting the birds on dowels maintains their attitudes and still allows them to be repositioned on the base. Bob says that the bird on the right is set and will help determine where the other two will be located.

The composition so far. Note that Bob has it on a plastic turntable, which allows him to see quickly the entire piece from different perspectives.

Bob starts changing the shape of what he describes as the middle bird.

Redoing the anatomy around the neck.

This is "sitting back and checking things out," Bob says.

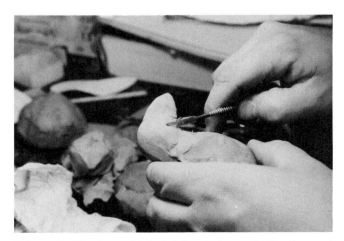

Bob says that the clay models look different when on the Styrofoam and will require more anatomical changes.

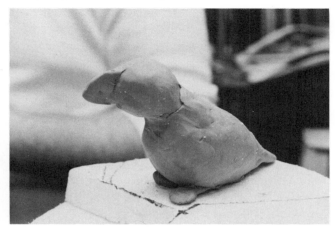

Bob has put the head of this bird farther forward as if to have it reaching out to grab something.

The angle of the upper bird is changed by tipping its head down more. Bob cut off the head and added some clay.

high or too overpowering, nor, as he puts it, "too big and blocky, though I want to show a massiveness, the barrenness of their habitat. This is where puffins spend their lives, on these big rocks. I want to show the height of cliffs, or at least the feeling of them." At this point, the Styrofoam rocks are covered with clay, a more easily worked "rehearsal" material than putty, and stand six inches high.

Bob spends about an hour working on the clay puffins. He refers to a stuffed puffin specimen. A tag on one leg reads that it was prepared by George Mischke Sutton, an American ornithologist and bird painter. The date is 1922. "I'm just finalizing my models," Bob says, "trying to get them a little more accurate. I've measured the beak of the specimen and got a little more than an inch and a quarter from the tip to the feathers. That's, ah, five eighths," he figures, making the measurement half scale.

He has put the clay puffins on small dowels. These hold the birds easily on the Styrofoam rock, and they allow the birds to be repositioned just as easily. He has put the rock sculpture on a turntable, which he rotates frequently. He thinks aloud about how to achieve the rough texture of the rocks, which he says should have pocked surfaces. But he has noticed more than once that the pictures of puffins in their natural habitat show a variety of rocks instead of a single cliff-like rock.

There is a lull in the progression of new thoughts on puffin positions, but he has reached some conclusions on the interaction of the three he is working with. Based on their respective heights, he has assigned the birds numbers. The puffin highest on the clay-Styro-

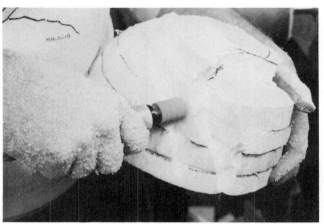

Using a cutter called a Karbide Kutzall, Bob starts to design the shape of what will be the rock by grinding contours into the Styrofoam.

The composition up to this point. Bob says this is almost the end of his preplanning. The major difference between this and the finished piece is that the latter will have a rougher looking rock with more angles and shapes to it.

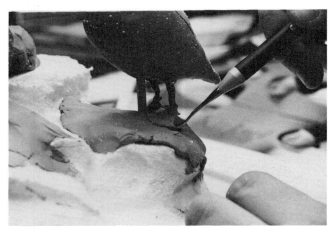

Covering the Styrofoam with clay, which can be more easily shaped and detailed.

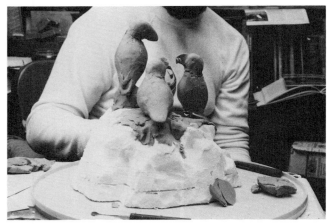

More clay on the Styrofoam.

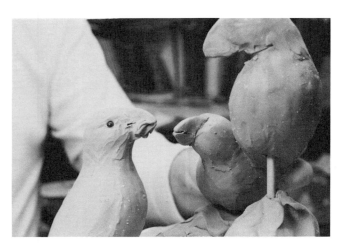

A close-up of the three birds interacting.

foam is number one, the middle bird is number two, and the lowest bird is number three. Number two bird is in a grabbing posture, reaching out to number three bird, which has fish in its beak. Number one bird has its body turned away from the other two, but its head is turned and tilted downward slightly. It looks inquisitive.

Bob decides that numbers two and three puffins should be on approximately the same plane, and he has moved number two to achieve this. Small elevation changes have been going through his mind. The turntable helps him alter the birds. He believes he has imposed a coherent structure on the piece.

As he moves the turntable clockwise, he says, "I can see shadows and how the birds and the rock relate to each other. There's a definite front to the piece because of the way the rock makes a big step up." This step up has given the needed elevation to puffin number three. "I think that kind of forms a wall, and the wall keeps you out. I might try to get rid of some of the clay," he decides, tapping a tuneless song with the knife he has used to move the clay around on the birds and on the rock on the edge of his worktable.

Within the next hour, he has removed some of the higher part of the rock with that same knife. He feels this lets more light into the center of the composition,

More clay being applied. Bob adds extra clay to give what he calls number one bird more elevation above the other two.

but the basic attitudes of the birds have not changed. He decides to use the clay models as patterns by tracing a pencil around their outlines.

He remembers he must finish a pair of goldfinches for a customer. That will take away time from the puffin composition. He estimates, however, that the puffins and their rock will take only four weeks to complete. He does not anticipate a repeat of the numerous false starts he had with a previous composition of three birds. He offers more exacting estimates of time. The birds will take three weeks to complete. The rock will be two days in the making. The painting will take less than a week. He recalculates. He feels he can finish the three birds in two weeks.

An Avian Anatomy Lesson

The hoatzin is not a particularly striking bird. Averaging 28 inches in length, the body is thin with a long, broad tail and a loose crest of head feathers. Its range is the northeastern part of South America, where it lives in dense woods by water.

Although the wings are by no means atrophied, the hoatzin is a poor flier, yet it never rests on the ground. The bird nests in the branches of trees or bushes near, or usually above, water. Chicks remain in the nests for some time, but if they are disturbed, they can rapidly abandon it, moving not only with the aid of their feet but also with claws at the tip of each wing. As the chicks become adults, however, these claws disappear without a trace. It should also be pointed out that the chicks are adept at swimming. Should they accidentally fall from a branch into the water, they rarely drown.

An equally unusual bird was first discovered in Southern Germany in 1861 in a limestone quarry, where it was preserved with remarkable clarity. *Archaeopteryx* had the fused clavicle bones known in birds today as the wishbone. However, it lacked a well-developed breastbone, suggesting that the large muscles needed for flight were missing. Also, its long tail would not have facilitated flight.

Smaller than a crow, *Archaeopteryx* had a short thumb and two longer outer fingers. These are found not only in the hoatzin but also in all unhatched chicks in which the bones are not yet fused.

Today's birds have an upper arm, or humerus, that corresponds exactly to the human bone of that name. And the two long bones of the human forearm are plainly represented in birds. In a human, the wrist is a flexible part of the anatomy, but a bird's extended wing presents a problem. Were the wrist at all flexible, the pressure of the air on the wing feathers would turn the wing tip around and make flight impossible.

Every flying bird has feathers called primaries and secondaries. The primaries can be described as the flight feathers, which are attached to the bones of the "hand." All flying birds have between nine and twelve primaries. Passeriformes, the largest order of birds, consisting mostly of songbirds of perching habits, have ten primaries. In some songbird families, how-

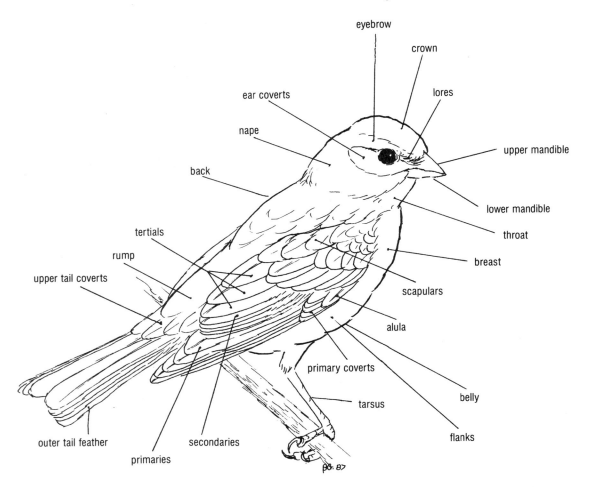

eyebrow
crown
lores
ear coverts
upper mandible
nape
back
lower mandible
throat
tertials
breast
rump
upper tail coverts
scapulars
alula
primary coverts
belly
tarsus
outer tail feather
flanks
secondaries
primaries

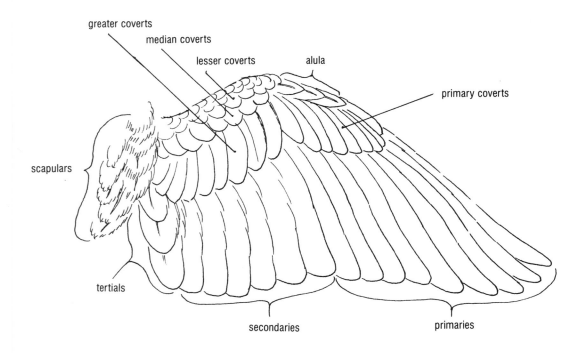

greater coverts
median coverts
lesser coverts
alula
primary coverts
scapulars
tertials
secondaries
primaries

ever, the tenth or outermost feather is greatly reduced. The flight feathers attached to the "forearm" or ulna are called the secondaries. Hummingbirds have as few as six, and some albatross species have more than thirty.

Another way of describing the attachment of these feathers is to say that secondaries sprout from the bone of the forearm while the primaries sprout from the fingers and wristbone.

Wings also have coverts, which are small feathers that overlap the bases of the flight feathers, and then each other. These are on the upper and lower surfaces of the wings. There are greater primary coverts, median primary coverts, and lesser primary coverts for the primary feathers. The secondary feathers have a similar arrangement. Covering both the lesser coverts of the primary and secondary feathers are the marginal coverts.

In addition, there are shoulder feathers called scapulars that overlap the bases of the wings. And there is a set of feathers called tertials, an alternate name for the three innermost secondary feathers of the wing. For some groups of birds such as ducks, tertials are shaped and colored differently from the other secondaries.

How is flight accomplished? When air passes over a bird's wing, the upper surface of which has a convex shape, it travels faster than across a hollow or concave surface. This creates pressure from below and a vacuum above. A bird's wing, with its blunt but rigid leading edge, is adapted to catching lift and then controlling it in opposition to the downward pull of gravity.

The forward motion of flight is produced by flapping. This is accomplished by the flexible primary feathers that form the wingtip. When the bird's main flight muscle contracts, it pulls the wing down for the power stroke. But the wingtip moves down and forward simultaneously. The primaries are held close together so that air does not pass through them, and the pressure that results bends them up and back. Then, the main flight muscle relaxes and another muscle contracts, pulling the wing upward. The primaries open up, and the wing returns to the top of its stroke.

The skeletal framework is well suited to flight. It is strong but light. The bones are hollow and air-filled, and a fusion of bones has cut down on the number of parts.

There are other features that set birds apart from other animals, ones which make flight possible. One such feature is a bird's respiratory system. A mammal's lungs change volume depending on how much air is inhaled or exhaled. But a bird has sacs adjacent to its lungs which hold the air. The lungs, then, do not deflate to take in more oxygen. If this were the case, especially with each breath, the bird would fly erratically in the air, increasing and losing altitude.

A larger heart is also needed. Proportional to size, birds have hearts larger than mammals as well as greater pulse rates. At rest, a house sparrow heart has a rate of 460 beats per minute; a hummingbird has a rate of 600 beats a minute.

Despite these major differences between birds and mammals, the difference in weights among various flying birds is far less than that among land mammals. Shrews weigh considerably less than elephants, but in comparison, a hummingbird does not weigh all that much less than a swan, which weighs around 30 pounds.

Feathers are more complex than the eye can see unaided by magnification. A typical wing, body, or tail feather consists of a central spine, the lower portion of which is hollow. Then it tapers slightly and contains a pithy core. The hairy parts that project laterally from either side are called barbs; there are some 600 pairs on a primary feather from a domestic pigeon. On each side of a barb, there are several hundred barbules. Possessing tiny hooks, barbules overlap and interlock each barb with an adjacent barb. This makes the feather flat and flexible. And although the barbs can easily be pulled apart for cleaning, they repair and close up because of the barbules.

Birds have six types of feathers. Contour feathers, which include the primaries and secondaries, form the outline of the bird's outer body feather, as well as the tail and wing feathers. Semiplumes grow along the margins and within the margins of contour feathers. These fill out the contours of the bird and aid in insulation. Down feathers are soft, fluffy feathers that may or may not have a shaft and are usually hidden beneath the contour feathers. Filoplumes are sparsely distributed over a bird's body and are associated with contour feathers. Hairlike, they grow around the base of the contour feathers and make up the underplumage of the bird. These are usually hidden underneath the contour feathers and aid in insulation. Powder down feathers do not resemble normal feathers at all. In fact, they are not even molted or replaced. Instead, their tips disintegrate, leaving a powdery substance. In birds that inhabit water, these feathers

After the initial shape of a bird is made with the band saw and grinding tools, Bob begins the feather layout. This is a miniature ruddy turnstone started for a competition in 1985.

Landscaping is a term Bob uses to describe feather layout and putting in the bird's muscles and bumps. He worked on this goldfinch for a seminar he conducted.

Feather tracts around the face of the goldfinch.

probably protect other feathers by soaking up water, blood, and other substances. The best developed powder feathers are in the plumes of herons. They may help the birds remove fish oil from their feathers. Bristle feathers are not found on all birds, but when they are, they are usually located around the mouth. Owls have long bristle feathers, and these probably help the bird in sensing nearby objects, since owls tend to be farsighted.

Except for ratites, which are flightless running birds, penguins, and the toucans of South America, birds do not have feathers evenly distributed over their bodies. Instead, they grow in tracts, separated by featherless areas. Because feathers normally overlap the bare spots, this arrangement is barely visible.

There are eleven major tracts. The capital tract runs from the top of the head to the beginning of the neck. The spinal tract is found from the top of the neck, where the capital tract ends, down to the beginning of the upper tail coverts. The ventral tract extends from the chin down the underside of the neck to the breast. The cervical apterium covers the bird's sides from the outer margins of the spinal tract to the outer margins of the ventral tract. The mid-ventral apterium runs from the breast to somewhere on the lower belly. The humeral tract is a narrow strip running across the wing bases from which the flight feathers and coverts originate. The femoral tract runs along the thigh. The crural tract covers most of the feathered portion of the legs. And the caudal tract is found from the end of the upper tail coverts around the tail to the base of the undertail coverts.

Just as the number of primary and secondary feath-

Bob says that feather tracts have to have a nice flow and not be stiff and sterile looking. Transitions are also important, from smooth to rough textures, for example.

ers differs, the total number of feathers on birds of different species differs dramatically. On a ruby-throated hummingbird there are in the order of 940 feathers. On a whistling swan, the number climbs to over twenty-five thousand. House sparrows have around thirty-five hundred and a blackbird has about five thousand.

Prior to the 1970s, birds, regardless of whether they were waterfowl, songbirds, puffins, or hawks, were carved with smooth bodies. A few carvers (such as the Ward brothers or Arnold Melbye) extended a wing off the body of a duck, but for the most part, birds were posed in a quiet posture. Gilbert Maggioni changed that. He inserted primaries and secondaries and even most of the coverts as distinct pieces of wood. One of his wings might have more than a hundred feathers!

The trend today is away from row upon row of inserts, especially for coverts. Those can be carved on the solid wing structure, obviously a less time consuming procedure. But a more valid reason for carving the coverts on the wing is that coverts are fluffy and lacy in appearance, characteristics lost when they are made as inserts. Carvers are still using inserts for the primaries and secondaries, however. This means laying out real feathers on thin wood, tracing them, cutting around their outlines, and putting the pieces into slots cut into the wings.

Flight feathers, however, do not lie adjacent to each other. Rather, they overlap and underlap. To make this possible, they have an S-shape in cross-section. This feature also helps them close up when the wing is on the downstroke, and separate—much like fingers on a hand—when the wing is on the upstroke, the solution to reducing air friction. Also, despite the presence of a rib, a flight feather is flexible.

Carving flight feathers from separate pieces of wood can have its advantages. The S-curve, which makes for a convex shape on one side of the rib and a concave one on the other side, can be carved into a reasonably thick piece of wood. The longitudinal bend that comes with wing flapping can be accomplished by lightly wetting a thin insert, bending it, and hot-air drying it so that it will hold that shape.

An interesting problem now arises. Can a wooden feather be carved with its characteristic S-curve and then be bent along its length? Unfortunately, wood does not have the same structural properties that feathers have, and carved inserts cannot be steam-bent into a compound curve.

Not all carvers do flying birds or ones with their

Crossed wings are difficult to create in wood, Bob points out. The levels have to stay the same while one set of feathers goes under the other set.

A finished goldfinch.

Bob wanted to use a single piece of wood to make his mantling kestrel. This is a view of the bird and one wing made from a single block.

Since the wood he had available was not thick enough to accommodate both wings, one of which was lower than the other, a carved wing had to be attached later.

The finished bird with its attached wing that was carefully placed under the secondary flight feathers to hide a seam line. The primary and primary covert feathers were carved separately.

Bob prefers to carve an entire bird from a single piece of wood as he did with this unfinished redpoll.

wings spread, as in mantling, a posture hawks often assume. Most carvers recreate the look of a perching bird. Its wings will be close to its body, its feathers compacted. Tail feathers may be close together or fanned out, displayed upward or straight out from the body. Does the carver insert separate pieces or not?

The answer would seem to depend on the size of the bird. It is rare for a carver to make inserts on a songbird, and certainly not for a miniature. When a bird's wings are folded against its body, flight feathers lie so close together their separations cannot be discerned. If they are discernable, a slight undercutting of the wood with a sharp knife or other tool can be used to indicate their outlines. Inserts become unnecessary and only contribute to breaking up the smooth transitions between the bird's anatomical parts. Tails are usually treated the same way. They are carved as part of the body, with slight separations carved on the surface of the wood to indicate individual feathers.

What is the strategy for larger birds? Can a single block of wood offer enough workable volume for a large bird of prey or gamebird? It could for a miniature puffin, even a flying one. But for other life-size pieces, carvers must opt not for inserted feathers, but for attached wings. Separate blocks of wood can hold the features of the coverts and flight feathers. As with songbirds, each individual feather becomes part of each wing but can be thinned considerably at its end.

In 1985, Bob was commissioned to create a flying bird. He convinced his customers to accept a mantling (or wing-spreading) kestrel, a raptor. It was a bird he had wanted to do for some time. One of the design problems he encountered was trying to carve it from

This blue jay was done from a single piece of wood.

Note how carefully Bob made the transitions flow from one set of feathers to another.

one piece of wood. A kestrel is about 10 inches long, a size not difficult to create from a large block of wood. But he could not find a block big enough to accommodate the spreading wings and the body. To solve the problem, Bob made the primaries and primary coverts from one wing out of a separate piece of wood. This was then inserted under the wing coverts, which were carved with the rest of the body. The seam was barely noticeable.

Although this wing piece was inserted, Bob does not like to make a practice of using separate pieces of wood when creating his birds. He says, "You lose the feel of the bird with inserts. I guess the continuity is lost somehow. And when people say they insert feathers because it's stronger that way than it is trying to undercut them or carve them from the body block, well, I undercut and cross my primaries without problems. Now I'll admit that the wood is fragile in that area, but then that's part of the art form. A carved bird is not meant to be played with."

Traditionally, waterfowl carvers have inserted the primaries of their ducks because of the difficulty in thinning down those areas. Either the wood would be too brittle, or their carving tools could not do the undercutting. Also, it is simpler to insert either a handful of glued-together, veneer-thin pieces or an entire primary group with the individual feathers layered on the wood.

The problems of wood grain would seem to have shaped early thinking on the use of inserts. Thin wooden pieces, with the grain running along their lengths, presented no structural problems. But now, carvers like Bob can insert a group of feathers. In fact,

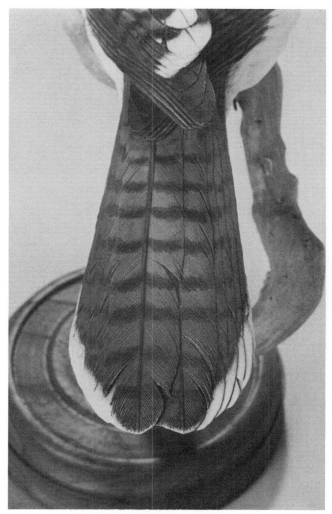

The tail of the bird and the crossed primary feathers.

Bob spends time studying bird anatomy and its movement using a study skin.

He demonstrates that a portion of a bird's leg is often hidden in the belly feathers. This is an indigo bunting skin.

the same strategy can be used for a flying bird. And, it is a solution to achieving the compound curve of flight feathers that are S-shaped in their cross-section and are flexible along their lengths. A somewhat thick piece of wood gives enough body so that both the S-curve and the bend of a feather in flight can be re-created. The results have been more realistic and anatomically correct birds.

Sculpture is a term more frequently used by carvers who want their birds accepted as artistic pieces. John Scheeler was a carver from New Jersey who, early in the 1970s, used inserted feathers. His techniques and innovations earned him seven Best-in-World awards from the World Championship Wildfowl Carving Competition. In his last years he preferred not to use inserts, claiming, "Without inserts, there are fewer seams to hide. It's hard to get a good transition from carved to inserted feathers. Without inserts, you keep the birds more consistent looking."

Feet are another interesting anatomical feature. Birds use their feet for a variety of purposes. With them, they can run, walk, hop, swim, perch, receive impact on landing, grasp prey, fight and scratch themselves or scratch in the ground. Some birds use them to hold or cover their eggs. Most birds have four toes, and the typical arrangement among song or perching birds is that the first or big toe turns backward, the other three turn forward. Except for cranes, rails, and pheasants, which spend most of their time on the ground, the big toe is at the same level as the other three. For the ground birds, that same toe is elevated above the others.

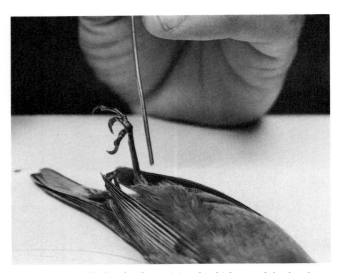

Bob uses the study skin for determining the thickness of the foot bone. This can be replicated using copper or brass wire.

Bending the wire to conform to the shape of the real leg and foot bone.

In what is becoming an obsolete method of making feet for his birds, Bob fashions the foot and toe wires as separate pieces and solders them together. The toes are stapled to a piece of balsa wood. Later, birds will have the toes that are made as individual pieces and glued together.

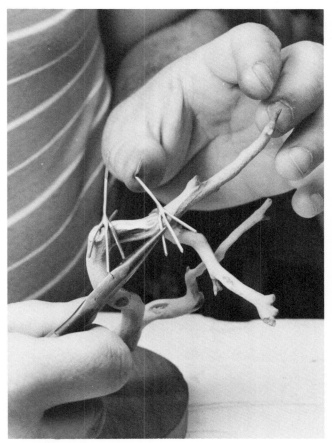

Bending the toes to fit a branch. Bob started out making soldered-together toes and feet. He remembers his father soldering feet together for a duck he was making.

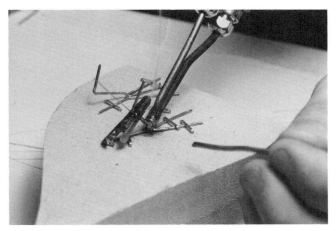

Soldering the wires together. These toes were made for an indigo bunting. Note how long the toes of a perching bird are.

The soldered joints.

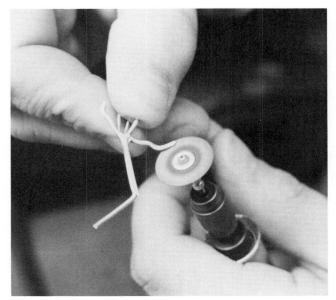

Shaping the nails with a small grinding disc.

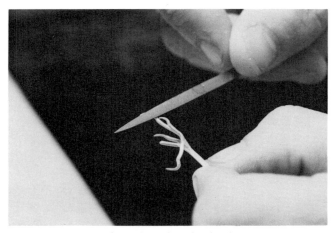

Refining the nails with a fine file.

Applying and shaping epoxy putty pads on the bottom of a bird's foot. These pads help the birds grip their perches better.

Interesting features of the burrowing owls Bob carved are their hairy feet and scaly toes. He made the hairy parts out of wood and the toes out of epoxy putty.

Ostriches have only two toes, while rheas, emus, cassowaries, some petrels, and most albatrosses have three. Regardless of the number of toes, however, feet are definitely specialized for different habitats. They may be webbed for birds, such as ducks and auks, that live on or near water. Feet may be strong, as on grouse and quail, for scratching the ground, or powerful for seizing prey, such as on owls and hawks. And, they are made to order for perching birds, allowing them to secure a strong foothold on a limb or other perch.

The roadrunner, a kind of ground cuckoo, has the fore and aft toe arrangement of its arboreal relations, but leads a terrestrial life. On the ground, it has developed remarkable powers of running and leaping. A typical roadrunner can outrace a horse for a hundred yards or more, and can leap ten to twelve feet upward unaided by its wings.

"You don't realize how similar the foot anatomy of a bird is to a human's leg," Bob says, pointing out that

A white-breasted nuthatch, a bird with feet that help it walk down a tree. In the collection of Mr. and Mrs. Stephen Keibler.

what seems to be the leg is still part of the foot up to the first joint. Making feet, he adds, is an aspect of bird carving he particularly enjoys.

"Stand in front of a mirror," he suggests, "and lift up one leg. It's going to be the same with the bird. The body will shift its weight over the one supporting leg. And this leads to a problem I see with birds at competitions. Carvers often have a bird standing on one leg without any compensation for the mass above. So you end up ruining the look of a bird because it is not balanced properly."

One way Bob recreates feet is to choose wire, the gauge of which will be equal to the diameter of the foot bones. Since there are tendons in the rear of the feet, he also selects wire with a smaller diameter for those, which will later be soldered to the backs of the feet.

"Depending on how the bird is standing, you will see a lot of leg bone, or very little. Also, that will depend on whether the bird is standing on an inclining

branch. What happens is that some of one leg or both gets concealed in the belly feathers."

The eyes of birds are not really like a human's. Fixed in their sockets, they cannot rotate as a human's can. A bird must turn its head to see. An owl has a field of vision of about 110 degrees, comparable to a human's. But it can rotate its head for almost 270 degrees, nearly three-fourths of a full circle. Another difference is that birds have both monocular vision and binocular vision. They can see independently with each eye as well as with both. Hawks have their eyes set more forward than do songbirds. Yet a woodcock's eyes have a field of vision that is almost 360 degrees. An added advantage is that its eyes are located near the top of its head, offering the bird the ability to see a predator in front of, behind, or above it.

Most birds, however, observe with only one eye, and consequently they will cock their heads from one side to the other, though shorebirds will turn only one eye and not the head skyward, to discern a threat. Yet

A well-designed piece that has the wood and bird reflecting the same shape.

Indigo buntings like to perch high up. Bob made this carving in 1986.

A close-up of the feet.

The back of the bird.

some birds seem to bob their heads when danger is near, apparently to get a quick double image of an object in order to gauge its shape and distance.

The color of birds' eyes differs as much as their field of vision. In most perching birds, or passerines, the irises are dark brown, but they may also be yellow, red, blue, green, and other colors. Most owls, and some hawks, have yellow eyes. Color may also change with age. Young crows have blue or blue-gray eyes, which become brown when they are adult. Immature red-tailed hawks have yellow eyes that gradually become red-brown after a year.

A bird's beak is an instrument for cleaning, caressing its mate, collecting nesting material, building the nest, threatening rivals, and obtaining food. It is then both hand and mouth for a bird. It also acts as lips and teeth. For some birds, it can bore holes in wood and in others it can pry open crustaceans.

The beaks of birds consist of two mandibles or jaws. These are usually covered with a hard, horny substance called keratin. They can be curved upward or downward—a flamingo has a bent bill, a tern has a straight bill.

In most birds, the beak tip wears away with use, especially with birds that feed on the ground, such as quail, sparrows, and meadowlarks. But the beak renews itself toward the tip.

A fascinating feature of birds is that unrelated species may have very similar anatomical features, and related birds might possess very dissimilar features. Hawks and owls, for example, are not closely related. Yet they have beaks and talons well adapted for preying on other animals. Striking dissimilarities are found among herring gulls, terns, and skimmers. These birds are closely related, yet they have very different bills. The herring gull has an upper mandible that overlaps the lower mandible slightly. The tern has mandibles that are fairly equal in size and come to a distinct point, but the skimmer has an upper mandible that is definitely shorter than the lower one by a quarter of the length of the lower. The bill is compressed laterally to a knife-like thinness. The lower mandible skims through the water in search of fish. When it strikes one, the upper mandible clamps shut.

A bird's neck has been compared to an arm. The number of vertebrae allows a great deal of movement. The small sparrow has fourteen neckbones and a swan has twenty-five; both a human and a giraffe have only seven. But the rest of the bird's body is quite rigid.

A bird's tail is both a lifting and a steering mechanism. On the one hand, it adds to the lifting surface of the wings; on the other, it can help steer the bird from side to side and lift or lower the bird in flight.

Long tails contribute to greater maneuverability. Crows and falcons can fly upside down and do somersaults. Ducks, however, cannot make such sharp turns.

In the songbirds, there are usually twelve tail or steering feathers. In most hummingbirds, there are ten. In a ring-necked pheasant, there are eighteen, and in a white pelican there are twenty-four tail feathers.

Tails come in a remarkable variety of shapes. Some are rounded at their ends; others, square. Some are graduated, meaning they overlap like scales from the rump to the tip. Others are forked, like those of the common tern, or come to a single point, as in the case of the pheasant.

Though in most birds the sense of smell is not acute, it is in vultures. These birds are highly adept at locating dead meat by the smell of decay. Some seabirds, such as the albatross, also have a good sense of smell.

It is difficult to study birds without an appreciation of their ability to reduce their visibility or remain con-

cealed using the surrounding environment. Feather colorations are used as camouflage. Shorebirds are white underneath, making them less likely to be seen by prey. On top, most are speckled, which reduces their visibility to predators. An ostrich, while squatting down, its head buried, may become an anthill to a lion. A bittern mimics the grasses around it by standing very erect and still.

Also remarkable are the distances birds can travel. Arctic terns travel about twenty-five thousand miles each year in their migratory flights. Even ruby-throated hummingbirds can migrate from Vermont to the Yucatan Peninsula in Mexico, a distance of some two thousand miles. When it comes to altitudes, some

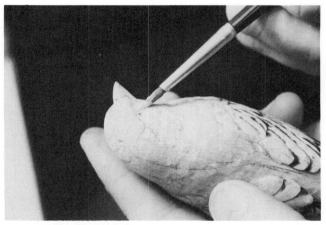

When Bob sets in the glass eyes for a bird, he makes a cavity that goes through the entire head and fills the cavity with spackle. He may have come up with the idea for this when working as a painter. Other carvers had been using a filler called Plastic Wood, but Bob found he had trouble shaping it.

A good view of the flight feathers.

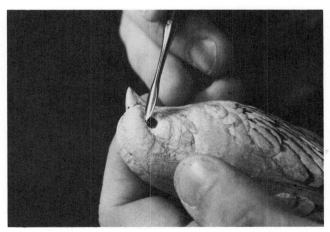

A dental tool shapes the spackle eye rings, though now he uses epoxy putty instead of spackle.

seabirds and shorebirds as well as hawks, eagles, and vultures fly at altitudes of over twenty thousand feet.

Bob says that bird-watching is his most important tool. "It's what I remember seeing, birds I've experienced. You need that reference to capture the personality of the bird. You need to know what it feels like.

"First-hand experiences, those are the ones that work the best. You need to view the bird in its life setting. I don't care how many specimens or photos you have."

He cannot codify exactly what he sees, though there are "looks" he adapts to his carved work. Most likely there are fleeting images of birds that are run and rerun through his thoughts as he develops a composition. He does have some ideas on what he describes as winter birds. They are stocky, sometimes fat. But the look is not due to diet. Birds puff up their feathers to create a layer of air under them. This acts as an insulator. "I've got a real good feel of what those birds are going through out there. I end up carving puffy birds

trying to keep warm."

One of Bob's most successful winter birds is his tree sparrow, which is posed simply perching on a nearly horizontal branch. The model for the carving had died on impact when it flew into his parents' picture window. Although there is a hint of cold imposed on the bird, it does not show the discomfort of cold. The look is one of confidence, perhaps a hint of defiance.

Bob has started visiting a nearby bird banding station. Here, he can study a hand-held bird, looking for details that are not available from any other source. In particular, Bob looks for facial details.

Study skins and mounted birds, however, are references that can be kept in a bird carver's shop, and are available for more than the fleeting moment of time that a live bird offers in its daily activities. Yet, the possession of a study skin or mounted bird may offer legal problems. The Migratory Bird Treaty Act protects not only most migratory birds such as songbirds and shorebirds, but also their skins. Fines can be

A male miniature cardinal in a winter setting done in 1983. In the collection of Dr. and Mrs. Stan Matusik.

The female displaying a posture that Bob says is often the way he remembers winter birds, "fat and puffy."

meted out for picking up even the feather of a robin, not to mention shooting it for a specimen.

This same treaty put birds into two categories: game and non-game species. Gamebirds include ducks, geese, brant, swans, doves, pigeons, rails, coots, gallinules, woodcock, snipe, and little brown cranes. Non-gamebirds include songbirds and shorebirds.

It is illegal to be in possession of a non-gamebird, whether it was intentionally or even accidentally killed and found. By the strictest letter of the law, picking up one feather from a songbird is a violation. Obviously, this would cover having a study skin or mount. Penalties can be a $500 fine and/or six months imprisonment per violation. Intent to sell a non-gamebird is a felony violation, meaning a $2,000 fine and/or two years imprisonment. For possessing a bird on the Endangered Species list, which would include such birds as bald eagles, California condors, peregrine falcons and a few others, the maximum penalty would be $20,000 in fines and/or one year imprisonment.

Study skins, often obtained from museums, are invaluable for a bird carver. This one of a puffin was preserved by the ornithologist and bird painter George Miksch Sutton.

One of the most important reasons for having a well-preserved skin is to have it as a painting reference.

Another view of the female. The snow for the habitat has been made out of plaster of Paris, a primer called gesso, and iridescent white acrylic paint. The result, says Bob, is an icy snow.

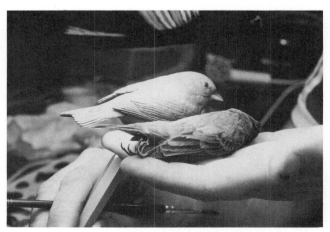

Comparing a carving to a study skin just prior to the painting. The bird is an indigo bunting.

Fortunately for carvers there are museums, colleges, and universities that have collections of dead birds, both as skins and as mounts. Bob explains that collections are not loaned out to everyone, but competent carvers and painters are usually granted access to them and sometimes are allowed to borrow them.

What does a study skin, such as the puffin's on Bob's worktable, offer as a reference? Bob took an overall measurement of it. That was compared with measurements given in several bird books. He can also measure feather tracts. The puffin's primary, secondary, and tail feather lengths can be determined, as well as their shapes, provided that the bird is typical of its species and not oversized or undersized. Bob believes what he has is a typical puffin.

Bill sizes, however, are not always reliable. A duck's bill shrinks considerably when the bird dies because its fatty substance loses moisture. This is also the case with the webbed feet. Yet, the beaks of songbirds do not suffer such shrinkage. Nor is this a problem with the legs and feet of most small birds.

But the primary reason a bird carver resorts to a study skin is its color. Photographs and personal observations cannot allow a carver to move feathers around and study the colors he needs to recreate close up.

Bob is already troubled with the coloring of the puffins. His photos offer almost no feather definition. The large areas of black and white plumage produce no discernible details. The puffin study skin solves the problem of finding feather tracts, but Bob has struggled with the color black before this project. It is difficult to reproduce without creating a solid black that obliterates the surface details.

He thinks, however, that in the next two months, he will solve the painting problems. He looks out the kitchen window, sitting at the oak table and observing the bird feeder. A black-capped chickadee has been taking seeds. He says, thoughtfully, "I think there are going to be a lot of puffins at The World."

Creating a Birdscape

A book that predates Bruce Burk's *Game Bird Carving* is *The Audubon Book of Bird Carving.* The birdsmith, as he is called in the book, is John Lacey. The tools Lacey recommends for a bird carver are an ordinary pocket knife; a sharpening stone called an Arkansas slipstone; a coping saw, which is U-shaped and used for cutting out intricate patterns or shaping a wood block (though Lacey says that with patience the knife will do the same job); a clamp, which should cost only 25 cents at a hardware store; sandpaper; a section of broom handle around which the sandpaper can be wrapped; a file called a rattail because of its shape; a nail punch, which will serve to make the eyes; and a tap and tap holder, normally used to make threads in metal, to be scraped across the wood to make feather delineations.

The woods Lacey suggests are pine, poplar, or basswood, but he puts knot-free white pine at the top of the list. For painting the bird, he advises using sable brushes and oil-based colors, which would be a mix of japan drier, linseed oil, and oil paints.

The book's first project is a miniature mallard drake, a bird which was Bob's first carving. The book offers a pattern and recommends starting with a block of wood $3\frac{1}{2}$ inches long, $2\frac{1}{2}$ inches wide, and $1\frac{1}{4}$ inches thick. The chapter in part reads:

> Don't try to finish any portion of your model with the knife. I know it will be a great temptation to carve on down until you have achieved the finished shape: but the rest of the modeling is to be done with sandpaper. Not only is this the safest way—for you can't put back any wood you've whacked off—but it is also the most effective means of bringing out the true shape of the bird. . . .
>
> If you have obtained the tools and materials called for in Chapter 1, you will have a No. 72 tap and tap holder ready to make the feather lines after you have finished sanding. Hold the tap as you would a pocket knife and scrape down the back of the head, down the neck, down the back, and along the top of the tail. Continue to scrape from front to back until the entire top of the mallard is marked off in lines to represent the feather pattern. . . . Do not scrape the bill: it is to remain smooth. . . .

There are all sorts of pedestals and mounts you can use for the mallard and other birds . . . but perhaps the most satisfactory is a knot or burl cut from a dead log. You can leave the bark on, or you can take it off and smooth-sand and varnish the wood. . . .

The mallard's legs are made of 4-penny wire brads or finishing nails about $\frac{1}{16}$ inch thick. . . . Consult a picture of the bird for guidance. If you make a mistake, plug the holes with plastic wood or some other wood filler, and make new holes.

Bruce Burk's first project is also a mallard, but this one is half-bodied. This means it is meant to be mounted within a frame, alone on a wall, or as part of a lamp or some other functional object. Burk's beginner's tools also include a pocket knife, a whetstone, a coping saw, sandpaper and block, a clamp, and wood filler. But he also suggests a knife with interchangeable blades, some carving chisels, and a rasp for removing and shaping wood. There is mention of a flexible shaft tool called a Foredom, which he says is useful for small details, but there are no photos of the tool in use. However, there is a picture of a high-speed grinder operated with a rotary cutter. The grinder looks like an electric drill with a pistol grip end. But the tap and tap holder have been replaced by a wood burner not much more sophisticated than a soldering iron.

Another major change is that glass eyes have replaced nail eyes. But when it comes to painting, the paraphernalia is about the same as that suggested by Lacey. Even the bases are pieces of forest wood sanded and sealed.

Fifteen years after Burk published his book, the typical carver cuts his block to size on a band saw, roughly shapes the body with the Foredom and bits called carbide cutters, replaces the carbide bits for ones finely covered with ruby grit, and then switches to sandpaper wrapped around a steel armature. If the Foredom is not utilized, then a Dremel Moto-Tool is

Creating a birdscape is the fun part for Bob. He says he can give the exterior of a bird "excitement, personality, and design."

Much greater detail is put on a bird today than at any other time in the history of bird carving. This is a birdscape for an indigo bunting.

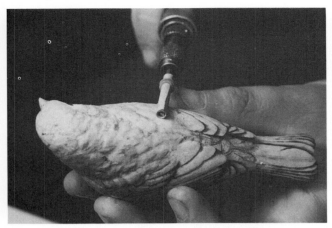

Bob uses a sanding roll, which is sandpaper and a slotted steel rod, to do the finished sanding after feather groups are ground into the wood.

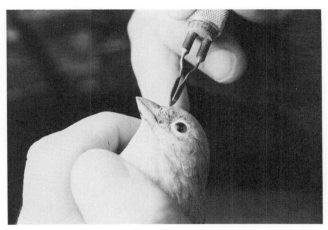

Many birds have short, bristly feathers around the beak. This burning tip has been ground down to a thin point for thin lines.

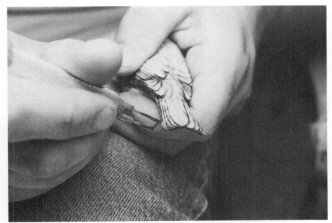

Putting burned lines on a bird to recreate barb and shaft lines is not new, but many carvers, like Bob, are limiting their burning. Here, Bob burns the tail feathers, using a standard burning tip for most of the work.

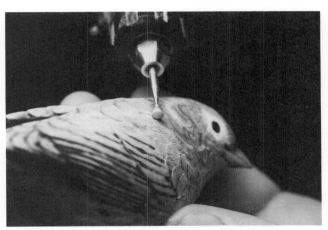

Stoning, Bob says, leaves a better surface for paint than burning. A stone, he says, actually rips the wood, leaving a rough surface. Burning, however, sears the wood, leaving a surface that is too smooth. For him, the rough surface allows the paint to adhere better.

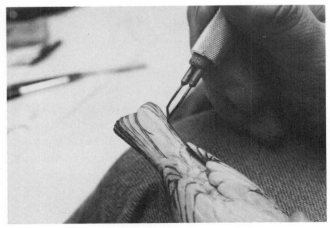

He explains that he burns backwards, pushing the tip away from him when working on this side of the bird. However, he always burns from the shaft out.

A rotary bristle brush used after stoning and burning. Run at a slow speed and moved with the texture lines, it cleans out dust particles.

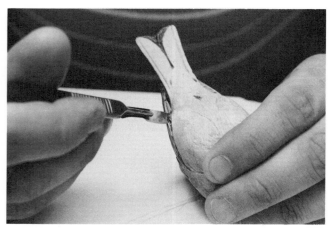

The dental and medical industries have given carvers dozens of tools that can be used for shaping a bird. Here, Bob uses a scalpel to undercut primaries.

The scalpel and some of the dental tools he uses.

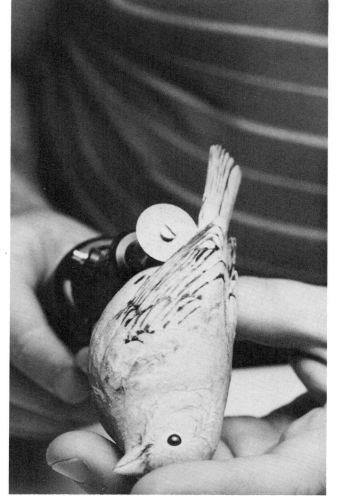

A small grinding disc made of aluminum with carbide grit on one side will thin the primaries and slice between feathers.

used, which is a grinder that has its motor in the handle rather than in a separate canister as the Foredom has.

A knife may be used, but only for making fine details such as feather separations or feather splits. Eyes are still glass, but copper wire has replaced the finishing nails used for the legs, and most carvers substitute acrylic paints for oils. A burning pen with a rheostat that controls the amount of heat generated in a finely pointed tip has replaced the wood burner, and it is highly improbable that a carver would even consider pine for a finely detailed bird carving, though Bob's first bird, his mallard, was in pine.

The wood favored by bird carvers in the United States for most of the 1970s was basswood. Known in Europe as lime and in this country as linden, the tree grows as high as one hundred feet with low-spreading branches. It has been grown as a decorative tree on avenues and in parks. Its range is from New Brunswick into North Dakota, south to Kansas and Arkansas, and east to North Carolina.

Light in color, it has creamy-white sapwood and pale brown heartwood, which is the old growth of the tree. About twenty-six pounds per cubic foot in weight, basswood is soft with a straight grain and no figure, which is common in a species like oak. In addition to being carved, it is used for boxes, venetian blind slats, and piano keys.

Basswood is fairly stable with a highly uniform texture. The European species is relatively strong compared with the wood found in the United States. The name of Grinling Gibbons, an English carver of the

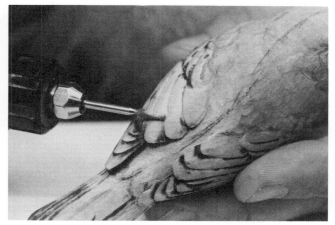

A blunt-ended stone used for layering flight feathers. The grinding tool is a Dremel Moto-Tool.

After the wings and tail have been shaped, Bob sometimes uses this Hot Tool burning pen to run along the feather edges to clean up any imperfections. Edges can be straightened or made wavy this way, he says.

seventeenth century, has become synonymous with profusely detailed work. A panel or frame done by him might include individual flowers, bouquets, fruits, vines, birds, hunting equipment, and cameos, all done with great depth and undercutting. Gibbons preferred basswood for the details it could hold. American bird carvers have favored the wood for the same reason.

But during the 1970s, carvers from Louisiana started coming north to enter birds at shows. They were using a wood known by a variety of names: tupelo gum, tupelo, sour gum, swamp tupelo, white gum, yellow and gray gum, and olive. It grows in a narrow belt about one hundred miles wide from southern Illinois through the Mississippi Valley to Texas and back along the coast up to Virginia. Growing best in swamps, it can attain heights of 100 feet and sometimes more, with diameters of four to five feet.

The Cajun people, who live in Louisiana, can trace their ancestry to Acadia, Canada, in the eighteenth century. Many settled in the swampy areas of the state where large stands of tupelo grow. Found usually in a foot of water, the bole or lower portion of the tree bulges out, giving it the appearance of a cypress tree.

The Cajuns, like carvers elsewhere, have used available wood for carved birds, though decoy makers have utilized wood that is light in weight, easily workable, and capable of accepting paint without pitch or resins bleeding through the finish, a problem in a species like yellow pine. Tupelo, the Cajuns have found, has merit in all three areas.

Cajun carvers do not go to lumberyards to buy tupelo. Instead, they go into the swamps to harvest

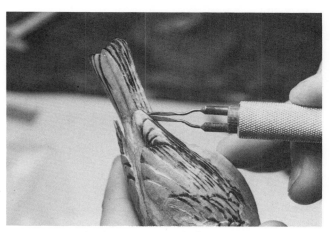

A thin burning tip can split feathers apart.

A truing stone for cleaning grinding stones.

When harvesting tupelo, a wood favored by many carvers for the details it can hold, Cajun carvers remove only the lower portion of the tree, which is found in Louisiana swamps.

The tree is sectioned and taken out of the swamps by boat.

the wood. This means bringing a shallow-bottomed boat, usually one called a mud boat, and a chainsaw into areas frequented by alligators and water moccasins. There, they cut down entire trees but return only with the bole, or first 4 feet. The rest is left lying partially submerged, like the reptile residents of the swamps, until time and rot return the trees to the murky soil below the water.

For a long time, Cajuns worked the wood green. This meant it did not go through either a forced or natural process of water removal. For cabinet or furniture-grade lumber, a six to eight percent presence of water in wood is acceptable. An unseasoned piece of wood, however, might be two-thirds water. Heavy, wet wood has a tendency to check or crack, owing to uneven shrinkage as the air comes into contact with

inner layers of the tree too quickly. This is a problem that increases as the thickness of the wood increases. Splitting did not seem to bother the Cajuns, who filled the cracks with wedges or wood fillers. What was important was that the wood could hold great detail, much like Gibbons' pieces done in English lime. The wood also held paint better than most other woods, so carvers could forgo the use of a primer and paint directly on the wood. But tupelo's biggest asset is probably that very thick pieces of it can be obtained. It is not uncommon for blocks 12 inches on each side to be seen in carver's shops. Especially for duck carvers, this means that a carving can be made from a single piece of wood. Pieces do not have to be glued together to accommodate the diameter of a body. And in most cases, a separate head and neck will not be necessary. Basswood, on the other hand, is rarely available in thicknesses greater than five inches.

A problem that relates to gluing up wood is the glue joint itself. Although some glues are advertised as creating a bond stronger than the wood itself, the glue can break down chemically over the years. It also can weaken as wood expands and contracts with the changes of humidity in the air.

Today, technology has caught up with tupelo. Artificial seasoning done in temperature-controlled kilns is now performed on most of the wood before it leaves Louisiana.

Tupelo is not without its shortcomings. The biggest is its lack of consistency. Over the span of 2 feet, the wood can run from soft and workable to a hardness comparable to rock maple. When a piece is being purchased, there is no easy way to ascertain the density of the wood. Very hard pieces are usually discarded as unworkable by bird carvers.

Bob has used tupelo, but most of his work is still done in jelutong. A Southeast Asian timber, it is found in Malaysia and in the Indonesian islands of Sumatra and Kalimantan. Rising to nearly two hundred feet in height, the tree grows with a straight, cylindrical stem. And though imported for its wood, the jelutong tree is also tapped for a milky latex, which is used in chewing gum.

Plain-looking and straight-grained, the wood's one fault is that it sometimes has cavities. These are latex traces that the carver must fill with an artificial substance.

The outstanding advantage of jelutong is its stability. Wood, because of its structure of thin-walled cells, expands and contracts as the moisture content in the

Bob has compared the workability of two of the three species of wood he has used. The wood at the top is basswood. At the bottom is jelutong, a Southeast Asian species.

air changes from season to season. This is why chairs wobble as rungs loosen up, and panels that are not firmly secured rattle in their frames. But jelutong, once dry, is subject to very little dimensional change. For this reason, it is the wood favored by patternmakers, especially those in the United States. Machinery parts in particular are being carved first from jelutong before being cast in metals. It also saws easily, and when ground down with rotary cutters, it has been said the wood disappears before the eyes.

Bob has heard that some of the wood is being harvested in Vietnamese jungles. Stories are spreading that the wood is contaminated with Agent Orange, a defoliant used during the Vietnam War. Bob wonders whether breathing in jelutong dust will be harmful. He is using a dust mask more often when working the wood.

— • —

The Lincoln Park Zoo is approximately fifty minutes from Carpentersville, barring excessive traffic. It is in the center of Chicago, close to the shore of Lake Michigan. Admission is free. It is Monday, February 17, and Bob needs to crystallize his thoughts on puffins before he moves from clay to wood.

Open every day, the zoo is small, but it has the traditional exhibits of giraffes, elephants, llamas, and tigers. Exotic birds are housed in one building. Seabirds are in another. Snow whitens the zoo, but a steady drizzle slowly dissolves it. Bob moves quickly. The seabird house is his first stop.

He watched a video of a program devoted to puffins the night before, when the children had left the family-room for bed. The program described an Atlantic seabird exhibit at the Lincoln Park Zoo. Young puffin chicks were removed from nesting sites in Greenland and taken to Chicago. The film shows a variety of puffin activities from swimming to flying to burrowing. Bob watched parts of the tape several times. Puffins made quick bumblebee-like flights to their nests and flew backwards with equal rapidity as he ran the tape fast-forward and in reverse. But he was most interested in how they behaved on land. He rewound the tape and continued to scan it for new information. He noticed a crease down the breasts of the puffins.

At the puffin exhibit, only one puffin is visible as Bob leans on the glass that separates the birds from the public. It sits unmoving on a ledge halfway up the clifflike face. A high wall of rocks is in the background with burrow holes discernible. White guano streaks the rocks. In a neighboring exhibit, the guillemots are more active and take to the water, which is also part of the exhibit. Their rapid wing-beating swim strokes are easily recognizable.

"I'm looking for some of the movements of the wings and the neck of these birds," he says in front of the guillemot exhibit. He moves back to the solitary puffin that occasionally moves its head. "It's amazing what they can do with their necks at different angles. It looks like they shouldn't work that way, but they do."

He points out that the puffin, now joined by another lethargic one, is an immature bird. The short tail and primary feathers indicate a young age. "The beak is

Bob at the Chicago Zoo looking at the puffin exhibit.

One of the puffins. Bob says later that its position is similar to one of the three finished puffins.

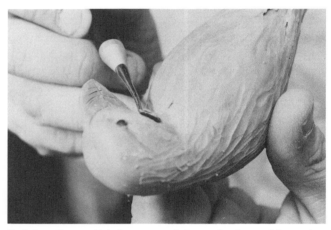

Back from the zoo, Bob does more refining on the clay models, particularly in the neck areas.

small," he adds. "It's not filled out. Beaks get thicker, taller as the birds get older."

As he gets ready to leave, he says, "The guillemots have the same kind of wings. They do the same things under water. They're all comical."

Back in his basement, Bob holds one of the clay puffins by the thin dowel that projects from the bottom of the bird. He has removed it from the Styrofoam base that is now gray with clay. The highest puffin stands on a portion of the rock that bulges out. It puts number one bird approximately 2½ inches above the lowest one and 1½ inches above the middle one, number two, that has the fish that attracts such interest. All three now have webbed feet shaped from clay and have been given stiffness with smaller dowels.

He says, at first running his words together quickly, "I learned that the puffins at the zoo have skinnier necks than the ones I have here. I did see enough movement and I got some good information." He also observed the size and shape of the beaks. "When birds are in captivity," he offers, "the beaks don't get the proper amount of bumping, scraping, pecking that they would in the wild. The beaks start to overlap and cross at their ends."

He returns to the clay. "My models are heavy and thick in all areas. But I'll use them as my patterns." He says he will do no more work with the clay. He must get to the wood. "I don't like to make patterns this way. You can end up with the wood looking stiff. But I've got to start somewhere."

With his free hand, he rotates the turntable that holds the clay and Styrofoam rock. He says, "I don't

Reference photos make up Bob's study board, which he can carry from one workroom to another.

The clay and Styrofoam composition and the study board.

A close-up of the finished models.

Another view of the models. Bob says these are "basic shapes without a lot of tight detail."

want the size of the rock to detract from the birds. But on the other hand, I want to show these little birds on a big cliff." He reveals that there are still slight elevation changes going through his mind. He decides to reduce some of the upper portion of the rock "to allow more light in the center."

He lays number two bird on his notebook, writes "TAKE 1" in one corner, and traces around the clay. He does the same for the other two. As he cuts out the pattern he points out that he will leave slightly more wood on the beak to work with than the outline of the pattern provides, despite the fact that the clay models are already slightly oversized. Ultimately, he says, the problems of anatomy have to be worked out in the wood, regardless of how accurate a clay model is. He also indicates that he will have to find a piece of wood that is thicker than the body of a puffin for number one and number two birds. "I'll add wood to the patterns in spots that might be subject to change. You can't add it later. Well, you can," he adds, perhaps remembering that wood fillers have corrected carving mistakes for decades. "But I want this to be all one piece of wood. And it's easy to take excess off. After all, these are small birds."

As he outlines number three bird, he says, "I'm just tracing the basic ideas here. It's not a real accurate outline. Do you see how breasty these birds are? The breasts seem to pop out at you."

He pauses to say, "You could lay down a piece of photographic paper, lay your subject over that, say a perfect clay model." He relates how this technique has been used by antique decoy restorers. "They have a bird with, let's say, a broken bill. Then they'll find a comparable bird with a perfect bill. Then they'll make

A rough tracing of the clay model for a pattern.

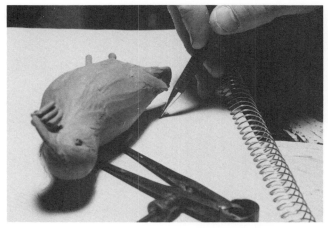

A high-intensity lamp overhead provides the shadow that he outlines.

Finalizing the sketch.

The finished sketch that will be a pattern.

Finalizing number one bird.

Number two bird being outlined.

a light image of it. But I still don't like to do clay copies. It would take an extra day to do a perfect clay model, and then do the same in the wood. I find that too confining. I like to adjust my wood as I go. I feel a tightness being stuck trying to duplicate an exact duplicate."

Drawing around number one bird, he says, "Even with clay models, I haven't taken time to shape these to their perfect half size or do fine detail work. I'll be doing that in the wood," he says evenly.

He recalls work he did on his three burrowing owls. First he did the heads in clay, then he did the bodies. When he started shaping the wood, it cracked, and he had to start a new set. Then he decided to try some attitude changes with the clay models. He discarded the wood and started a third set, which satisfied him. He thinks he might work with more than one set of puffins. "They're small," he points out, "so there's no problem with more than three birds. And once you have a basic shape, it's easy to start another one. I know what the shape is supposed to look like," he says with certainty.

He has taken the clay models and the reference board of puffin photos to the band saw and grinding area.

Sitting down in a chair that has its back to the Styrofoam-padded wall, Bob starts to reflect on the type of wood he will use for the puffins and the rock. Removing an electric drill plug and replacing it with that of his Foredom, Bob says he likes tupelo but has reservations. "I like the way it works, but I don't like the grain. You get hard and soft spots. That tends to create some problems when putting a surface on it. That grain will show up in rows. Basswood doesn't show as much grain." But he is comfortable with jelutong. He has used it for nearly all his primitives.

He decides to eliminate the tupelo and make a comparison between basswood and jelutong. He will grind the surface of both with a small carbide cutter and judge the effects on the grain. He complains that he hasn't used basswood for a long time. "This is just to get a feel for it. Jelutong is kind of like tupelo in that it comes hard and soft. But it fits into a general soft category," he says loudly over the sound of the Foredom. It makes a funnel of dust, spewing most of it on his pants. "I'm familiar with the smell, the feel, the texture of jelutong." He lowers his voice as the grinder comes to a stop.

He pouts. "I don't know what to do. I can't get the real fine, feathery, hairy cuts with jelutong. And I can't raise the tips of the wings," he adds, noting that jelutong, structurally, will not hold very fine detail. "Basswood is so much more solid. It's going to be hard getting detail around the legs with jelutong. There's a lot of down on these birds." But his thoughts continue to sway from basswood to jelutong. "Basswood has a fuzzy grain," Bob says, shaking his head. "It rips if you go against the grain."

He had decided on basswood for the underwater birds because of their open wings. "Jelutong can break and chip easily. Basswood holds up a whole lot better."

Bob points out that both woods hold burning lines well, "but jelutong burns faster. I guess that's because it has small pores. But they create problems. Basswood burns more precisely."

Bob makes his decision. He will use jelutong for both the birds and the rocks. He has it in thicknesses that will require no more than two pieces to be glued together for the rock, accommodating either a horizontal or a vertical seam.

The band saw quickly cuts the profile of number two bird made from the paper pattern laid on a 2-inch-thick piece of jelutong scrap. Bob has a variety of thicknesses in this room, from 1 inch to almost 4 inches. He holds the block up and examines it. "Some people draw out the side and a top view. But I make only a side-view pattern."

He goes back to his painting room and returns with a book. It is Roger Tory Peterson's *Field Guide to the Birds*. The book is probably the most popular field guide for bird watchers in the United States. Bob chooses it not for its references but instead for its size. It is approximately one half the thickness of the bird

Before he goes to the band saw, Bob puts a few more details on the clay models, especially on the beaks.

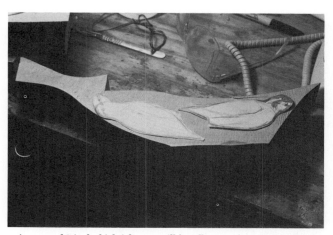

A scrap of 2-inch-thick jelutong will handle two of the bird patterns.

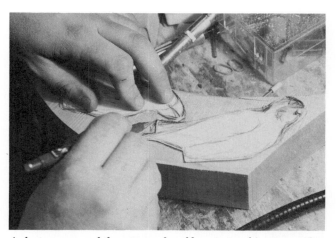

As he traces around the patterns, he adds some wood in areas such as the rear of this bird. Since he isn't positive whether he will raise the primaries or cross them, he wants the extra wood. He also adds some wood around the head area. Bob says emphatically that though he may begin with a pattern, he will not be regimented by its shape.

Establishing a centerline on each cutout. Here, he uses a book that is half the thickness of the block. The pencil is held stationary and the block is turned.

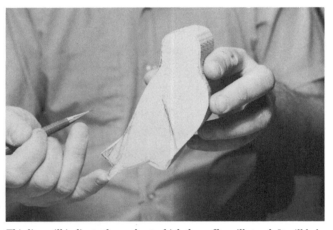

This line will indicate the angle at which the puffin will stand. It will help him visualize how the bird will look as he carves it.

Comparing the block to the clay model.

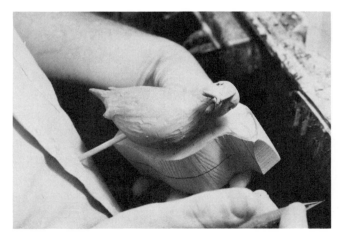

Another comparison to try to visualize the turned head in the block of wood.

block. He places the wood puffin profile on the band saw's steel work surface, the book next to it, and lays a pencil on top of the book. Holding the pencil stationary against the wood, he rotates the block until a line girdles the wood. This is Bob's centerline.

Centerline references are used by most bird carvers. They allow wood to be removed on either side to affect the roundness of the body. The actual pencil line is usually ground away only at the very end of the shaping process.

"A centerline is a point of reference. These birds aren't going to be completely symmetrical, but it's a point of reference during the roughing stage, at least until I find the angles of the heads in the wood."

He goes back to the bench, lays the clay model on top of the wood block and make a quick outline. The puffin's head turns some 30 degrees to its left.

He puts a ⅛-inch-diameter dowel into the underside of the wood cutout. This will enable him to shape the wood without his hand being in the way. He next puts a larger carbide bit into the Foredom. It is barrel-shaped and ¾ inch in diameter. Its surface is covered with small needle-like bits of extra hard steel. He presses the foot petal but releases it long enough to say, "You have to determine where the angles are when you're roughing. But it's not hard. You just do a little bit at a time." He puts on a pair of goggles. "You have to see the bird hiding in there, in the wood. Trying to teach somebody this is hard," he says, picking up the Foredom handpiece.

In many respects, the tools are as informative as the birds being copied. Carvers contend that hand-held grinders like the Foredom have made sculptors out of

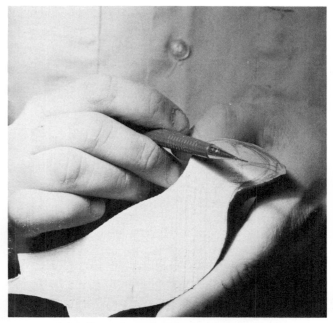

Bob indicates the angle of the head with the pencil.

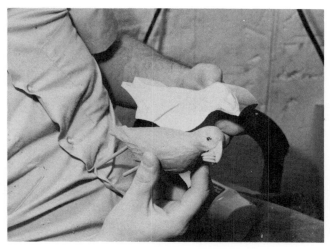

A comparison of the clay model and the cutout.

Bob draws a line that will indicate how the head will be turned.

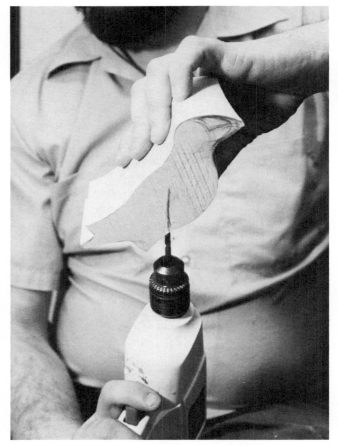

Drilling a hole for a dowel at the same angle as the line. The dowel can then be put into a scrap of wood or the Styrofoam.

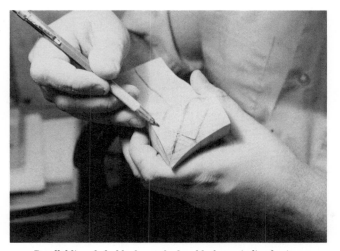

Parallel lines help block out the head before grinding begins.

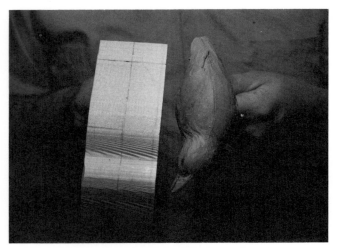

Showing how the puffin will lie within the block.

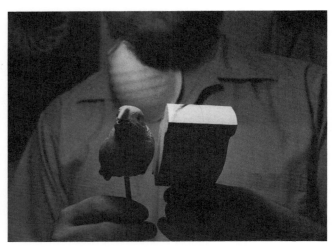

Another view.

whittlers. The tools also make wood behave in more predictable ways. With the right cutters, then, order is quickly imposed on shapeless wood.

The Foredom has been described as an oversized dental drill. The ⅛ horsepower motor is housed in a canister that can be put out of the way by hanging it on what looks like a stand for intravenous equipment. Between that and the handpiece, which comes in different sizes and has prelubricated ball bearings, is a flexible rubber shaft about 3 feet in length. An accessory used by most carvers is a rheostatic foot speed control. The more pressure exerted on it, the more torque and the greater the speed. The maximum revolutions per minute for a Foredom is 14,000. The speed is low enough to accommodate even the sizable bar-

rel-shaped carbide bit Bob uses to rough-shape his birds. Greater speeds would cause metal fatigue at the point where the shaft meets the tip. This has sometimes been a problem with thin-shafted bits, such as ruby carvers, in grinders with a higher rpm.

Within the year, Bob will switch to a Gesswein. This tool has its origins in the metalworking industry. The Gesswein is a "high-tech" grinder with very high rpm. Its range is from 10,500 to 45,000 without the optional foot rheostat. Control is achieved with a simple lever on a control box. The handpiece is lighter than those adaptable to the Foredom, but it cannot deal with large cutters. Its biggest advantage, however, is that it is controlled through a flexible, lamp-wire-thin cord that extends to over 6 feet.

The price for a Gesswein is about three times what a carver would pay for a Foredom with a foot petal included. But carvers appreciate a unique feature of the Gesswein: the motor can reverse itself. Since wood grain is layered, it has a tendency to tear if the layers are pushed against. This might find a parallel in an open phonebook; if a finger is run from the back page toward the open middle, pages will be lifted up. Something comparable happens with wood when a carving tool, even a grinding bit, is used against the grain. With chisels, the result is often a chunk of wood lifted and separated from the block. With a bit that can have its rotation reversed, the tearing problem is neutralized. This is particularly advantageous to carvers who use basswood, which, despite its featureless grain, tears at its layers easily.

The Foredom is not the power grinder that will help shape the puffin birdscapes. Instead, Bob will use the Dremel Moto-Tool. This drill is probably more familiar to non–bird carvers than its larger counterpart. The Dremel is different from the Foredom and the Gesswein because the motor is in the handpiece. This makes for a bigger tool to hold. The standard Dremel handpiece is 8 inches long, compared to the Gesswein's, which is only 5½ inches. But it is more closely allied to the Gesswein in that it has a simple cord with a plug on the end. There is no rheostat box, though one is available for it. Also, like the Gesswein, it runs at a higher speed than the Foredom, with a torque of 30,000 rpm.

After he switches to the Gesswein, Bob will say, "It's unbelievably fast, and it's not real loud like the Dremel. It's good to spin in different directions around beaks and eyes because it spins so fast, it doesn't want to run away from you," which has been a problem with the Foredom. "I don't know how we did without it. You can use it like a pencil. It doesn't get hot or whiney like a Dremel. I couldn't handle that after a while. It has a little bit of a whine, but it's not annoying. It's a good tool."

Bob did not begin carving with a grinding tool but with a knife. Unlike the pocketknife recommended in Lacey's *The Audubon Book of Bird Carving*, Bob's first cutting tool was an X-acto, a steel handle with small, interchangeable blades. But he soon purchased a Dremel, then a diegrinder, then a Foredom.

Switching off the Foredom, Bob nods approval at his clay puffins. "It was an eight-hour day to put this whole piece together. But I got a feel for the birds." He creases his forehead. "I might come back and work on the clay models if I have trouble with the wood. It's sometimes easier to solve the problem with clay, and you're less likely to make a mistake with it."

He says that for a species with which he is familiar, a sparrow, for example, he will ignore the clay altogether. But if the pose is unusual, even for a bird he does know, he will make a clay model. He did this for an indigo bunting. "I wanted a bunting with its wings out. I went with the basic clay body and some metal for the wings."

He continues transferring data from the clay puffins as he returns to shaping the wood. "I've started to block the head in," he says through his dust mask. "I've drawn two parallel lines at the widest point of the head just to block it in. I'm at the point of no return," he shouts above the Foredom.

He emphasizes the importance of the centerline while he works. Yet he might change the direction of the centerline slightly if the head is not at quite the right angle.

"I'm stalling mentally on this project because I was ready to do the underwater piece. But I'm happy with what I've come up with so far."

In addition to blocking out the head, he will also determine the position of a bird on its base and then

Bob uses his basic tool for roughing out birds, whether they be big or small: a Karbide Kutzall that measures ⅜ inch in diameter and 1 inch in length.

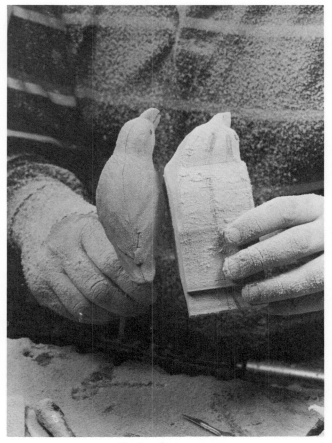

Checking his progress.

More shaping around the head. Bob points out that he seldom uses more than one view of a bird. In most cases, he uses the side profile.

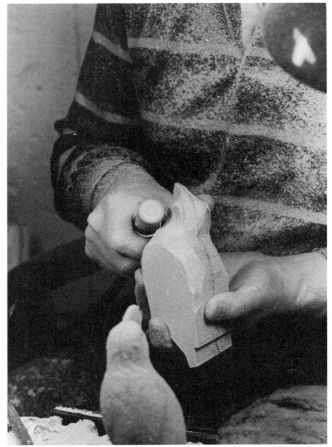

Shaping of the neck area.

draw a line from the top of the side profile down to where its feet will rest. This will maintain its proper stance, he says.

Bob holds up a wood puffin on its dowel holding device. He removes his dust mask and inhales deeply. "Conceptualize how the turning of the skull will affect the neck and feathers. This is where observation of a live bird is important. Later I'll sketch in the feather groups on the head to get a better perspective on the shape of it. That'll be the eyebrows, the cheeks, small feathers. On most birds I'll leave extra wood around the eyes for the bristly feathers you find there."

For the next two months, Bob will create birdscapes using a variety of small tools. John Lacey would have been astounded with the detail they can achieve. A small carbide bit will give shape to wings, while main feather groups will be defined with grinding stones called ruby carvers.

Oxide stones have been available for many years to carvers and predate ruby carvers, but they could do little more than give some smoothness to what had been left after carving, usually with a knife. Rotary files have also been around for some time but they left a coarse and chattery surface with dig marks. Even the carbide bits perform better. The ruby carver carves, as its name suggests, but also leaves a fairly smooth surface, at least on the macroscopic level.

High-speed bits with differently shaped heads impregnated with ruby grit, these cutters came directly from the dental industry. Made in Europe, they were designed to shape dentures, caps, and bridgework.

No one is certain when ruby carvers were first introduced. One story has a Pennsylvania carver named Ernest Muehlmatt bringing them to a carving demonstration in San Francisco around 1980. Muehlmatt says he got them from a dentist who carved birds. He

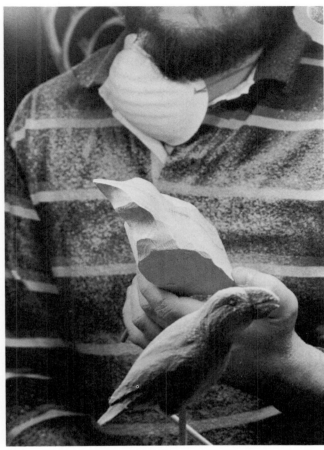

Progress so far.

The three puffins roughed out.

A close-up of number three bird. Note the crossed primaries.

came across them in a dental catalog. Muehlmatt used them with jelutong, the wood he favored at the time, and he was pleased with the results. A tool dealer at the demonstration decided to include them with other carving accessories. Now nearly every bird carver working professionally or actively uses ruby carvers, with their shapes ranging from pear-shaped to pointed to ball shaped.

New bits impregnated with diamond grit have recently been introduced to bird carvers. These probably will not replace ruby carvers, but they will achieve finer details in the wood.

Bob has a recipe for resurfacing the bird made somewhat smooth by large cutters. He uses the term "landscaping" to describe a process that breaks up the surface. He sees a bird as a biological metaphor of muscles, feathers, and tension. The bird's surface becomes a compositional narrative of subtle changes.

Bob sketches in the details that will have to be cut into the wood.

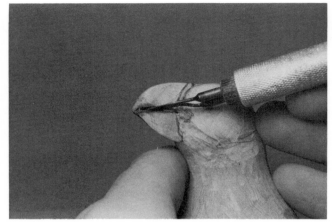

Using a burning pen to create the split of the beak.

Bob says a mirror is very helpful for shaping because he can see both sides of the bird at once.

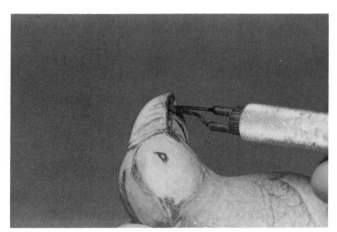

More defining of the two mandibles, or jaws.

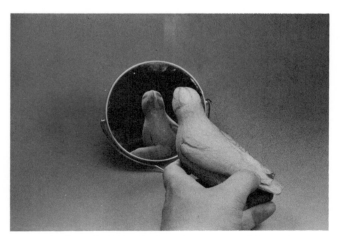

A mirror also helps check on the symmetry of the head.

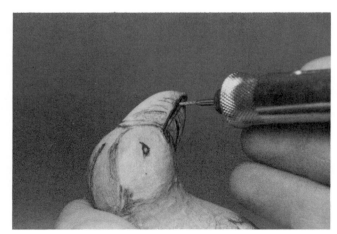

A finely pointed diamond bit opens an area where the fish, which Bob has decided will be herring, are to be placed.

A close look will show that a wide opening has been made in the beak.

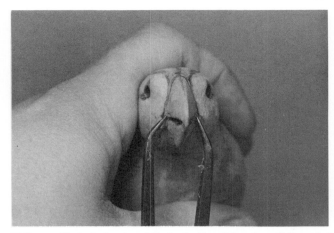

Calipers will check the size of the beak. Everything else will be scaled from this part of the anatomy. Note that these are half-size puffins.

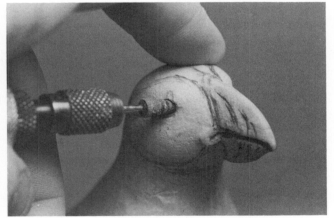

Putting an eyehole in the bird. Bob uses a simple tapered stone. He says that he tries to burn some of the wood with the stone so that a dark area is left. This makes the hole easier to see as he continues to work on the head.

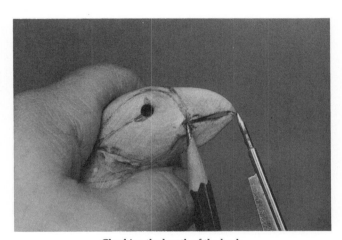

Checking the length of the beak.

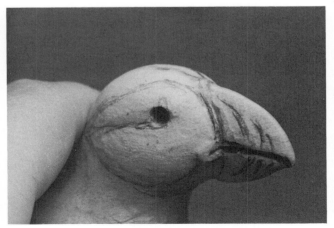

The eyehole.

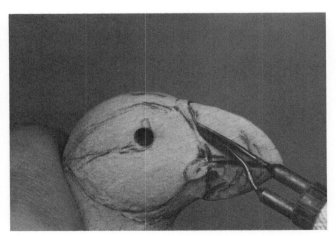

With a burning pen, Bob runs a line around the base of the beak.

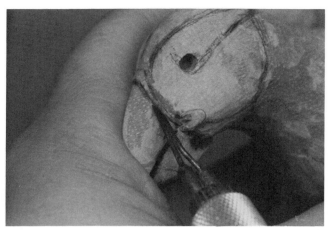

Another view of defining the base of the beak with the burning pen. The pen is not set at a high temperature for this kind of work.

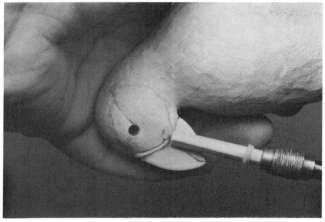

Sanding the beak with a sanding roll. This is sandpaper wrapped around a mandrel.

Bob spends a lot of time sketching on his birds. The beak of this bird has its final shape.

Cutting in the wing and scapular area with a ruby carver.

"I'll landscape the rest of the bird with muscles and bumps," Bob says, removing the dust mask he had put on when grinding. Exhaling, he says, "You want everything to flow from the head back." Landscaping does not begin until the head has been shaped. "But," he says, "what I draw on the bird is my own design. On the back of a puffin, I'll start with some rows of feathers. Even though it's a solidly colored bird, you can still see individual feathers on the specimen. Some I'll carve, others will be burned in place, some will just be painted. But let me point out that the lines I draw are only a rough draft to follow. I may change them or see something differently as I'm working."

He says he varies the depth of the feathers as he removes wood, working towards a basic overlap. He advises, "As you move to smaller and smaller feather tracts, you go to smaller, rounded stones, maybe another ruby carver or a small oxide stone." He becomes adamant on the next issue. "You don't want harsh edges. One group has to blend into another. Your eye

Checking the measurements of the wings. The study skin helped determine the length.

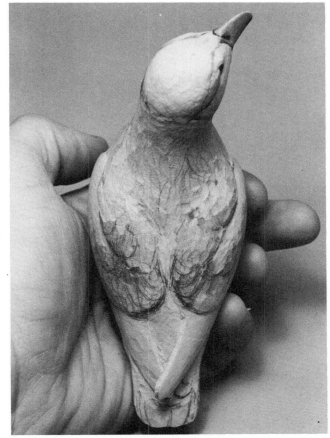

Bob begins landscaping the birds, finishing the feather groups.

should go from the head and slide along to the end of the tail without going down steps."

He comments on various parts of the anatomy. "There's usually more order to back feathers. I'll spend more time laying them out. The cape or back feathers are usually more defined as opposed to the breast, where the feathers are big and flat and fluffy."

The tail, however, requires a different strategy. "You don't want that too flat. That means you don't want to start out too thin. So I start out curving the top. I'll draw in the top feather and raise it by cutting the edge with a square-ended stone."

Bob depresses the Foredom foot pedal, but stops. "The wings come out from the body and hang back when the bird is relaxed. Otherwise they're tighter and further back." He inhales deeply. Speaking rapidly, he continues, "The wing has a double curve. After that's in position, you draw in the main feather groups. The primaries are the longest ones, the secondaries are where the color starts. The top three of

those are the tertials. These cover the secondaries. There are the greater wing coverts, the median wing coverts." He stops abruptly and returns to the puffin.

Wing feathers are not unlike tail feathers. They will have to be defined with definite edges. Yet Bob will still avoid sharp divisions. Many carvers will make stop cuts, which are straight-in penetrations made with a sharp tool to define an area that will be carved higher or lower than an adjacent one. Bob avoids stop cuts. "I don't like to make them because once you do, there's no changing your design. And if you should try, there could be a small line in the wood to contend with." What Bob uses is a small, thin stone that he has modified by bending slightly. He explains, "It's just enough so that one side is hitting the wood with each revolution. Believe it or not, it gives me more control and cuts faster." Without the stop cuts, then, he is "shaping feathers with one motion, eliminating the extra step of the stop cut."

Bob has also adapted a carbide coated disc, one

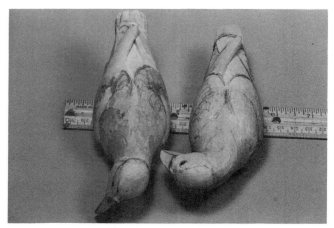

A comparison of two birds so far.

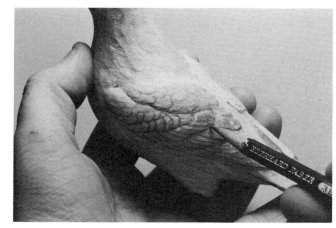

Sketching individual feathers.

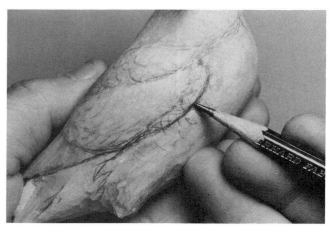

This wing will be partially tucked in. The lines will help Bob visualize how the wing will look.

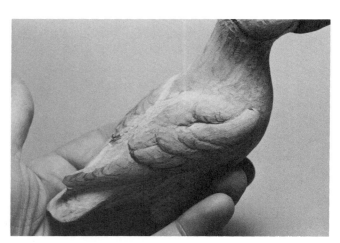

Final wing groupings: primaries, secondaries, and tertials.

adaptable to a grinding tool and only one inch in diameter, for feather definition. When run along a feather edge, it actually separates one feather from another, though not so deep as to weaken the strength of the wood.

Also useful for defining individual feathers, especially their edges, is what Bob calls a sanding stick. Its core is a ⅛-inch diameter steel rod, the top portion of which has been cut down its middle. A strip of sandpaper is then inserted into the slot, wrapped around the shaft, and held with a rubber band.

The burning pen is yet another tool Bob uses for defining feathers, particularly those on the tail and around the beak. The connection between this tool and bird carving goes back to New Mexico in the early 1960s. A minister named Jack Drake took an interest in carving birds. He made a connection between feather barbs and quills and the lines created with a tool that was little more sophisticated than a soldering iron. A waterfowl carver named Larry Hayden independently came up the idea in the early 1970s, and soon nearly all carvers were burning birds.

But carvers discovered they needed less heat than that given off by standard woodburning pens, which have made their way under Christmas trees for decades. They needed something to control the heat and consequently developed a primitive apparatus to do so. Instead of the small rheostat box featured with today's burning tools, they used a wooden box that had a socket on its top to accept a lightbulb. Different wattages dictated the amount of heat generated in the pen.

But even with the heat under control, the pen itself,

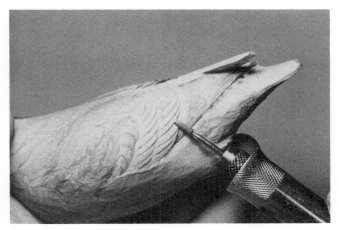

Cutting in, or layering, the feathers with a small, tapered stone that has a blunt end.

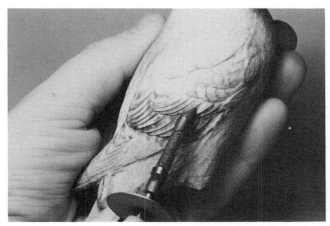

A burning pen called The Hot Tool cleans up the edges of the feathers, making them "crisp," Bob says.

which had a heavy steel tip, created lines too wide and too deep. Today, bird carvers are going after realism by burning a closer approximation of the actual feather. To do this, many burn a minimum of 80 barb lines to an inch, and at least one carver has attained over 220 lines per inch.

To make this all possible, burning tools or pens were developed without light bulbs and with finer tips. In the last few years, manufacturers of "burners," as they are known among carvers, have offered a variety of tips. Some are skewed; some have long, thin tips for getting under the long primary feathers that extend off the back of a duck; some are blunt-ended; and at least one ends in a small circle.

A multiline burning pen with razor-edge elements was in vogue among a few bird carvers. The design was rejected, however, because the lines it made were stiff-looking and too precise. Carvers wanted twists, curves, and S-curves to their barb lines, with barbs coming together at their ends, especially on waterfowl, or splitting apart randomly.

Burning tools have such names as The Detailer, Detail Master, Super Pro, Feather Etcher, and The Hot Tool.

Though Bob prefers what is described as "stoning" to burning, he will resort to a burning tool for defining wing or tail feathers. He admits that some other feathers, those around the beak, for example, are too fine to be achieved with a grinding bit.

When burning in detail, Bob indicates that feather separations are barely visible at the base of the tail and at the base of the secondary feathers. In fact, one feather can barely be differentiated from another.

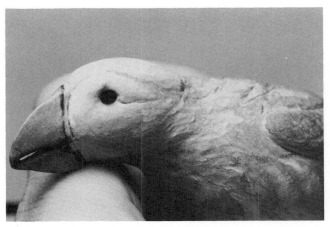

Feather groupings on the neck and how they look with a stretched-out neck.

To set in the glass eyes, Bob first drills through the head, fills the cavity with spackling paste, and then sets the glass eyes into the paste. He uses 4-millimeter brown eyes.

Using Duro two-part epoxy, Bob creates the eye-rings. The tool used is a dental instrument for modeling wax impressions.

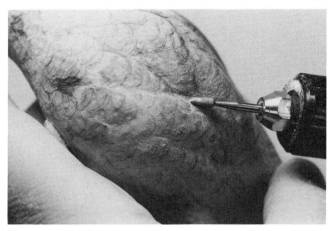

With a small, ball-nosed stone, Bob cuts in the breast feathers, defining each with a soft edge.

At the base of the puffin mandibles is a soft, fleshy area. Bob also recreates this with Duro epoxy.

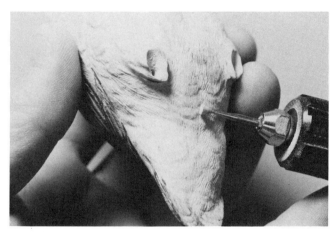

A small, inverted cone-shaped grinding stone creates the body texture.

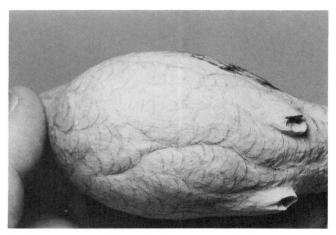

Back to landscaping, Bob puts the feather tracts on the lower parts of the birds.

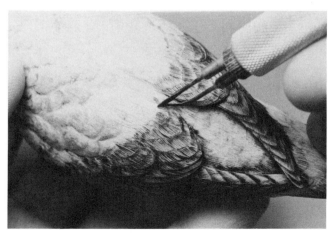

Bob burns all the flight feathers, which he describes as "stiffer, stronger feathers." The body feathers will be textured with a stone.

They at first blend into each other and then spread out into individual feathers.

He also points out that texture that has been stoned in holds paint better. Stoning—detailing the surface with an aluminum oxide stone—ripples the wood, making it conducive to accepting paint. Burning, on the other hand, sears the wood, creating a rather flat surface.

Bob concedes that there is more to burning than just using it as a substitution for stoning. Finely done, close-together burn lines will appear, microscopically and cross-sectionally, as if they were minute points on a saw blade, or hills and valleys that rise to points or descend into sharp grooves. Carvers have found that fine burning with a sharp tip creates a multi-beveled, reflective surface, which will reflect light, shadow, and color, all combining to achieve a liveliness in the carving. Despite the overlap of paint, these hills and valleys will create an illusion of softness. Grooves with planes between will create a hard look. This helps explain why granite looks hard and hair or feathers look soft. Bob's burning strategy is to burn fine lines close together.

"You notice how I crossed the primaries on one of the three clay models." He has switched the Foredom off and removed his goggles. "I do a lot of birds like that," he explains. "It's not that I cross them for any reason in particular. But it does break up the bird, and it gives a little more design." He does not do this on all his birds. A notable exception is his tree sparrow.

He discusses his notion of feather inserts and the loss of continuity. "I don't like inserting feathers any more than I like to cut a head off, turn it, and glue it back on the body. I think you lose the feel of the bird, the continuity. One block of wood feels better to me than putting things together. But if I have to, I may slide a single set of primaries and secondaries under the scapulars." He did this for a mantling kestrel completed two months before he started the puffins.

"But if you're doing bigger pieces, you have to insert." He introduces John Scheeler's name. "Scheeler got away with it." Scheeler, who died in 1987, had been an icon to professional bird carvers, leaving footprints across the entire development of bird art from its aerial theatrics to its serious poses. "But Scheeler did it well. There aren't many people who can do inserts well."

He adds that he had to insert the thigh feathers of his burrowing owls. The bodies were jelutong, and the thighs, with stiff copper wire acting as armatures, were shaped from an epoxy putty.

He makes a stoic face as he holds up one of the puffins again. He leans back in the chair. "Well, its not my original idea of a plastic block, but it's shaping up." He has 66 days to finish if he is to enter them in the World Competition.

East to Maryland

Bob talks of the children and of anticipated projects before he leaves for Ocean City, Maryland. It is 8:15 on the evening of April 23. It will take nearly eighteen hours to reach the resort town on Maryland's Eastern Shore.

A suitcase has been packed, the puffins and their base rest in an open box of Styrofoam, and his paints and dental tools have been laid out in the back of the Chevy van, which is outfitted with a bed, captain's chairs, and carpeting. Bob won't be going alone, for his brother-in-law, Blake Woods, has offered to help with the driving.

Bob says good-bye to each of the children, gives Jody a kiss, and hurries out the rear door. Hoisting himself up into the driver's seat for the first part of the journey, he says he will do most of the mileage at least until daylight of the next day. By daybreak, when he will be into Pennsylvania, he hopes to be working on the puffins in the rear of the van. Assembly must be completed on the sand eels, and the birds still need

their coats of white primer. He now has approximately thirty-six hours to finish the composition before it can be entered into The World Competition.

The engine console has a place for a coffee mug, and Jody has given him fresh coffee. He squirms a bit, finding a comfortable position in the seat before he attaches his seatbelt. The night is clear, and the Fox River, which he passes over on his way to the Illinois Tollway, reflects the moonlight.

He relates the events of the last several days. "I just didn't sleep. Well, one night I slept two hours, four another night. That was out of four days. But I had to get most of it finished. I'm pretty sure I'll sell it at The World if it doesn't win."

As he approaches the Tollway, he says, "I had a preconceived notion of what a puffin looks like, and I found out what I thought they looked like is completely different from what they really look like. It was frustrating trying to decipher from so many different photos. So I had to concentrate on one or two

To make the feet, each copper toe has to be stapled onto a piece of balsa wood.

as reference." He explains further. "There were so many things going on in all the shots, it was just confusing me. Normally, I go with my instincts on a carving, what I remember in my head. But in this case, I saw that my instincts hadn't been quite right."

Other frustrations emerged. "I had been spending a lot of time on the heads and beaks. But I decided to turn the other way and work on the bodies for a while." As he starts to merge into 290, which will, in part, take him on the outskirts of Chicago, he says, "You tend to be so critical, and you don't see what you're really doing. You have to get away from an area and come back to it and look at it with a different perspective." He brings the van up to sixty miles an hour. "I just had to stop to work on other things and make some money. It was frustrating having to stop and then try to get started again."

He recounts the trouble he had making the feet for the puffins. These he made out of copper wire. For the webbing between the toes, he used a two-part epoxy. To do this, he first put aluminum foil on the rock with

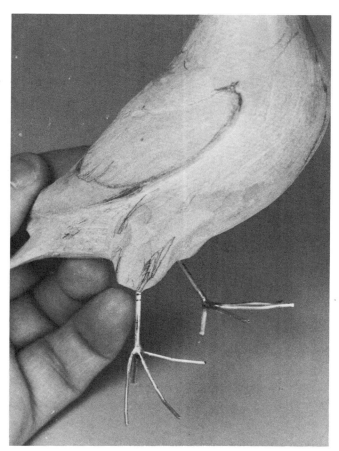

The soldered-together feet.

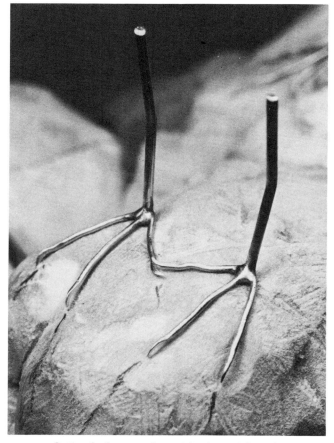

Getting the feet to conform to the shape of the rock.

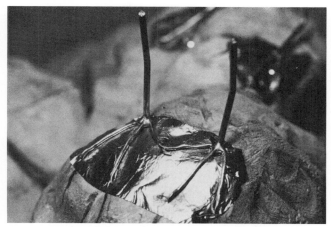

Glued-down aluminum foil will allow the webs, which will be made from epoxy, to conform but not stick to the rock. The bird and its feet can then be removed.

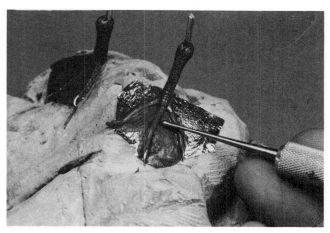

Modeling the epoxy webbing.

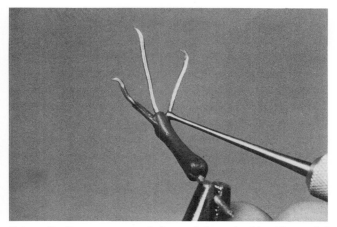

Bob applies Duro epoxy to each foot and shapes it with a blunt-ended burnishing tool.

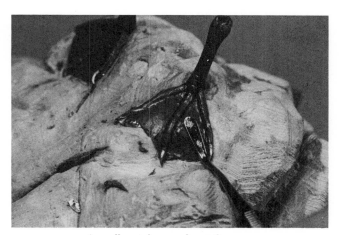

A small spatula spreads out the epoxy.

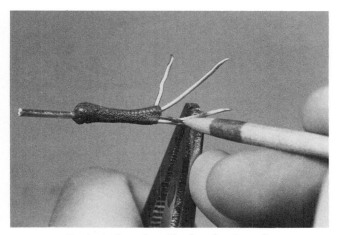

Putting in the scales with a hypodermic needle.

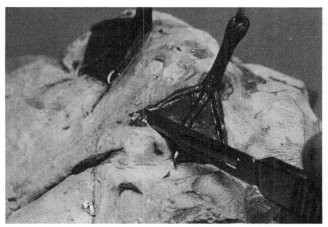

A scalpel cleans up the areas around the toes.

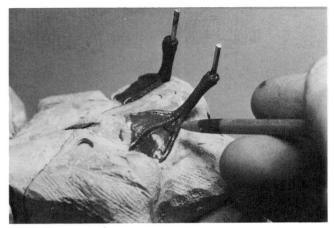

A hypodermic needle set into a dowel makes the scales in the semi-wet epoxy.

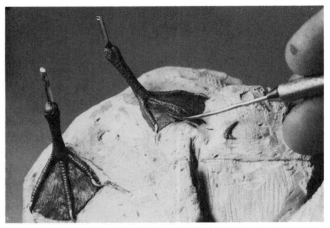

Bob drags this bent dental instrument across the webs to give them a wrinkled look.

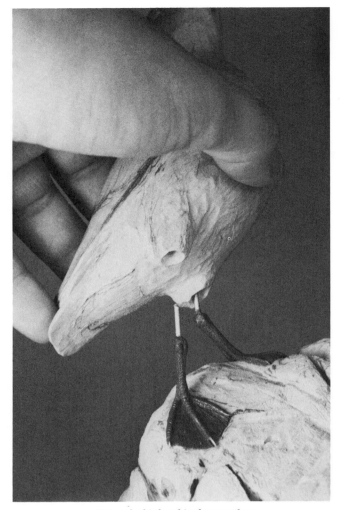

Fitting the bird and its feet together.

wood glue to hold it in place. He put the toes on top of that and built up the epoxy webbing in between the toes. He explains, "When I was done, it conformed perfectly to the rock. The epoxy stuck to the foil and the wood glue let go. Then I trimmed the edge of the foil around the feet and I was done. It's a real nice way of getting the feet to conform to the rock."

But the feet presented other problems. At one point, the epoxy was getting unworkable by the time he was ready to do the final shaping. He had to tear away what he had applied and start again. Then he had to stop to have some photographs of him taken by a local newspaper photographer. Again he had to tear away the epoxy he had applied. He shrugs indignantly. "I keep a block of wood on the floor that I rest my feet on. I dropped a puffin foot and thought it had fallen behind the block, so I rolled the block over toward

me. It rolled over the foot and crushed it," he says with a forced smile.

He remembers one step that was problem-free — making the scales on the feet. He used a hypodermic needle pressed into the putty he had put around the copper armatures.

The radio is playing an Elvis Presley song. Inhaling after taking the last mouthful of coffee, he says, "I had originally carved the puffin lips where the mandibles come together. But I cut those off and redid them with epoxy. That gave a nice fleshy look." He remembers it was a Duro product. "I used epoxy to form the bony eye ring. That worked real well," he says loudly.

The eels presented a problem. How was he to insert them in the one bird's mouth? One solution that came to mind was to cut the lower mandible off, lay the eels on top of that, and glue the lower jaw back in place.

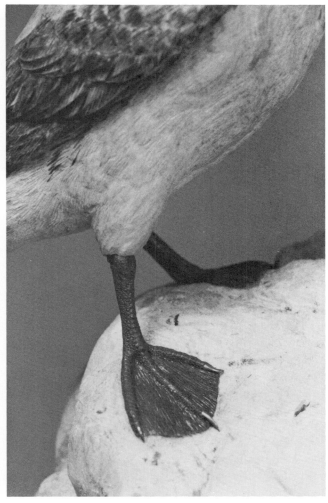

The textured bird and the feathers around the feet are completed. Bob will use very little epoxy to fill the area between the feathers and feet.

The gessoed puffins.

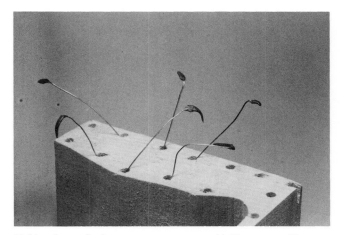

Making the sand eels on copper armatures with Duro epoxy. These are the tail halves.

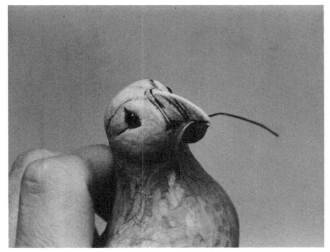

The sand eel wires are pulled from either side through the beak to give a tight fit and the illusion of a continuous eel. This is done before the epoxy is dry.

He decided, however, to make the eels in two parts. They were formed of epoxy putty molded around copper wires. These, in turn, projected on either side of the beak, giving the illusion of a continuous eel. But they have yet to be put into the puffin's mouth.

As Blake sits back with his eyes closed, Bob says, lowering his voice, "I've been continuously concerned that I get done on time, but I didn't cut any corners. I didn't really want to." He allows nearly a minute of silence before he speaks again. "I have a chance of winning, or a chance of selling it." He frowns. "It's hard putting so much time into a piece when you don't have it sold already." He exhales deeply. "I hope someday to be far enough ahead that I won't have to think about money at all."

He tunes the radio to a string piece with vocal accompaniment. "The puffins are a competition piece all right. I don't like it as much as my original idea of the birds in a block of plastic, but I think it has what it takes." He pauses before saying, "That depends on what it's up against. But it should be good enough to justify a win."

He reflects for a few moments. The news has come on the radio. "The painting is what's going to make it or break it, with just two main colors, black and white. Those are the two toughest colors to deal with, especially the black."

He does not know what any other carver is going to enter in the miniature division. He is certain that there will be other puffin compositions, as well as some gulls, terns, and perhaps cormorants. His friend Barth has been working on a pair of flying terns. He does not know that Barth will occupy the room next to his in the Ocean City hotel where they will both work on the painting of their pieces.

He has crossed into Indiana on Interstate 90. He feels like talking about competitions. He cannot accurately tally how many he has been in. He figures, though, that it has been over fifty. But he is critical of competitions. His tone gets sharp when he says, "It's hard to judge. It shouldn't be done in the first place. What right do I have to tell you whether you carved a good bird or not? It just doesn't make a whole lot of sense."

Still, he is not prepared to stop competing. In fact, he has even acted as judge at fifteen competitions. "It's fun," he says of judging, then, more hesitantly, says, "It's hard sometimes."

He explains that at most competitions there are three judges for each division. "I guess three's the best number so far. They need an odd number in case two get deadlocked. And one isn't enough to judge. So three is the next odd number."

Bob has his own criteria for judging bird carvings. He uses a three-point system with one point each for composition, overall design, and accuracy. He says it is easier that way, that there is an odd number to deal with.

They have come as far as Ohio, still on Interstate 80 and 90, just south of Toledo. He says that the competitions are meeting places for carvers who are his friends. And they are places where he can win money. His mourning doves earned him $5,000 in 1985. "The purchase award at The World is OK if you're the guy getting purchased. It's not bad for miniatures. But the guys who do the life-size pieces may have to spend too

much time on a piece." Barth had spent nearly a year designing and carving a snowy owl and bonaparte gull for the 1985 World Championships. It was given the Best-in-World title and Barth took home $20,000. Bob had entered his three burrowing owls that same year.

Larry Barth's owl and gull started as clay models, though sketches preceded that to establish the pose of the owl and its prey, which was held under one foot. Barth says he was looking for a gesture in the clay, while surface details would be worked out in the wood.

He saw the lakeshore setting as one that a snowy owl might visit on its way south during the winter months, and he traveled to Lake Erie, not far from his home, to research the habitat. What he decided on was a base that would capture the essence of a beach. There would be grasses, a sizeable piece of driftwood actually taken from Lake Erie, and a surface of sand that gave an expansive feeling. What he arrived at was a wooden dune coated with sand that feathered out and away from the two birds.

Bob has misgivings about the miniature division at the World Championships. "They state half scale or less. The carving can't exceed eight inches." His puffins stand about 5 inches in height. "But you can't have anything less than four inches in length. So that squeezes you into a mold. And there goes the art." He accelerates slightly. "I can buy the eight-inch maximum height. If you took a half-size eagle and compared it to a half-size cardinal, it wouldn't be fair." A typical eagle carved half scale would be about sixteen inches in height. A half-scale cardinal would be one-quarter that size. "I guess the half-scale thing is a good idea. Otherwise people would do nine-tenths scale. Or they'd be doing microminiatures. Those are real tiny and don't justify the prize money."

Blake offers to do the rest of the driving if Bob wants to sleep. Bob answers that he does. He asks Blake for another five minutes. He wants to talk more about miniatures. He says he keeps most of his birds within the limits of 4 and 8 inches. But he foresees problems for the 1987 World Championships. The theme will be songbirds. Many popular songbirds are less than 8 inches in length. Half that size would disqualify that species.

Bob sleeps for two and a half hours. They have just entered Pennsylvania. Sitting in the passenger seat, he blinks back sleep. "You know what I'd really like?" he says, trying to release a yawn. "Well, my first choice would be to work when I want and do what I want. My second choice would be to be under contract to someone with a weekly paycheck. With an artist, it's feast or famine. But it would be really nice to have three or four days a week for myself where I could spend time to do what I want for me, for gifts, for my collection."

Yawning, he continues, "I wouldn't want all my time tied up with one guy. But I would want the security. If someone told me what to do it would be drudgery, it wouldn't be a bit fun."

He talks about the people who buy his birds. What he calls his "good birds" go to a great variety of buyers. Bob refers to a husband and wife who bought nine good birds. He is an airline pilot, she a physical therapist.

"A lot of dentists seem to enjoy this kind of work. Other carvers will tell you the same thing. I sell very few good birds through galleries. And I don't do consignment work."

Blake asks him if he takes telephone orders. "If you asked for a cardinal," Bob answers, "I'd probably tell you I wouldn't want to do one." He coughs out a laugh. "I would either be that honest or I'd tell you it would be a long time because I'm not inclined to do cardinals now. Well, I might tell the person what I felt like doing in the near future or else I'll call when I have something. Very few people go away unhappy. But I will tell you I don't enjoy doing ducks. Oh, I guess if you called for one, I'd try to talk you into something else. I try to make everybody happy, but most of all myself."

The sun starts to emerge above the horizon. Bob tells Blake he wants to work on the puffins. He stretches and snuggles back into the seat, as if resisting going to the back of the van. "People ask me to justify what I do as art," he says, swinging his legs around. "I may tell them to look up some definitions of art," he says gruffly. He seems to be processing his thoughts, saying nothing for nearly a full minute. Finally, and slowly, he continues. "Although I've had to learn how to work a piece of wood, which can be considered a part of a craft, I consider my ideas that come from inside of me as art. But there's good art and bad art. When I started, I was nothing more than a bird carver, a craftsman, whatever. But I was blessed with a talent. Yes, there's a certain amount that has to be learned, but that's true of any art form, whether you're a stone carver, a moviemaker, a photographer, a painter. Working with just tools is a craft. Taking

pictures for no reason or taking pictures of your family isn't art. But when the person tries to produce a feeling, a mood, you turn to art. It's that thing that's coming from inside of you."

He relates these notions to his bird carvings. "I feel ideas, shapes, things I want to show people that come from deep inside of me. This whole field started as a craft or folk art, but it's developed into a fine art form."

Wildlife art has had a relatively short history. "Critics say it's a copy of something that's already there, but I don't know what that means." He moves to the back of the van with three quick strides. "Even an illustrator who just painted a picture of a bird might be a craftsman, but if he paints what he feels, that makes him an artist." There is impatience in his voice. "It's the approach that counts."

On the stationary table, Bob lays out puffin number three, made starkly white by the primer, and the sand eel halves. He also puts tweezers and dental probes on the table.

Holding one of the sand eels, he says that some critics claim that birds assembled from inserts and separate pieces, such as feet, keep bird carving from being an art form. Still holding the sand eel, he says, "This one-piece art doesn't make sense. How can it be when I have to be a painter, a metal sculptor, a wood sculptor, and who knows what else I might have to use in doing a piece? I had to sculpt the feet, didn't I? Why would anyone not want to accept that?"

The sun begins to penetrate the van through the windows. Bob is able to work without the overhead light on. The sand eels have been glued into place with a two-part epoxy. He says he has been groping for new compositions. He thinks a future project will be a painting with a carving emerging from the canvas. He had seen a painting of a hawk over a ravine. It was filled with vegetation, he recalls. But a ravine can't be carved, he points out, though it can be painted. The carved hawk would somehow have to emerge from the canvas, he says. Breathing heavily, he explains, "You'd still be able to enjoy the sculpted part and enjoy the background. That would be an interesting mix. I've never seen that, but people have told me it's been done."

He asks Blake how he feels and starts to prepare the paints he has brought along. He will paint only the sand eels. "Some carvers have tried carving habitat in a wood like walnut. Larry did that with a kingfisher looking into walnut water. I've seen that kind of thing at shows for years. Years ago I saw a goose in carved water." He frowns. "It doesn't do to me what it used to do. There are very few new ideas anymore," he says precisely. "I'm looking at the whole process. I started out as a simple bird carver, and I'm growing. All aspects are changing."

He stares out the back window for about a minute. He tells of teaching a five-day seminar at Jim Sprankle's home on Kent Island, Maryland. Sprankle is a waterfowl carver who added to his income by giving intensive carving seminars to a limit of ten students per five-day session. Sprankle teaches duck carving and painting while guest instructors teach their own specialties. Larry Barth was also there as a teacher.

Bob had his students carving and painting a goldfinch. Barth had his ten students working in clay. They had a choice of creating a cardinal, a saw-whet owl, or a kestrel. Bob recalls that one of the nights they were there Barth worked on sketches of a peregrine falcon chasing shorebirds and a goshawk chasing a grouse. There were some twenty pages of drawings. Most were accurately rendered. Bob daubs some paint on the sand eels and says, "Few can sketch like Larry and make it right the first time." But Larry wants to carve, not paint canvas. He's a true artist who does what he wants when he wants.

"I can't afford to put the amount of time he puts into a piece. Maybe someday I will when I don't have to consider paying the bills next week. Money for me comes in and it's gone again. Now Larry works to that

final point where he can't do anything else to make the piece look better. I envy him for that. He's been working on a piece for The World show doing a pair of flying terns. He has a real good chance of winning. That's $20,000 up front."

Bob's face shows signs of pressure as the inside of the van receives the light of the morning. There is a Dali-esque incongruity as he sits, in a crouch, working on puffins at sixty-five miles per hour.

His thoughts are still sharp, despite days with little sleep. A stretch of grooved highway makes the puffin with the sand eels vibrate slightly. He decides to announce his plans for the summer. He will be going to Alaska for the last week in June and the first week in July. He calls it a field trip, a time to watch birds without the company of his family. He says he needs fresh ideas. Accompanying him will be Frank Russell, a friend from Vermont, and John Felsing, a wildlife painter. A car will be available to them once they arrive. There will also be a house to stay in, though the three plan to spend most of the time camping.

Having found a reasonable round-trip air fare of $430, Bob thinks there will be few other expenses. He expects to spend one week in Denali National Park and another week on the Kenai Peninsula. He covers a yawn with the hand holding the brush. He offers a serious theory concerning the extended day in Alaska. "We'd really get three weeks because the sun doesn't go down until about midnight, and it's back up at about 3:30 A.M." He giggles, "I'll just forget about sleep."

The World Championships

Bob and his brother-in-law arrive in Ocean City shortly after one on Thursday afternoon. Ocean City is a retreat for tourists with beach frontage on either side of a long peninsula that extends twenty-five miles along the coast of Maryland, with the Atlantic Ocean on one side, and the Assawoman Bay on the other. The main road is called the Coastal Highway, and in Ocean City it is crossed by 146 streets. The plentiful bars and restaurants provide nightlife, and hotels rise upwards to twenty stories.

The World Championship Wildfowl Carving Competition is scheduled for three days, April 25 through 27, at the sizeable Convention Hall on 40th Street.

Bob and Blake will stay at The Castle in the Sand Motel until Sunday evening. It is almost directly across from Convention Hall.

The furniture has been shifted to make the desk into a worktable. Bob has set up a pair of high-intensity lamps that he clamped to the edge of the desktop. The stark white puffins are on their habitat, a hairdryer to warm-dry the thin layers of paint he will apply is next

to the rock, and next to that is what Bob calls his wet palette.

At one time Bob mixed his colors only on glass with white paper underneath—the glass being a smooth and easily cleaned surface, the white imitating the color of the paint primer. He still uses that method, but he has added the wet palette, which consists of a special paper that is placed on a foam pad. The foam is soaked, and the paper wicks up the water. The biggest advantage to the wet palette, Bob feels, is that it allows paint to stand for days without drying out. This is a long time, considering that the watered-down acrylic paints he uses can dry by themselves in less than an hour.

Exterior painters of the 1920s mural movement were influential in hastening the need for more durable paints than were available. Linseed oil, the vehicle for oil paints, is chemically unstable and becomes porous. A breakdown occurs within the paint, and a process takes place not unlike the one on the surface of the aging human body. The plastic acrylic paints

Bob working in an Ocean City, Maryland, motel room. He must finish painting his puffins before he can enter them in the 1986 World Championship Wildfowl Carving Competition.

resist this and provide a cohesiveness to the surfaces to which they are applied. Acrylics also dry far more quickly than oil paints, which can take days. Bob has approximately eighteen hours to paint the puffins.

He has been squeezing his colors onto the wet palette. Without stopping, he says he changed the surface of the rock from what he had envisioned in the clay model. He decided to have a chipped and broken surface. He compares it to a fallen cliff face.

"As I worked it, I decided to make it rougher, giving it more angles, which gave it more character. I've seen rock like that. It was just more interesting. And I could give it a distinct grain like real rock."

Putting together three different pieces of jelutong as if they were slices of bread and gluing them, Bob ran their grains vertically. Once tightly bonded, the laminated piece was hollowed out from its bottom to relieve the stresses of expansion and contraction and to keep it from cracking. This is always a possibility for wood that has not been thoroughly seasoned, a fact woodworkers usually learn too late.

He then rough-shaped the wood with a large carbide cutter and Foredom. To create the look of grain and a chipped surface, he went over the wood with a chisel and broke away pieces. He then took a defuzzing pad, a spongy material held at the end of a steel shaft, to the surface. This, he says, softened the rock slightly.

The last step was to seal the rocks with a lacquer sealer and a mix of gesso and gray acrylic paint. The first application was a very pale gray, which he stippled. This is a process of using a dry, stiff brush to

The wet palette that Bob sometimes uses when painting birds that may take a long time to complete. A foam rubber pad is soaked with water and a special palette paper is applied over the pad. The paper wicks up the water and prevents the paint from drying out.

Acrylic blobs of paint on the wet palette.

Bob chose jelutong for the puffin base, which was made up of two 4-inch-thick pieces and one 2-inch-thick piece. Bob has the grain running up and down. The boards will be epoxied together.

Bob hollows the bottom of the rock to reduce the risk of cracking and splitting later on.

press the paint on the surface. After the first coat dried, Bob applied a second coat of gesso with more gray in it. After the second coat dried, he put on a third coat of what he describes as a "brownish black, muddy glaze made up of burnt umber and ivory black." He made the third coat watery so it would get down into the cracks of the surface. The final step was to go over the painted surface with a defuzzing pad and remove some of the medium gray areas of the second coat. At that point, Bob explains, there were three colors showing. But he did come back with small quantities of a mossy green color and some yellow. These would help make the black birds stand out in even greater contrast to the gray rocks.

His paints are ready to be applied to the three puffins. "This was a different kind of bird for me," he says, applying a coat of black over the back of number one bird. "Puffin feathers are different, hairlike, with almost squared-off edges on their bottoms. Not a lot of definition to them." He is quiet for a few moments, the black color going on quickly. "On the specimen, the feathers looked clipped off. I tried to get that on the breast and belly feathers. And I tried to get a lot more feathers on the birds when I was landscaping them without getting too lumpy and bumpy.

"I guess puffin feathers have to be more rigid and tighter because of their diving. So I didn't want to get real fluffy with them. Most of the time I deliberately go overboard on landscaping. It's fun to do, but for puffins I thought it was more important to keep that down a little bit."

Trial-positioning the birds on the rock.

Another view of the composition.

Bob says that Larry Barth is in the room next to his painting his pair of flying terns. He has told Bob that he will stop by within the hour to give encouragement.

"I apply black and then white, and then I'll apply color on the feet and beaks as soon as I can. I guess I can mentally balance all the colors out and see how they relate to each other. A lot of guys carving do one small place at a time. But it's obvious I'm not doing that."

The explanation for his procedure lies, he says, with blending. Rarely are there sharp divisions between colors on a bird. One of the reasons for this is that the barbs of feathers of one color will splay out and run into an adjoining color. The eye sees a blend. Another reason is that colors will vary in value or intensity, which also gives the illusion that there are few sharp color boundaries.

Grinding off excess wood on the rock. Bob uses a round Karbide Kutzall that eliminates sharp edges.

Bob chisels sections of the rock and lets them chip away. This, he says, gives the rock a grainy look.

If Bob were to paint one feather at a time, without a base coat of color, he would have difficulty balancing different color areas. "The color you're applying might not be right, though it will look fine by itself or against a white background like on a piece of glass over a paper towel. But when you get it next to another color on a bird, it might be way off. By having all the basic colors there, even if they're not quite right, I get a better feel for the different values I'll apply later."

Finding different intensities is important for the puffins, Bob points out. If he did not mix different shades of black, he would have a solidly colored bird. In fact, he did not take his black directly from the tube but instead mixed it with a color called burnt umber. "A warm black is what I used for the base coat. This was ivory black and then burnt umber to warm it up. The outer edges of puffin feathers tend to be a cooler black. For that I'll use a Mars black. The white is

The finished, but unpainted, rock.

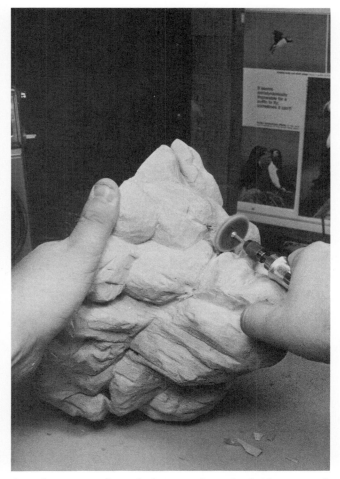

A rough contour sanding pad takes away sharp edges but leaves enough of the grainy look.

The puffins on the rock.

Brass leg armatures have replaced the dowels.

titanium white and a little bit of burnt umber and yellow ochre to dull it up a bit. But the white on puffins is quite bright. Maybe I'll use some straight titanium to give that effect. The beaks will be basically cadmium red and cadmium yellow."

Bob stops painting so that he can gesture at the backs of each bird. He feels it is important to justify the textures and shapes of the birds. Only the flight and tail feathers were burned, he explains. The rest of each body was stoned using a small one-eighth-inch-diameter stone shaped like an inverted cone. He did each pair of primaries differently: number one bird has its primaries comfortably crossed; number three bird, with its catch of sand eels, has only the tips crossed; and number two bird, who reaches out for the prize, did not have them crossed at all, though one wing is dropped slightly and pulled out from the body.

Returning to the painting, he says that at one time he would take his paints directly from a tube, perhaps varying them with an umber. Now, however, he enjoys using different combinations of colors when mixing. Since the human eye is not built for spectral analysis, the same color sensation can be created by different stimuli. With paints, this means that a mix of colors such as red and green will appear as yellow, though it does not contain light of the wave lengths corresponding to yellow. Any color sensation, then, can be duplicated by mixing various quantities of the three primary colors, which are red, green, and blue.

Bob has found that the browns he wants can be gotten by mixing reds and greens. Many painters, however, use tube colors called burnt umber and burnt sienna for their browns.

"Color theory depends on what school you're from," he says as he puts color on the puffin beaks. Some carvers use what has been called a limited or muted palette. For one carver, Bob's friend Ernest Muehlmatt, this would consist of only four colors—ultramarine blue, burnt umber, yellow ochre, and burnt sienna. If Muehlmatt required a red, he would open a tube of cadmium red. Many of Muehlmatt's birds have earth tones or brownish plumage. Much of that he achieves with a mix of burnt umber and ultramarine blue.

"Most carvers," Bob says, "start out with earth colors like burnt umber and burnt sienna and try to find what they need right out of the tubes rather than going to the trouble of mixing." His hands are starting to spot with the paints he is using.

"I wish I knew what I was doing when I paint." He forces a laugh. "Seriously, how do I tell someone how to paint? I take a little bit of this and that and, if it doesn't look right, I take more of this and that. A lot of this is instinct. If it looks good, it is good. I guess that's why I don't paint two birds of the same species the same way. I just don't know all the color theory, so I want to trust the way I feel at the time I paint."

Blake, who has been sleeping, swings his legs off the bed and offers to bring in coffee. Bob waves a paintbrush in a gesture of goodbye after he points out where the keys to the van were left. It is getting close to five, and Bob says he'll have dinner with friends. He thinks he can take himself away from the puffins for a few hours.

Bob does not return until nine in the evening, having left the room at six-thirty. He now has eleven hours to finish the puffins.

It is fifteen minutes past midnight, and Bob's face shows fatigue. Though his sentences will turn to fragments as the late hour turns to early morning, he wants to talk about techniques.

For one, each of the puffins has its own holding device. Decoy carvers often employ a keel or scrap of wood temporarily glued to the bottom of a duck, allowing the wood scrap, and not the bird, to be held. Bob has devised a holding fixture that is nothing more than a dowel with a screw epoxied into one end. The threaded part is then inserted into the bottom of the bird. After the painting is finished, ordinary spackle is used to fill the hole which in turn is painted over.

Spackle has another use. Bob sets the glass eyes of the birds into it. Glass eyes originated in taxidermy work, and birds' eyes can be purchased from taxidermy suppliers. The use of these realistic glass eyes on carvings is relatively new, for old-time decoy makers either carved or painted in the eyes, used tacks, or applied buttons. Today nearly all bird carvers and decoy makers use glass, though there are a variety of techniques for setting them into the wood. Some carvers use clay as a positioning base and then seal over that with a two-part epoxy or wood fill. Others use only a wood filler. But Bob apparently is the only carver who uses spackle.

When he cuts in the eye holes with a cone-shaped stone, he makes a continuous channel instead of shallow depressions. He then fills this through-cavity with spackle. When the eyes are set into either side of the head, he can get them perfectly balanced, for pushing one in will squeeze the other out. However, he limits this to small birds such as the puffins. He feels a large bird filled with a water-based material such as spackle would loosen up eventually. Also, with small species, the spackle that squeezes out around the eyes can be shaped to make eyelids.

"Jelutong is very porous," he offers out of nowhere. "The pores are very visible on the wood," he says, adding that they will show through even heavily applied paint. But when sanding the surface, the pores become filled with minute particles of sanding dust. "I want to leave that dust where it is," he says. "I'll use a rotary bristle brush to remove some of the roughness left by the texturing process, but not enough to lift the dust from the pores."

He remembers to explain that he does not put gesso immediately onto the wood after the texturing and sanding. The wood is first sealed with a mix of two parts satin lacquer and one part lacquer thinner. Fast drying, it leaves no brush marks, and it soaks evenly into the wood.

The puffins are completely covered with the blacks and whites, though the blacks have a grayish cast. The coats he has applied have been greatly thinned out with water. These go on as cellophane-thin washes. He talks about color transitions, whether between the whites and blacks of the puffins or between similar colors. He calls his method a wet-on-wet technique. It allows colors to blend into each other without sharp transitions. The trick, he says, is to keep the bird fairly wet when applying colors. A wet surface will have adjacent colors flow into each other at their boundaries.

He talks about different light sources and their effects on different surfaces. "Take a study skin and put it under incandescent light, which is your household bulb, and then under a cool fluorescent. The differences are extreme. Incandescent light projects a yellow tone. Fluorescents project blue or some cool color. So how do you decipher colors?" he asks.

It isn't easy to coax the answer out of him. Finally, as if annoyed with his own silence, he says, "I make my birds to look good under artificial light, basically incandescent. That's the way I look at the study skin. That's the way most art is displayed. From a single light source."

He tries to stifle a yawn and fails. "I paint transparently. That means I keep my colors thin. I let the gesso show through. To help create the colors. I don't like my pieces shown in daylight. Too much of the white would show through. Sure, I could paint over and over until I got a nice solid color over the gesso. But it sometimes gets too shiny."

Larry Barth has come through the glass doors. He has climbed over adjoining railings, for his balcony is next to Bob's on the third floor.

Twenty-eight years old, Barth is considered to be almost a supreme artist among bird carvers. With a unique background, Barth's formal training has given him what could be called a college degree in bird carving.

His interest in birds developed early, and during his first years in high school, he began to carve birds in a smooth, stylized fashion. In 1975 he enrolled at Carnegie-Mellon University's College of Fine Arts to pursue a career in illustration because, at that point, his carving did not seem to offer a feasible career.

The factor that would sway him toward carving birds professionally came during his freshman year of college while he was on a trip with his family that took him through Salisbury, Maryland. There, the Ward Foundation's Wildfowl Carving Exhibition, a fall show, was being held. He saw an entire convention hall of bird carvings, some similar to his own style, others highly detailed.

At the university, however, there were no courses on how to carve birds. But he managed to build a repertoire of artistic skills by studying design, composition, color, and anatomy. His senior-year thesis included a sculpture of great horned owls—an adult and two young. The same year, Barth entered the birds at the World Championship Competition, where it took second place in World Class Decorative Life-size. He graduated a week after the show and has been carving ever since.

He is young looking and studious, with a face that would seem to suggest a bird watcher—eager, sensitive, curious. He speaks with such erudition about birds and their counterparts in wood that many accept his words as gospel.

His home is in western Pennsylvania, where birds have great tracts of woods and banding stations exist. His living room is also his studio, in a house that was acquired in part by the sale of the great horned owls. What has also helped with the mortgage was the purchase award of $20,000 for his snowy owl and bonaparte's gull. He is hoping his terns will be equally rewarded.

Scrutinizing the puffins, Barth says, "What is it about Bob's work? How to sum it up. What I keep coming back to over and over again is personality. He's able to capture the personality of a bird. The work itself convinces you he knows what that bird looks like. You can tell that he knows the birds he's doing. He's sensitive to them. That comes through."

Barth continues the analysis, putting the words together. "He keys in on the subtleties that I always like to see. Say he were to carve five different sparrows—a song, a chipping sparrow, a field sparrow, a white-throated sparrow. I'm running out of sparrows," he says with a hesitant smile. "If he were to carve those, I would be able to identify them. You would see them all as different and identify them as species without his having even painted them. He wouldn't carve a generic sparrow and slap the different birds' paint jobs onto them. He would pick up a white-throated sparrow having such a massive head in proportion to its body. He'd catch that small-headedness of the tree sparrow. He's real good at getting the attitude and the essence of the species."

Barth refines the analysis. "Bob captures nothing of the bird's disposition, whether it's happy or not, but some birds just look happy, some have kind of a heavy-browed fierce look to them. He gets those consistently," he says persuasively.

Barth points out that the finish Bob puts on his birds is similar to the one he uses. "I found myself looking at a certain area and finding myself remembering doing that area, though I didn't actually do it. His finish is so similar to mine that I can practically remember having carved the bird myself. That's probably one of the reasons I enjoy his work so much. Technically we're keying in on the same things."

Barth seats himself on one of the unoccupied beds. Blake is on the other. His glasses seem to frame a pensive inner inquiry. He finds himself captured by detail, be it feather definition or plumage rendering. He argues that an almost inevitable process occurs. "Once you go to a certain level on one bird, there's no turning back. You find yourself feeling like you have to put that same degree of workmanship and thought into every bird you do. But I think it's human nature to go down that road. Yet, it doesn't have to, artistically."

He finds himself envying Bob's line of primitives. Bob nods in agreement. "Bob has a hard time some days wishing he was not doing them. But I almost envy him that outlet. It almost seems like it would be therapeutic to turn out a whole batch of birds in one day." Barth admits to frustration "putting all the detail into these birds." He adds, "Though with his decorative birds he may be looser and freer than I, he is no less precise.

"I think we complement each other, each drawing on the other's strengths. He's encouraged me, by example, to loosen up a little. There's a tendency for me to be too tight. Bob can stay loose without sacrificing what is essential."

Barth spends a few moments processing his thoughts. He switches his thoughts to artistry. "I also enjoy that Bob is thinking all the time. He's not blindly doing the same thing over and over again. He's concerned with the artistic direction of his own work and of bird carving in general. That kind of outlook is healthy." He rises from the bed. "It causes you to struggle with what you're really after. It's that internal conflict that an artist needs if he's going to grow. He has constantly to be trying to find his direction, though it doesn't mean he's lost or wallowing around. It's healthy to be questioning what we're doing."

He seeks his words more precisely. "It's not that he's found what sells, and doing that over and over again. He's doing new things. That's what I see as being needed."

"Five hours to The World," Bob says.

Barth says he can't stay much longer. It is three in the morning. His terns are nearly painted, though they have to be assembled in flight. Barth offers to stay a few minutes longer to talk briefly about competitions. He sees them, The World contest in particular, and the field of bird carving as inseparable. However, he believes strongly that there must be a shift, a moving on in the field. He suggests that what has already been accomplished is a foundation, but only that. There must be growth, even if it means moving away from the competitiveness.

Barth has a theory that says, in essence, that bird carving will recapitulate the history of art itself. He thinks that the same reenacting of the process is true for the individual artist and even for the competitions. He explains, "As you start out, you have to lay a foundation. You have to put in your apprenticeship, get ahold of the techniques, practice just to get to where you're familiar or good enough in the technical practice so that you can effectively and competently express your ideas. In our case, three dimensionally. There are a whole lot of skills to be mastered before you can get people to look at what you've done, whether your thinking is sound or not. You have to have the technical skills to back that up. I think that's what an individual artist has to do and I think that's what bird carving has been doing. I see bird carving as having gotten to a point where our technical skills are sufficient, and now it's time to start the artistic process. There are many who will say that's been happening all along. And there are those who will say that it hasn't evolved yet."

He asks for a moment to regroup his thoughts. The only sound is the hairdryer that hums incessantly as it dries the paints applied to the puffins.

"In my own case, I can say that I have gotten the techniques of bird carving under control. I don't need to be able to burn any finer. I don't need to paint any better. It doesn't mean I can paint perfectly. I've gotten to a point where I'm good enough that if I don't get any better at burning and painting and carving, that'll be okay. It's the ideas I want to focus on now."

Still, he hopes to better his techniques. "I should be able to notice an improvement in my future works. They should get technically a little better every time, but for the average person, there isn't going to be a tremendous jump in quality from one bird to another."

Barth smiles. He has made a new metaphorical breakthrough. "The techniques are on the back burner. They'll continue to simmer there. But when you get to a certain level, the last frontier is composition."

The puffins get progressively darker. Bob interjects the word sculpture. He seems too fatigued to generate complete sentences.

Picking up on this, Barth says, "For bird carving to make the jump from being called bird carving to sculpture, I think that's a mental jump more than a technical jump."

He speaks of his own evolution as an artist. His original interest in birds was their colors. That, he says, translated into two-dimensional work, which in turn moved him to three-dimensional art, where his interest manifested itself in shape and form, not necessarily colors. His last two major pieces, his snowy owl and bonaparte's gull, and his two common terns, are, he describes, "clean-lined and patternless. They are not heavily vermiculated birds like woodcocks that used to be my favorite kind of bird – brown, very complicated, complex plumage. That's changed to birds like terns and snowy owls where you don't have the patterns camouflaging the form.

"The terns are really no different from any of the birds I've been doing for years as far as the finish. It's the presentation that I'd like to think makes the piece look different." He describes its pedestal as being a tall but narrow square-sided block painted black, with a suggestion of waves seen far away carved on the top of it. "You have built into that pedestal a classic sculptural presentation. It's already on a pedestal whether you put it on a card table or another pedestal in a museum or art gallery."

The base, Barth says, was designed with minimal detail and clean lines. "It doesn't get bogged down in all the trappings that are so easy to get mixed up with in bird carvings." Some of these trappings have included not only stones, grass, leaves, branches, pine needles, snow, mud, and sand, but also dragonflies and even houseflies. Barth says, "There's nothing wrong with doing leaves, branches, stones." He is interrupted by Bob calling out rocks. Barth adds sand with a slight laugh. "To step back one year to the snowy owl, there was sand and grass and all the components that are real typical to a bird carving. But again I'd like to think the presentation of those elements was what made it different.

"Bird carving is incredibly bogged down with techniques, because there is so much involved in making things in three dimensions," Barth says. "Two-dimensionally, you can sit down and draw a bird, and people know exactly what you're thinking. On paper you can do that in moments. In the loosest three-dimensional material, which is clay, it would take you much longer to achieve that same level of refinement and definition, but certainly not as long as it would take you were you working wood.

"That's inherent in the three-dimensional process, the time it takes to develop detail and precision. You can get so totally immersed in that, you can't see your way past all the details." He pauses, as if preparing himself for a pronouncement. He says, finally, "I think that carving has gone as far as it needs to go with detail for detail's sake. It must now deal with the foundational considerations of design and composition."

Bob, who is still painting the puffins, says, in effect, that this is not the case with waterfowl.

Barth nods a barely noticeable agreement. "I see the decoratives and the decoys getting further and further away from each other each year. They have a common ancestor, but I wonder if they've evolved to the point of being totally separate species. At this point, I don't think they can interbreed much longer.

"As carving is moving toward a more sculptural approach, I see the difference becoming more and more pronounced. As the work gets more sculptural and less bird carving, it will become less faithful to the medium of wood, which is at the very heart of the decoy heritage. However, I foresee in a year or two a new category at Ocean City, one that will attract the stained and naturally finished carving. It's a natural outlet for those who want to do more purely form studies. And at the same time, it's not bound by all the rigors of the highly refined decorative work."

Barth glances at the clock Bob has set up in the room. Blake has stirred from an interrupted, fully clothed sleep, and he and Barth exchange greetings. But they say nothing else.

Perhaps speaking for himself, Barth foresees more carvers moving away from competitions. He sees this as a process, however, rather than an expedient to some new stage, and he has an analogy to describe it. "There is the hunter who has a reckoning with himself one day and ceases to pull the trigger. This is analogous to the carver or artist who no longer needs that blue ribbon.

"This is the hunter who needs only to spend that day in the field without bringing home the quarry to have a fulfilling experience." Yet, he admits that there are hunters who will hunt all their lives, as there are carvers who will always compete, and there are people who will never hunt, as there are carvers who will never compete. "These have their own comfort zones in or out of competitions. But there are some who will enter to a certain point and discover that the reward comes from within."

Painting Notes

Painting has often been described as the most difficult aspect of realistic bird carving. Avian colors rarely come directly from tubes. Instead, mixing is necessary, and then there must be a careful application that requires close attention to feather plumage. In addition, colors often blend one into another, making distinct separations in many areas unrealistic.

An entire book would have to be devoted to the intricacies of painting even a single bird, and no less so for a miniature of that species. However, basic guidelines can be offered that attempt to take some of the mystery out of coloring a bird. The following painting charts and instructions provide the essentials for achieving the colors used and how to apply them. These notes, both written and pictorial, are not the final say in painting the seven species illustrated. There clearly are differences between one bird and another, even of the same species. Granted, to many observers all robins look alike. Yet there are many variations between individuals, not to mention the coloring differences found at various times of the year. But these seven species—puffin, bald eagle, gray partridge, cardinal, sanderling, mourning dove, and eastern bluebird—are in their best plumage and represent what might be called generic birds.

The charts give the patterns for the birds and some of the stages of color buildup after a primer coat of gesso has been applied. Particular parts of the anatomy are enclosed in circles. Each chart shows the final color mixes and the colors used to achieve each blend. The sizes of the color dots indicate the proportion of the paints mixed: small dots, small amounts of paint, for example. In a few cases, colors are used straight.

Proportions, however, are still approximate and may not give the exact colors indicated. Experimentation may be necessary and is recommended.

The paints recommended are acrylic pigments contained in tubes. Most of the names referred to are available in Liquitex Acrylic Colors. The exceptions are noted. Other paint manufacturers may have identical or similar names and colors.

Carvers, both novice and professional, are encouraged to refer to photographs, study skins, and mounted birds whenever possible and ultimately to develop their own plumage colors.

Puffins

Begin with the basic body color, 1, which is a mix of ivory black, raw umber, and a small amount of titanium white. Referring to Figure A, apply thin coats. The belly, face, and under the tail of the bird are Mix 2, which is titanium white and very small amounts of ivory black and yellow ochre (Aquatec Acrylic).

While the bird is still wet from the previous applications, go over the base of the flanks and down onto the leg area with Mix 1 and blend the white and black body colors together. Refer to Figure A.

The final body color is achieved with 4, which is straight Mars black. This is used starting from the edges of all the body feathers, but apply less toward the centers of those feathers. Refer to Figure B.

The head is shadowed using Mix 3, which is titanium white and small amounts of raw umber and ivory black. Refer to Figures C and D.

The beak and feet are primed with 5, which is straight cadmium yellow medium. Figure A shows the beak primed. The feet are gone over with 6, straight cadmium red medium. This should result in a reddish orange color, as in Figure E. The beak area is done the same way, as in Figure D. The blue-gray area at the base of the beak is done with equal amounts of titanium white and ivory black. Also, the eye-rings of the bird are a cadmium red medium, and the body area above and below the eyes is a blue-gray mix of titanium white and ivory black. Refer again to Figure D.

Puffin

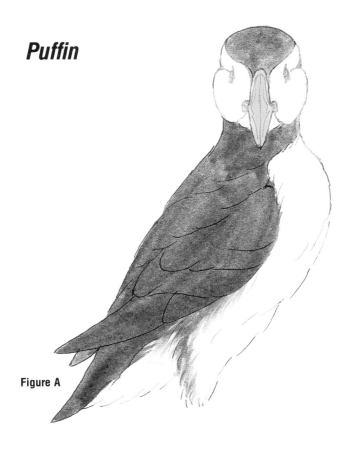

Figure A

1	●	=	● ●	body base
2	○	=	○ ● ●	underparts
3	○	=	○ ● ●	head
4	●	=	●	body
5	●	=	●	beak and feet
6	●	=	●	beak and feet

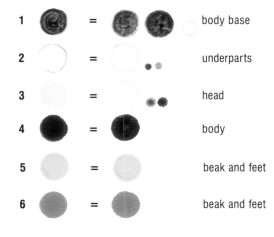

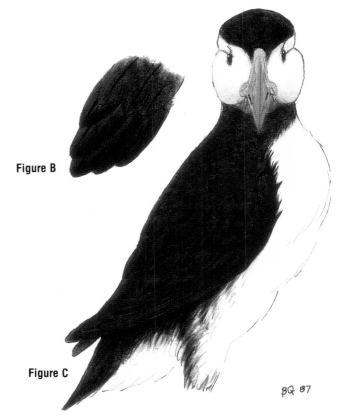

Figure B

Figure C

BG 87

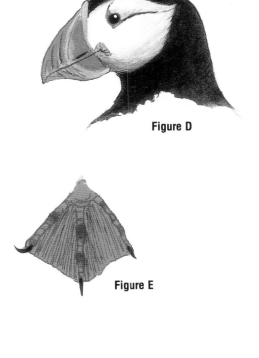

Figure D

Figure E

115

Bald Eagle

The basic body color, Mix 1, is applied in thin coats as in Figure A, working toward the color intensity shown in Figure B. The mix is made from a combination of burnt umber, ivory black and much smaller amounts of cadmium red medium, permanent green light and a small amount of titanium white.

For the primaries, Mix 2 has equal parts of burnt umber and ivory black and a small amount of titanium white. This darker color is blended along the front edges of the wings and across the secondaries. This should be applied in several coats.

The head and tail areas will be painted with a base coat of Mix 4, which is titanium white and a very small amount of raw umber.

In Figure D, more of the basic body color, Mix 1, is applied to the feathers. However, little is applied at the feather edges. In fact, each successive coat is applied farther back from the edges. What is left is light borders.

For the head and tail in Figures C and E, highlights and shadows are used. The shadows are titanium white and a very small amount of ivory black, as in Mix 3. Shadows are applied to the bottom of the head, the brow, and the edge of each feather. Higher areas on the head such as its top and cheeks and the edges of the tail feathers are highlighted with Mix 5. This is titanium white and a very small amount of yellow ochre (Aquatec Acrylic).

The beak and feet color is begun with 6, a straight cadmium yellow medium. Adding white will make the color brighter, and adding raw umber will make it paler. Also, there is a small amount of yellow above the eyes. Again, use 6.

The baby eagles are given a thickened coating of gesso, applied with a stiff brush.

Bald Eagle

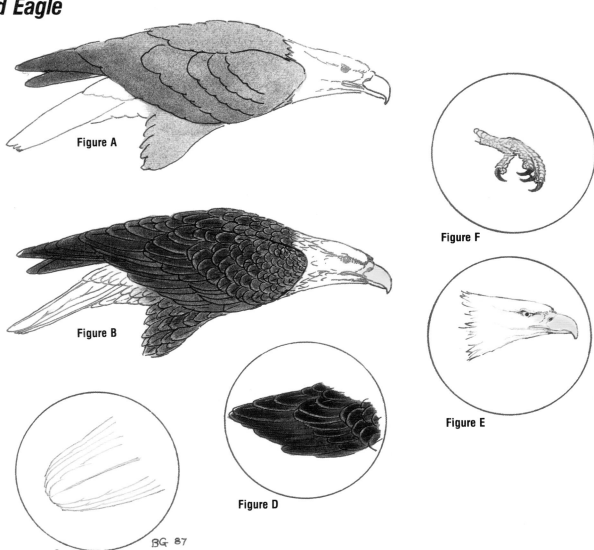

Figure A

Figure B

Figure C

BG 87

Figure D

Figure E

Figure F

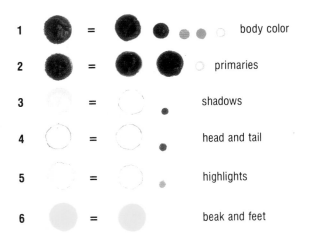

1	● =	● ● ● ● ○	body color
2	● =	● ● ○	primaries
3	○ =	○ ●	shadows
4	○ =	○ ●	head and tail
5	○ =	○ ●	highlights
6	● =	●	beak and feet

Gray Partridge

This bird starts with three basic colors, all blended together on a fairly wet surface. The rump and back are made with Mix 1, which is titanium white and smaller amounts of raw umber and yellow ochre. The breast color, Mix 2, is titanium white and smaller amounts of ivory black and raw umber. The flanks, Mix 3, are titanium white and smaller amounts of ivory black and raw umber. Refer to Figure A. Avoid sharp edges by using thin washes. Figure B shows the three basic colors built up in intensity.

The next step is putting in the barring on the flanks, as in Figure B. This mix, 5, is burnt sienna and smaller amounts of burnt umber, titanium white and raw sienna.

The final colors on the head and face are also established. This mix, 4, is raw sienna and smaller amounts of titanium white and burnt umber. Refer to Figure B.

In Figure C, all the barring has been established with Mix 5. Also, the coverts and scapulars have been colored with Mix 5.

To achieve the breast coloring as in Figure E, Mix 2 is used with a small amount of titanium added. Note that each feather is lighter at its base. This accentuates the puffiness of the feathers.

Vermiculating the bird is next. The areas to be done are in Figures C, D, and E. This is done with Mix 6, which is burnt umber and ivory black in equal proportions. A #00000 technical pen can be used.

The flank feathers are given a white edging, as in Figure C. This is done with Mix 3, with more titanium white added. The same color is used for the feather shafts on the flank feathers.

The beak can be done with a mix of white and yellow ochre and the red eye patch is straight cadmium red.

Gray Partridge

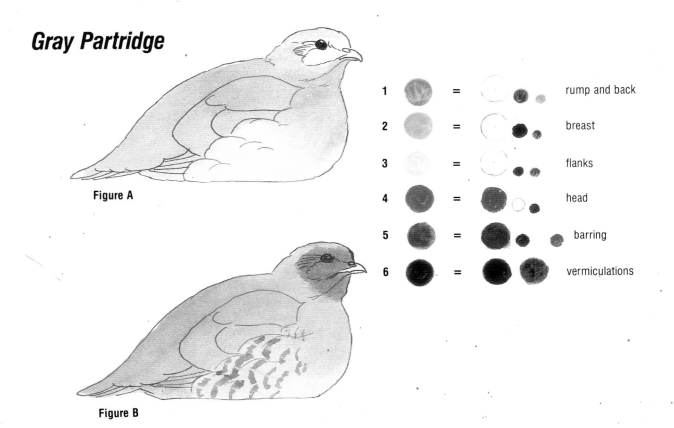

Figure A

Figure B

1	=				rump and back
2	=				breast
3	=				flanks
4	=				head
5	=				barring
6	=				vermiculations

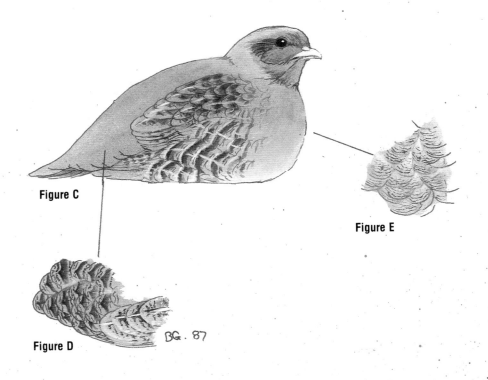

Figure C

Figure E

Figure D

BG. 87

Cardinal

The basic colors are blended on a fairly wet surface, as in Figure A. This begins with the breast color, Mix 1, which is cadmium red medium and smaller amounts of titanium white and burnt umber.

The back and tail are Mix 2, which is cadmium red medium and smaller amounts of burnt umber.

The primaries, Mix 3, are burnt umber and smaller amounts of ivory black and cadmium red medium.

The head and upper breast, Mix 4, are straight cadmium red medium.

Figures B and C show the buildup of the basic colors. For the area around the face, cadmium yellow medium can be added to cadmium red medium to give the area more orange. This is the same mix used for the beak.

The tertials can be edged with straight cadmium red; secondaries, coverts, and outside edges of the primaries and tail feathers are edged with 6, straight cadmium red medium.

Mix 3 is used along each feather edge and down the center of the tertials. Refer to Figure C.

Mix 8 is titanium white, ivory black and raw umber. This is applied to the edges of the secondaries, tertials, primaries, and greater coverts. Refer to Figure C. This same mix, with Payne's gray added, can be put on the back of the bird.

Build up the intensity of the beak with Mix 5, which is yellow ochre and a smaller amount of cadmium red medium.

The area surrounding the beak is straight Mars black built up with thin coats. Refer to Figure C for the final color.

Paint the feet with Mix 7, raw sienna, a smaller amount of burnt umber, and a very small amount of cadmium red medium. Over that is applied an ivory black wash.

Cardinal

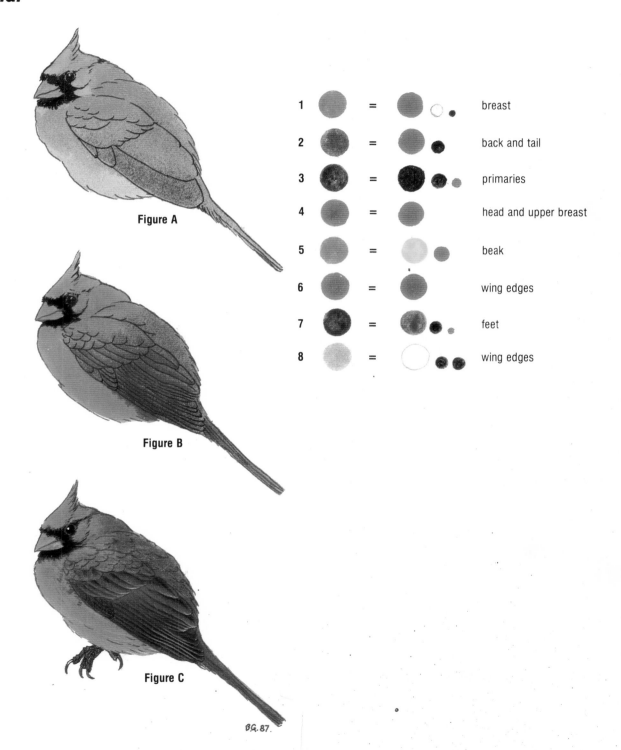

Figure A

Figure B

Figure C

BG. 87.

1 ● = ● ○ . breast

2 ● = ● ● back and tail

3 ● = ● ● . primaries

4 ● = ● head and upper breast

5 ● = ○ ● beak

6 ● = ● wing edges

7 ● = ● ● . feet

8 ● = ○ ● ● wing edges

Sanderling

Keeping the bird fairly wet with water so that the basic colors flow together, begin with Mix 1, which is titanium white and very small amounts of yellow ochre (Aquatec Acrylic) and ivory black. Apply Mix 3 for the back as soon as possible. This is titanium white and small amounts of raw umber, ivory black, and yellow ochre. Refer to Figure A for the intensity of colors. Start on the head with Mix 3. Again, refer to Figure A.

The primary colors are the next to be applied. Mix 4 is ivory black and raw umber in equal parts and a smaller amount of titanium white. This is blended into the rear of the bird, with the primary and tertial feathers darker than the others. Refer to Figure B.

In Figures C and E the tertial, secondary and covert areas are enlarged. Using Mix 3, paint over these areas, but leave light edges on the feathers. Apply each successive wash of color farther back from the edges.

The dark centers of the feathers are made with Mix 4. Refer to Figures C, E, and F.

The final step is to apply Mix 2 to highlight the feathers with a light color. This is used even on the underparts, as in Figure D.

Sanderling

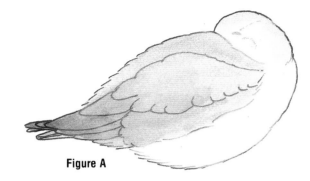

Figure A

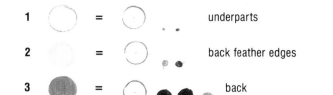

1	=		underparts
2	=		back feather edges
3	=		back
4	=		primaries and dark areas

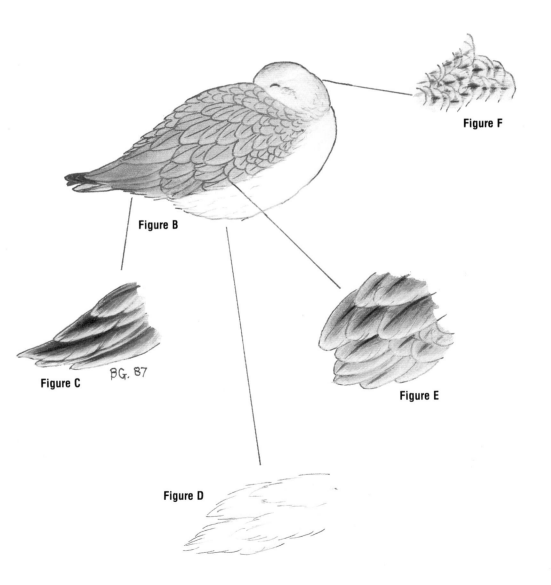

Figure F

Figure B

Figure C

BG. 87

Figure E

Figure D

Mourning Dove

The base coats are blended on a wet surface. This can begin with the lower wing color, Mix 1, which is equal amounts of ivory black and titanium white.

The primaries, Mix 2, are done with ivory black, raw sienna, and a smaller amount of titanium white.

The upper body and tail colors, Mix 3, are raw sienna, ivory black, and smaller amounts of raw sienna and titanium white.

The head, Mix 4, is raw sienna and smaller amounts of white and raw umber.

The lower tail coverts and flank area, Mix 5, are white, a very small amount of cadmium yellow medium and dioxazine purple. Refer to Figures B and C for the final colors.

The breast, Mix 6, is permanent green light, cadmium red medium, raw sienna, titanium white, and smaller amounts of dioxazine purple and cadmium yellow medium.

The belly color, Mix 7, is raw sienna, titanium white and a smaller amount of cadmium yellow medium.

Refer to Figures A and B for the buildup of these basic colors. Note that more of Mix 1 is brought up into the inside of the lower wing feathers and more of the body color, Mix 3, has been brought into the outside of the feathers. The edges of the secondaries are lightened with Mix 1, with more titanium white.

There is light edging along the breast as in Figure D, achieved by adding raw umber to the breast color, Mix 6.

The eye-ring, done with Mix 8, is titanium white and smaller amounts of cerulean blue and a very small amount of permanent green light.

The feet and base of the beak are done with Mix 9, which is alizarin crimson (Aquatec Acrylic) and smaller amounts of titanium white and burnt umber. Refer to Figures B and D. Apply a thin wash of titanium white and raw umber to the feet.

Mourning Dove

Figure A

Figure B

Figure C

BG. 97

Figure D

1	=							lower wing
2	=							primaries
3	=							upper body and tail
4	=							head
5	=							lower tail coverts
6	=							breast
7	=							belly
8	=							eye-ring
9	=							feet and base of beak

125

Bluebirds

The base coats for a bluebird, as in Figure A, must be blended on a fairly wet surface. The basic body color is on top of the bird. This is Mix 1, cobalt blue, ultramarine blue, and smaller amounts of titanium white and alizarin crimson (Aquatic Acrylic).

The breast color, Mix 2, is burnt sienna and smaller amounts of burnt umber, raw sienna, and titanium white.

The belly color, Mix 3, is titanium white and very small amounts of ivory black, raw sienna, and yellow ochre.

The primaries' color, Mix 4, contains equal amounts of burnt umber and ivory black.

Refer to Figures B and C for the buildup of intensity of the four basic colors.

The insides of the secondaries and tertials and the primaries are recolored with Mix 1 to achieve a darker blue. Refer to Figures D and F.

Mix 3 is used to lighten the edges of the tertials and secondaries and the edges of the primaries. Refer to Figures D and F.

The undertail is done with Mix 1, with more white added to achieve a grayer color. Refer to Figure E.

The beak and feet are straight ivory black.

Bluebirds

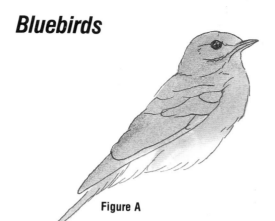

Figure A

Figure C

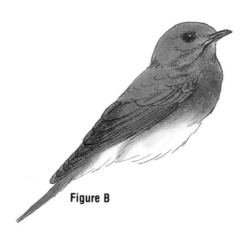

Figure B

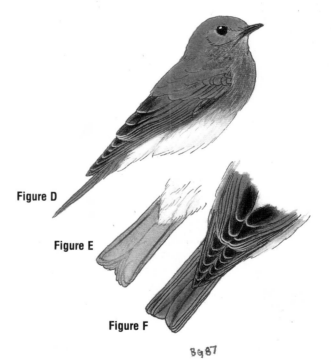

Figure D

Figure E

Figure F

BG87

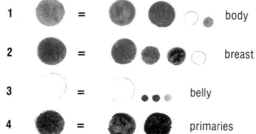

1 ● = ● ● ○ ● body

2 ● = ● ● ● ○ breast

3 ○ = ○ ● ● ● belly

4 ● = ● ● primaries

127

Puffins with sand eels

Bald eagle with its eaglets

Bald eagles

Gray partridge

Gray partridge

Gray partridge

Cardinal

Cardinal

Cardinal

Sanderling

Sanderling

Sanderling

Mourning dove

Mourning dove

Mourning dove

Mourning dove

Eastern bluebirds

Eastern bluebirds

Eastern bluebirds

Eastern bluebirds

Best in World

World Championship Wildfowl Carving Competition rules, 1986.

World Class Rules

1. Open to all master carvers and Best of Show award winning carvers.
2. Divisions are:
   A. Competition Grade Decorative Floating Waterfowl.
   B. Decorative Lifesize Wildfowl.
   C. Decorative Miniature Wildfowl.
3. Entries are limited to one per person, each Division.
4. Entries entered in World Class are not eligible for Professional, Amateur or Novice Classes and vice versa.
5. The species for Division A, Floating Waterfowl Pairs, will be cinnamon teal. Full body is optional. Action-like poses will be expected. Extra points will be given for full body, extended legs and action poses. Listing or sinking birds shall be eliminated. They must float perfectly regardless of pose.
6. Division A, B and C carvings will be constructed of wood and/or cork with necessary fillers, etc. Cast metal or plastic bills, legs, feet, etc. are barred on any entry. Handmade metal beaks, bills, legs, wing parts, etc. will be allowed only if part of a structural necessity for support.
7. Decorative Lifesize and Decorative Miniature carvings (World Class) this year will have the theme of seabirds. Official designation is loons, grebes, auks, cormorants, shearwaters, petrels, pelicans, frigates, tropic birds, jaegers, gulls, terns, skimmers, boobies and all others that are sub-species of the same families. There must be at least TWO seabirds with anything else in nature to set the scene in summer or winter plumage.
8. Division A, B & C will be judged on eye appeal, originality, the degree of difficulty in carving and painting, life-like settings, natural poses using the "Live Bird" as your model.

The finished puffin composition, winner of the Best-in-World title for miniatures in the 1986 World Championship Wildfowl Carving Competition. In the collection of the North American Wildfowl Art Museum, The Ward Foundation, Salisbury, Maryland.

9. Decorative Lifesize & Decorative Miniature carvings will be full and freestanding and viewable from all sides. If encased in glass it will be removed by carver prior to judging.

10. All carvings in the World Class will be new work made for this contest. No prior judged carvings are eligible!

11. World Class Divisions A, B and C are designated as three-dimensional fine art, and we give the carver the freedom of originality in composition. It is not our intent to dictate but will advise judges to deduct points for "non-carved," manufactured components, i.e. natural grass, leaves, branches, fence posts, etc. instead of handmade objects.

12. Division C, Miniature Wildfowl (1986-Seabirds) will be ½ scale or less with 8" maximum per subject, from base of bill to base of tail. Carvings with open and extended wings and long tails shall not exceed an absolute maximum overall of 12" per

subject. Decorative Miniature carvings that exceed the overall 12" maximum will not be considered in this class. Any carvings exceeding can be placed in the Pro, Amateur or Novice Classes, where ½ scale or less is the only rule.

13. The definitive formula to equalize the scale of miniatures has not been settled upon yet. We leave it to the carver's discretion to create his scene with his seabird species that will do best in this contest.

—— • ——

The Convention Center is set back approximately the length of two football fields from the Coastal Highway. An electric signboard announces the competition and alternates that with the dates. It is one o'clock and the filled parking field discourages any new visitors. Two trucks, one from Virginia, the other from Maryland, sell blocks of basswood and tupelo in the lot. But inside, there is a great deal more business.

Tools, wood, and books have become as much a part of carving as the birds themselves. The dealers are not readily visible from the entrance to the main hall, however. The area is filled with rows of white-clothed tables displaying birds of several hundred species. On either side of the exhibit area there are curtained-off areas in addition to the north and south halls, where the retailers of the carving accessories can be found.

A man in his thirties in bib overalls is selling study bills. Made of epoxy resin, they are impervious to most abuse. The retailer will in fact strike the edge of his table with a bill from a cinnamon teal, a mallard, a black duck, or one of a dozen other species. Near him is a waterfowl carver who has replicated birds to sell, ones cast from polyester resin. There are two men who sit quietly with a simple display of their burning tools. A tall man with tinted prescription glasses has a table display of books for carvers. Placing an expansive hand on a book with a canvasback hen on its cover, he guarantees to his customer that its contents are invaluable. Near him is a man demonstrating duck calls. A husband and wife from Connecticut sell bases with a variety of shapes. Most are made of walnut. There is a new magazine for carvers and there are artists selling prints and original watercolors. A man with a Southern accent demonstrates a new grinding tool and another merchandiser talks about the difference between carving basswood and tupelo, using Scheeler's name twice in the conversation.

In the main arena, the area around the tables is clogged by many of the several thousand visitors present that afternoon. They move unrhythmically past the ducks and other birds that already have blue, red, yellow, and green ribbons near or on them. The Open Class, Intermediate and Novice carvers have been judged and can return home to celebrate or plan revenge for the following year. The Ward Foundation will announce later that there are over twenty-three hundred entries in the competition.

Also in the main arena, a man with a clipboard wearing a short-sleeved sports shirt has been perusing the tables. He will take back to his home in Michigan many of the best pieces, including a pair of life-size standing Canadian geese.

A group of onlookers forms an irregular circle around the geese. The man who carved them talks about the preliminary clay models, the sense of balance and power he wanted to impart to the geese, the

wood he chose, the problems he had working it, the oils he employed, and the eleven months he spent on the birds.

A carver who lives in Vermont is telling a group of people about his five life-size puffins. He explains how he wanted one of the rocks to "spill over" the walnut base. On it is a crab. "The crab is an interloper," he says, "so the puffin closest to the crab and lowest in the composition is balanced on one foot, ready to jump up and away. Another bird, higher up, is curious without the tenseness of that other puffin, and he is assured that there is no threat."

Cigar Daisey is there without his cigar, and a boy from Wisconsin is looking for his father, who will later be announced the winner of the World Class Floating Decorative Waterfowl Pairs. A contingent of carvers from Long Island move together along the tables, pointing out the fine points and flaws. One of them photographs the others as they talk to well-known carvers. A book editor whose publishing house is in Harrisburg, Pennsylvania, talks with Barth about

Another view of the puffins.

A close-up of birds number one and number three.

Number two puffin.

Number three bird.

his terns, and a Cajun talks in French with another carver from a nearby Louisiana parish.

It is two in the afternoon. Bob has already judged Novice Miniature carvings. Asked to do this at the time he entered the puffins, he was able to return to the motel for only a couple of hours of sleep. He looks bewildered with fatigue. He manages to carry on a conversation with a carver who will attend one of his seminars held in Salisbury that summer.

At the miniatures table, Bob's birds are at one end of the long table that has more puffins, pied-billed, least terns, pelicans, gannets, and others.

Three judges have spent over an hour walking around the miniature pieces. John Scheeler is one of them. He is slow, laconic, almost avoiding the other two carver-judges. Lynn Forehand of Virginia is another. He won Best-in-World in 1979 for a pair of

life-size jungle fowl in conflict. The third is Robert Ptashnik of Canada. His pair of miniature avocets won the 1983 Best-in-World competition.

A writer has been talking to Bob about his puffins. Bob talks about the work in the van, the painting in the hotel room. Scheeler appears almost unnoticed. Offering his thin hand to Bob, he lets his eyes drift back to the miniature table. His jaws work for a moment, as if practicing the sentences he needs to make. Barth has called him a Zen master of bird carving, a man to whom many carvers brought their work for approval. He says a few words about the workmanship of Bob's puffin composition. But he drifts off, and is joined immediately by other carvers who want him to see their work.

One hour later, Bob is announced as the winner of the 1986 Best-in-World prize for miniatures.

North to Alaska

The screen shows a sprawling mountain, most of which is whitened with snow. Surrounding mountains are dwarfed by its presence. It is so overpowering that it might be missed altogether as one sees the regular line of peaks below it.

"The closest I got was twenty-five miles to Mount McKinley," Bob says as he makes a slight focusing adjustment on the projector. He has been home for slightly over two weeks, after an equally long visit to Alaska. Vivian and Roy are seated on one of the sofas. On the floor are Caleb and Joshua, and under the opening that leads to the kitchen stands Jody with Asher.

Bob calls this trip, during which he spent the last week in June and the first week in July in Alaska, a field trip to look at birds. Bob's companion for most of the trip was John Felsing, for Frank Russell had to cancel five days before they left Illinois. Despite Russell's absence, Bob and Felsing still had access to a car and spent a few days with a biologist who works for the United States Fish and Game Service.

Alaska has been called an untamed Eden and earth's final chapter. It is a landscape of glaciers, mountains, and tundra, a concert of beauty that offers a glacier the size of Switzerland, and a mountain that stands 20,320 feet tall, the highest in North America. An Indian tribe gave Mount McKinley the name *Denali,* meaning the Great One. So imposing is it that it can be seen from Anchorage, more than one hundred miles away.

Denali is also the name of the mountain's surrounding national park, in which Bob and his companion spent a good deal of the two weeks. Nearly four million acres make up Denali National Park and Preserve.

Those who never enter Denali can still find in Alaska nearly three million lakes and fjords that offer nesting grounds for two hundred million birds. Among them are more bald eagles than all the other states combined.

Nearly half a million people live in Alaska, and nearly half of them live in Anchorage, where Bob landed after a seven-hour flight from Chicago.

Roy asks Bob what he really got out of the trip. The answer, Bob says, begins with 120 species of birds he

Mount McKinley, 20,320 feet tall, the highest peak in North America.

identified in Alaska, many of them shorebirds and seabirds. The species include kittiwakes, glaucous gulls, murres, auklets, and puffins. He spotted a gyrfalcon, watched plovers on the tundras, and heard warblers that he could not see. In all, he saw thirty-five species he had never seen before. One of them was a Townsend's warbler, which he calls a rare find.

Many species of ducks nest in Alaska, for food is plentiful and there are more daylight hours to find it in. Bob remembers seeing harlequin ducks, scaup, and barrow's goldeneyes.

"I gained what I thought I was striving for," Bob continues as a slide falls into place, one of him sitting on a grassy slope with McKinley beyond him. "That was to get out and experience nature. That sounds corny, but it's not. It worked out well.

"It's seeing animals in their natural habitats. Take a robin, for instance." A slide of him and Felsing takes the place of him and McKinley. "Everyone around here looks at a robin that's out in the yard with a worm in its mouth. Up there, you can't get near a robin. They're all wild birds, they're not backyard birds."

The next slide shows a mew gull. Bob explains how it came right to his feet. The following slide shows it next to someone's hiking boot. "The other extreme is that sparrows that are hard to see around here are everywhere. You get sick of looking at them. They'll come up to you in the middle of nowhere. In Alaska, most birds will welcome you, come to check you out."

Slides of wildflowers and lichen follow. There is a photo of a bird eating food Bob holds in his hand. He says it's a gray jay, nicknamed a camp robber. Another of the species also took a cracker from his mouth.

A picture of Anchorage provides the stimulus for unusual recollections. He saw well-kept, expensive houses with yards of junk, ranging from partial automobiles, to parts of airplanes and helicopters. Bob's theory is that Alaska lacks spare parts for almost anything mechanized. Yards, then, become storage areas for much needed components.

"Seeing this stuff in people's yards was the norm as you drove down the main highway of Alaska. People drive their cars until they break down and let them sit around for junk scavengers. Things are hard to come by."

Another bizarre sight was seeing a framed but unsided house that was furnished.

Most of the remaining slides he has taken are in Denali Park, which is five hours from Anchorage. There were more experiences there than counting birds, some of which put Bob and Felsing in danger. A slide of a grizzly bear appears on the screen.

Bob and Felsing knew not to run from the bear, which would have triggered a chase reaction, Bob explains. "Bears have bad eyesight, and we thought we'd be safe taking a picture. But he stuck his nose in the air and looked right at us. He then charged a hundred yards. He went into a grove of willows where we couldn't see him. Luckily a bus came by a couple of minutes later."

At home on the same day Asher suffered convulsions. "There are no phones in Denali. I had a weird feeling one day. It was five days since I had spoken to Jody. I took a bus out of the park and called her from a bar. I found out that the baby was in the hospital."

A slide of a kittiwake colony comes into view. These members of the gull family nest in colonies on precipi-

Bob came to the Alaskan tundra to observe its unique bird life.

A mew gull, common in the tundra area, encountered on the trip.

A gray jay spotted about seventy-five miles from Mount McKinley.

A kittiwake colony. Bob says he learned not only about birds, but also about rock textures and grain. He plans to carve a pair of kittiwakes and particularly likes the way these birds build their nests on the steep sides of rocks.

tous cliff faces usually overlooking the sea. The nests, Bob says, are plastered together and lie on narrow ledges. "What keeps the young in the nests?" Vivian asks. "I guess they know, but I don't," Bob answers.

Other slides of sea lions, rocky cliffs, tundra, and a few more views of Mount McKinley take turns on the screen. The slides appear not to be in any order, for photos of Anchorage houses vie with a picture of a tug, a sunset, and a glacier. Glaciers are moving masses of ice in high mountains or high latitudes where the snowfall rate is greater than the rate of melting snow. They are usually bordered on their sides by zones of rock debris. The rate of advance or movement varies greatly. Most glaciers move downward a few feet per day. But observations of the Black Rapids Glacier in Alaska during 1936 and 1937 showed that it was moving more than one hundred feet per day. Thicknesses also vary. The glacier Bob photographed from a cruise ship is, he estimates, three hundred feet high, though glaciers can soar as high as nine thousand feet.

In the middle of the photo is a pair of kittiwakes.

A braided river about two miles across.

An Alaskan glacier seen from an excursion boat. Bob was in the Kenai Fjords looking at seabird colonies.

"We had twenty or more hours of light. It gets twilight but never really dark, but you lose six minutes of light a day. It's a real long sunset and a real long sunrise with the sun going just below the horizon."

Small, dark forms appear in the middle of the slide. They stand on the very top of a chunk of the glacier that has fallen into the sea. They are a pair of bald eagles.

Bob saw many golden and bald eagles during the trip. Juveniles were also plentiful, and he remembers one young bald eagle sitting in the middle of a kittiwake colony. The birds moved away from the eagle in

an almost symmetrical circumference. He compared the scene to a magnet repelling iron filings.

There are more slides of the tundra and several of "braided rivers." Woven tapestries of criss-crossing streams, these are rivers generated by melting glaciers. Bob says they are unique to Alaska and have beds that are deceptively wide. The distance across is difficult to ascertain on the slide. One he photographed is two miles wide.

Roy asks if Bob did any sketching. Imitating a buzzing sound, he says that the mosquitoes were everywhere, especially in the park. Drawing was impossible, Bob responds. He remembers a woman he met in Denali who, without a mosquito net around her face, had hundreds of welts. "There's stagnant water everywhere and permafrost in the ground," Bob says.

Permafrost runs deep. In Barrows, Alaska, it is one thousand three hundred feet thick, though in parts of Siberia it is as much as five thousand feet thick. "So nothing drains. Water lies in one spot. If you put your hand down into the earth, water comes out."

Despite the soggy soil, vegetation and even trees are part of the ecology of Alaska. The shallow-rooted black spruce tree, which can survive provided that the permafrost is no more than eighteen inches in depth, is common.

Bob saw a forest of dead black spruce trees along an area called Turnigut Arm. The ground settled over seven feet. Salt permeated the ground, resulting in wholesale death of the trees. Bob remembers how the branches hung down on the trees, "all withered, skinny, small, with most of the growth at the tops."

Eagle Nest and Rock

"It would be a great to win the World Championships for the third time," Bob says, stretching out his legs in his steel swivel chair. He is relaxed, rested, and smiles expansively enough to reveal his teeth.

The children are rarely in the basement, except in late afternoon and evening, spending their summer days on the lawn and sidewalk facing South Lord. The basement is cool, and the radio is tuned to a baseball game. It is July 23.

He has already planned to do towhees for the World Championship Wildfowl Carving Competition of 1987. The theme, he has known for some time, will be songbirds. He also plans to enter the life-size division with a pair of juncos and bittersweet branches with fall berries.

The juncos, he says, are steel blue, "a fantastic color, with the orange of bittersweet. I'm thinking of maybe marble or a black slab for the base. Maybe a semiporous stone that doesn't shine when polished. Maybe granite. The bittersweet is gnarly and twisty. It'll be a small piece, maybe 18 inches. The bittersweet will have berries and leaves."

For the miniature class, he plans to do a pair of towhees. He describes them as ground feeders. They are large enough so that the half-size rule would not result in birds that are too small. He sees them as ground feeders, and he foresees the piece having autumn leaves.

He says Larry Barth has a theory for winning championships such as the Best-in-World title. One win is luck. Two wins suggest coincidence. And three wins make a true world champion.

"I'll put enough time and effort into the miniature piece to justify a win, but the junco piece is life-size. I just know I'm not going to put enough into it." He remembers the amount of time he worked on the puffins.

"People came up to me and said they weren't black enough. But on a black bird I would rather have it much lighter and be able to see contrasts." He still has the puffin study skin. Taking it out of a plastic bag that has kept it separate from other borrowed study birds, he holds it under the flexible arm lamp over his worktable and spreads the feathers apart on its back. He

The first design idea for an eagle and nest composition, a miniature model of base, cliff face, and tree, made of clay and a scrap block of wood.

says that living black and painted black are different colors. He moves the bird around under the light to allow for highlights to appear, areas that are almost grayish black. Feeling he has proven his theory, he says, "I still think I put enough time and effort into the puffins."

Putting the puffin back into its bag, he says, "I'd like to put more detail on most of my birds, as I did with the puffins, but I can't afford to. So sometimes I go just far enough to get the point across." He leans back and puts one foot on the edge of the table that has been freshly surfaced with a clean piece of white paper. His shoe leaves a smudge of dirt that will stay there through the next project. "It's the same with painting. If it looks like a goldfinch, I'll stop putting yellow on the bird, though I could work longer and make it look more accurate."

He adds that some of this curtailing of effort comes from being bored, or from the need to do a variety of different birds. But he remembers that the tree sparrow was, in the minds of his peers, an exceptional piece. Yet it took only three days to carve and paint. He calls the bird a fluke. "I wish everything worked that well. It jelled. It fit together. I started it, and all of a sudden it was finished. It was knowing the bird that made it work. I studied several tree sparrows that had been frequenting the feeder. One hit the window of my parents' house, so I had a fresh specimen to study. And I saw one being banded the day before I started the piece. Everything just fell together. That doesn't happen often. It should have been a week's work."

He has come up with a new composition. It is a commissioned piece. The buyer requested that it have a bald eagle, a nest, and chicks. Both he and Bob accept that it will have to be miniature in size, but Bob wants to pursue an approach that will emphasize habitat and composition rather than the birds.

He envisions rocks with a tree coming out of them and a nest on top of the tree. That he doesn't have an eagle mount or skin doesn't bother him. He has seen bald eagles in Alaska, and he has paintings and photographs of them. Springing forward in his seat by dropping his foot, he says rapidly that he is not particularly excited about doing a bald eagle. He later admits that he would prefer to carve a golden eagle for the adult. "I'm thrilled with the idea of the nest, of the rocks and tree."

He thinks he will recreate a dead-looking tree. He also likes the idea of old wood. "A lot of times you see an eagle's nest in dead trees," he points out. And a nest might remain for a century, even being taken over by another pair of eagles if the original pair dies.

What he thinks will be unique about the composition will be the rocks. Instead of a tall pile similar to what he had composed for the puffin piece, he will have a cluster of rocks with a sculpted back. The design is identical to a technique used with busts made of marble or clay. The lower part of the chest is carved concavely and smoothed so that the upper torso does not disappear abruptly into the pedestal.

He does not make too much of this design and abbreviates his comments. He says, simply, that he couldn't figure out how to portray a cliff face without making it look like a rounded pile of rocks. Nor did he want a tree growing out of the middle of a base without rocks.

Eagles nesting in trees along cliffs and fjords are frequently seen in Alaska. Seeing this, he thinks, helped shape the composition. "When I thought nest, I thought tree for a bald eagle. The two go hand in hand. I don't know where else they would nest. Then I had to concern myself with the rocks. Rocks are a nice way to get some mass on the base, some weight, to balance the mass of nest and eagles on top of the tree. And I could get by with a shorter tree on top of a mountain. I guess seeing nests in Alaska helped. The black spruces I saw in Alaska are fairly short trees, and they can be high up off the ground when they protrude from a cliff face."

Having a sculpted back for the rocks would suggest that much more rock was involved, he feels, perhaps even a mountain's worth.

The wood armature for the cliff face.

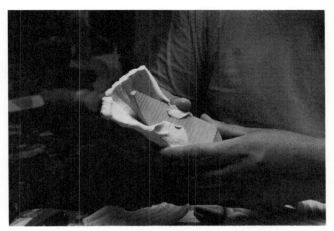

The first layer of Sculpey applied to the armature.

"At this point, the birds are still secondary. I can see them mentally, but I can see stronger shapes to the rocks and the tree. I see roots growing out of the rocks. I could even get color by putting some lichens on the rocks. But I have to work out the proportions first." This, he says, will be done in clay.

Bob takes a piece of wood to the band saw and returns with a fruitlike shape that leans over to one side. Around this he starts to mold thick sheets of modeling clay called Sculpey. Once done, he rolls out a thin length of the material to represent a tree and places it on the clay rock. He then fashions a crude, saucer-shaped nest and places that on top of the clay tree.

"I want to get a feel for this thing. I've got to get a balance between the height of the rock and the length of the tree or height of the tree," he says, removing the clay tree from the rock. "That will be my first concern, the proportions of the rock to the tree to the bird. Once I get that, it won't make any difference how big I make the piece."

Putting the unsupported clay tree on the table, Bob goes to the other work area and finds some heavy gauge copper wire, and returns with two pieces of it, each about two feet in length. He drills a ¼-inch-diameter hole into the wood rock. He then twists the ends of the two wires together and inserts them into the hole. He starts to twist the wires around each other, working the twist toward their outer ends.

About halfway along the lengths of wire, he stops and applies a few drops of Super Glue, an epoxy adhesive, mixed with baking soda. He also applies this to where the wires enter the wood. He explains that the

The clay responds as Bob's ideas take shape.

Applying more clay to build up the cliff face.

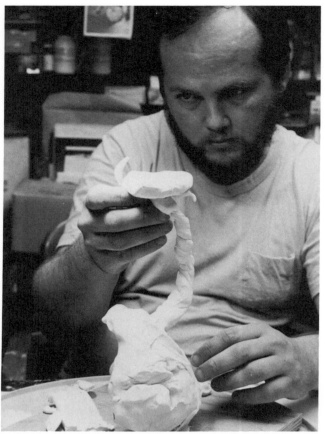

Some clay is roughly shaped and twisted up to give the look of a tree and nest. This will help determine where the tree will come out of the rocks.

baking soda "cures" the glue and hastens the hardening. The mix will not only secure the strands in the block, but it will also prevent the wires from separating. The mix is also a good filler, Bob adds, and will help disguise a glue joint where there has been a break.

He then covers the twisted portion with Sculpey. The next step is to fashion an eagle shape out of the clay. This he places, after bending one of the wires horizontally, about one foot above the rock. He puts the nest he had fashioned earlier on the newly bended branch, as well.

"This ought to be called rock and nest rather than bald eagle," he says, taking some kinks out of the wires. Pushing his chair back as far as it will go, he looks critically at the composition. "There will be a bald eagle." Then, as if an afterthought, he adds, "and two nestlings.

"It's nice to talk about an eagle and nest and young ones," he says, doing some modeling on the clay that surrounds the rock. "But when it comes right down to

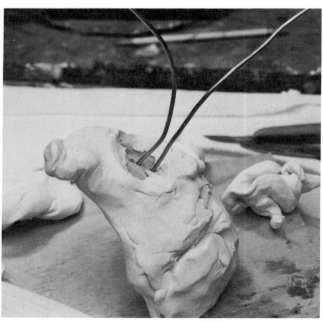

Inserted copper wire will be the armature for the tree.

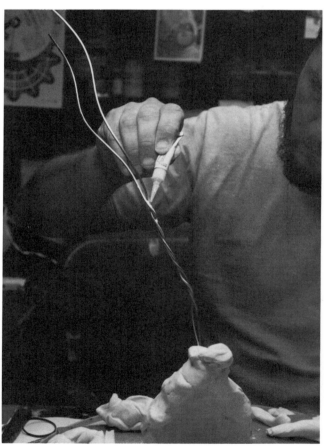

The wires are twisted together for strength, and Super Glue is applied for more strength.

it, where are you going to put the nest so it's going to look good? It won't work stuck on a block of wood."

He explains the terms of the commission. "A local veterinarian asked me to do an eagle and two babies. I gave him some ideas that could be done using a nest and tree. He liked the idea I came up with. It was easy to talk about it without seeing proportions and feeling more strongly about getting a nice design that will be real appealing."

He still feels confident with the shape of the rock. He says it is an appealing way to deal with a sea cliff. "It reminds me of a bronze or a bust. Rather than cutting it off at the back, you open it up. It's pleasing to me anyway, for whatever reasons. As an artist I do what feels good to me. That's important."

He studies the composition for a few minutes. Several times he bends the wires to point in different directions. With a modeling tool, he describes the roots of the tree in the clay that surrounds the wood armature.

Joshua and Caleb come in, cautiously at first, and

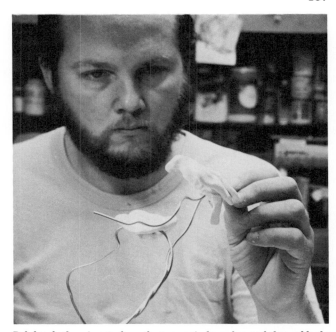

Bob bends the wires to form the two main branches and then adds the clay nest.

A quick eagle model to help get the height and shape of the tree.

Modeling on the clay cliff to give an idea of the root system of the tree.

then breathlessly ask questions about the piece. Bob explains to them the nature of the eagle, the nest, and the babies. Caleb wants to make eggs. Given some clay, he rolls small marble-size balls and puts them into the nest. Bob himself takes up a piece of clay and rounds it out until it is almost an inch in diameter. Joshua wants his father's egg to have a face. Bob obliges and squeezes and depresses the surface to create eyes, nose, and mouth. With a wide smile, he finds some small-gauge wire and needle-nose pliers. Quickly, he creates a miniature pair of glasses. These he puts on the face. The children beam with delight. Bob applies the head to the clay model.

After the children leave, stomping up the stairs and then overhead until the slamming of a backdoor brings quiet to the house, Bob says he might make a somewhat detailed model in Sculpey and heat it to make it a permanent sculpture. Bob says that Sculpey is a nontoxic substance with an odor that reminds him of a glazing compound. "It must have some kind of oil

in it," he adds. "It leaves a residue on your hands but washes up with soap and water. I like making birds out of Sculpey and just cooking and painting them." He remembers that when he and Barth were doing workshops at the Ward Foundation, Barth had made a cardinal out of the clay and Bob had shaped a tree sparrow. The birds were exchanged.

Bob lets out a loud laugh. He pats his stomach and says that Sprankle has a swimming pool on his property. When Bob and Barth were in the pool, Sprankle had called them white walruses. The joke gave rise to a retort. Bob and Barth fashioned walrus tusks out of Sculpey and made them to fit into their mouths. They hardened them in the Sprankles' oven. When it came time to swim again, they made sure the tusks were at the pool's bottom. When Sprankle was present, they dove to the bottom and fitted the tusks into their mouths; the "white walruses" then returned to the surface, barking and making walrus-like noises.

Bob continues to make slight alterations in the posi-

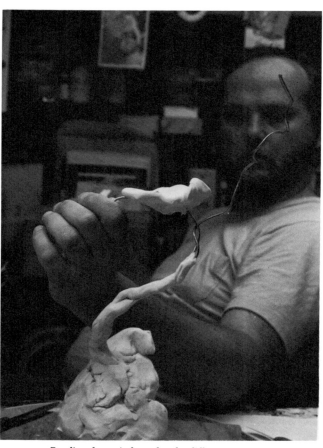

Bending the main branches for different positions.

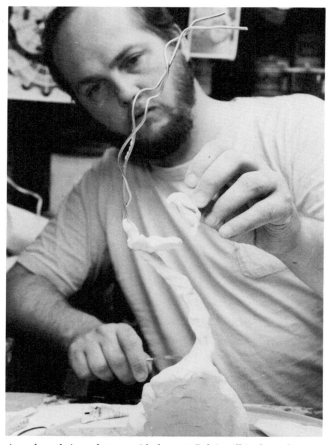

A crude eagle is made to go with the nest. Bob is still in the preliminary design stages.

Bob makes sketches to see how the shapes will work with the wood base. He is also trying to finalize the shape of the rock sculpture.

More modeling on the roots to get the tree to work with the shape and flow of the rocks.

He adds eagle and nest to the original design idea to see how all components will relate to each other.

Modeling tools, all obtained from dental catalogs.

Bob balances the tree with the rocks and tries to create a series of arcs. He also wants to see how the rocks and tree will relate to a square base.

tion of the eagle that now wears glasses, the nest, and the tree. He says he has been toying with a cliff face for a long time for birds such as kittiwakes, which he had seen on his Alaskan trip. He wondered how to do a cliff face and make it pleasing from different views. The sculpted back concept, he feels, will work well for the eagles.

But he thinks the rock and tree will not be enough. There should be a base, though not the round base used by many carvers to display their birds. The idea of a square block appeals to him. He sees the rocks coming out of that. "I see the whole thing growing out of a square block turning into rocks and boulders."

Suddenly, fresh ideas are generated. He might do an entire bird coming out of a block of wood, the bird textured and painted, rather than having it added to the block. He uses the example of John Sharp's work. Sharp, a one-time patternmaker, spurns the use of grinding tools, burning pens, and paints. Instead, he carves his birds and other wildlife, including fish and even snakes, from stumps. Animal and base are one,

and the essence of the wildlife is captured through abstraction and simplicity rather than exacting detail.

"Sharp does his stuff out of a base of a tree and turns it into an animal. But mine would be a transition to a completed bird, not a natural, wood bird. The art critics wouldn't be able to complain that it was not art because it was made out of a lot of little pieces. My idea would say sculpture."

The idea of a single piece of wood containing more than one component is not new for Bob. Earlier in the year he made a miniature kestrel and goldfinch out of one piece of jelutong. "I wanted to show prey, and I didn't want it to look gory. The people who wanted the bird wanted prey. I just decided to hide most of the goldfinch under the kestrel. It was simpler not to use two pieces. I might do a hawk or falcon and carve the bird and rock out of one piece or a bird and a tree together."

He talks about another miniature project he has in the planning stages. This would have two separate bases and two very different birds, though the habitat would suggest prairie or desert for both. One would have a burrowing owl, possibly at the entrance of, or partially in, a burrow. What he describes as a sister piece would have a roadrunner. The base would be elongated with cactus as part of the habitat confined to one area. The roadrunner, however, would be at the end of the base with one foot off the edge. This, says Bob, would suggest speed.

"The roadrunner is running, obviously. I might have the two bases the same shape. I could put the two pieces together, the roadrunner on one side, the burrower on the other. But with the roadrunner, I definitely see the stretching, the speed building up. I've never seen anything like it."

Returning to the eagle-nest-tree composition, Bob reflects on the black spruce trees he saw in Alaska. "These trees will get kinky, grow at weird angles, and the permafrost underneath will give way and the trees will tip. And then the frost will freeze through a number of years and a whole forest will look drunk." Twisty, weird angles, he repeats.

Rotating the plastic turntable the clay model is on, he says with a wrinkly frown, "The problem isn't going to be the size of the bird, it's going to be the size of the nest. And this one isn't big enough." He recalls reading that first-year nests can be small, but each year the returning eagles will add to it. He says that a nest can be as large as a small car after years of build-up.

He twists the wire-tree a bit, then puts more shape into the eagle. He first has it outside the nest on the limb, then on the nest itself. The turntable again gets rotated.

"I'm not going to make this real accurate." He smiles slightly. "I like the shape of the clay now. I don't think I'll go any bigger with the eagle."

Bob decides to support the rocky surface with a simple block of wood. He finds a scrap of two thick pieces of glued-together jelutong in the other room and cuts them into a cube shape between 3 and 4 inches on each side.

"A bigger block would take away from the piece, but bigger might be better. Maybe that's what it's going to take. The birds are almost secondary in this case."

Suddenly giggling, he says, "This is a bird on a stick on a rock on a block."

Seriousness returns, and he starts revising his thinking rapidly, saying at first that the eagle should be smaller, that the tree should be shorter, then that the entire composition should be bigger. "I don't mind the concept of a bigger piece either," he says to himself, "but it's going to be a tall, skinny piece." He rotates the turntable once more and decides, "There's too much mass below the tree. And it makes it too high."

Before he makes any changes, he picks up a piece of clay and quickly shapes two baby eagles. They are joined like Siamese twins, heads up and mouths open in expectation of food. The parent bird is above the nest on a piece of uncovered wire. He makes a series of free associations as he inspects the composition. "I like this design. I still feel the eagles are secondary to this piece and they're going to be whether they're big or small. I can now see the proportions, but I still have

Bald Eagle

⅛ scale

BG. 87

Young Eagles

¹⁄₈ scale

B.G. 87

work to do on the tree. I'm pretty close on the eagle, I think." A long pause. "The problem is going to be this nest. It's just got to be bigger." He remembers what Barth had said about a composition he made with a flying screech owl above a branch of pine needles. The needles offered mass without weight. "The nest will be large but airy where the sticks hang out. It'll be mass without weight around the outside edge."

More reflections: "The problem with the nest is this. It gives size to the whole thing. Without the nest and babies, the tree could be smaller." The rock begins to bother him. "I'm going to add to one side of the rock, take some off the other side."

After doing more shaping on the roots of the tree and the craggy rock, Bob admits he is still having trouble with the eagle. "I like the sculpture at this point, but I don't like the bird. I don't want to do an eagle. That's the whole problem."

At one point, to please Caleb and Joshua, he gave the adult eagle a large, vulture-like beak and calls the composition a vulture on a nest on a tree. Later, he spends a few minutes refining the look of the adult eagle. "The rocks balance off the tree. They give mass

or weight to the base. They balance the height of the tree and nest."

Jordan comes into the room hesitantly and in tears. She articulates precisely that someone had hit her and names the offender. Bob assures her that she will be all right. She retreats to her dolls and seems to lose interest in the injury.

He refers to several books that contain paintings of eagles and magazines that have photos of the bird. He indicates with a finger that eagle feathers are scaly in appearance. He feels this characteristic lends itself to a miniature scale because it will be fairly easy to define those edges while not making them too sharp.

Other children have joined Jordan in the family room. Seth and Joshua have brought out drawing tablets and markers. They have been taking private art lessons and both have taken ribbons at a local children's art show.

He begins to see a series of arcs in the tree and its branches, in the rock face, and its sculpted back. He leans back as far as he can go in the chair, hands folded over his stomach. "Everyone wants to be an artist in our field," he says, while his feet feel for a

The final design after it was hardened in the kitchen oven.

Putting together reference photos for the eagle composition.

A bald eagle. Photo by Larry Stevens.

A close-up of the head. Photo by Larry Stevens.

The scaly feathers on the back of the bird. Photo by Larry Stevens.

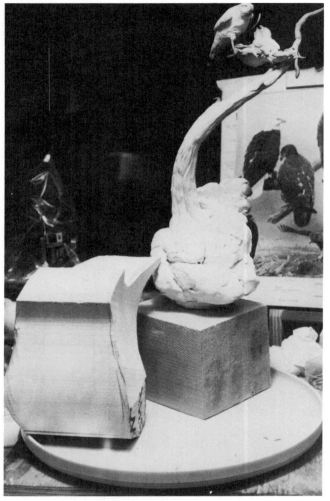

This is the rough-cut block of tupelo for the cliff face.

place on the edge of the worktable, but fail. "But that's just ego. There's no legitimate reason for it. If people are buying your work, what's the difference? If you call me an artist instead of a carver, what benefits do I get from that? Does it make me any better? I'm still doing the same thing, aren't I?

"I'm putting a lot of thought into this piece. It's going to be a sculpture in my mind. The birds will be secondary to the other things. It will still be a bird carving, but it will look comfortable to me."

He tries to explain his comfort zone. "A lot of times I have a preconceived notion of what I want with a mental picture. But if the piece, in wood or in clay, doesn't match up to what I'm expecting, then it feels wrong." He adds that he has mental pictures of most birds he has seen, and those become his final references.

It is after five. He has made some decisions. One is that he will not burn lines on the adult eagle. Instead, he will use a small grinding stone to put in all the texture. Another is that he will carve the two chicks out of one piece of wood. A third decision is that he will heat the model in the oven and keep it as a permanent reference. He then wonders whether a more thoroughly worked piece could be used for casting bronze replicas. He decides to find out more about the bronzing process.

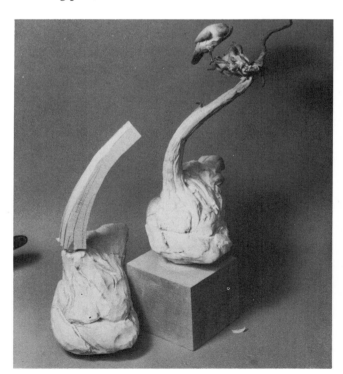

Bob starts to shape the rocks and added the main stump of the tree.

Another view of the block before shaping begins. Note the eagle references in the background.

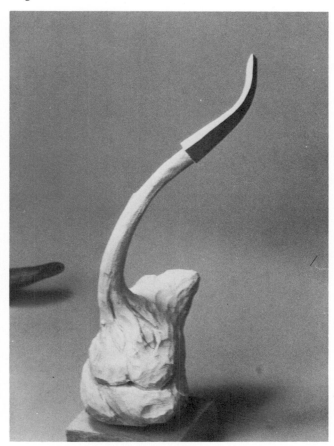

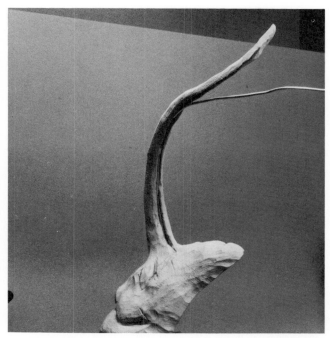

A piece of brass, inserted up the groove for strength, will also become the main support for the adult bird. A smaller branch will be soldered to the main support.

Two more pieces have to be added. The pieces are glued with epoxy. He then V-grooves, or notches, the perimeters of the butted-together joints and adds a material called Tuf-fil, a polyester resin.

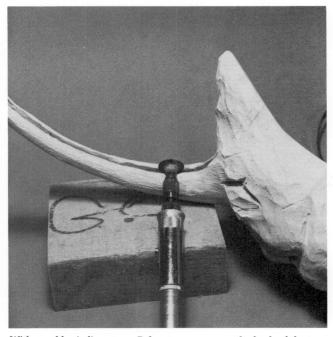

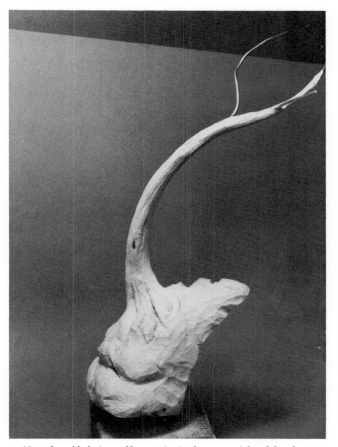

With an old grinding stone, Bob cuts a groove up the back of the tree.

Note the added piece of brass wire in the upper right of the photo.

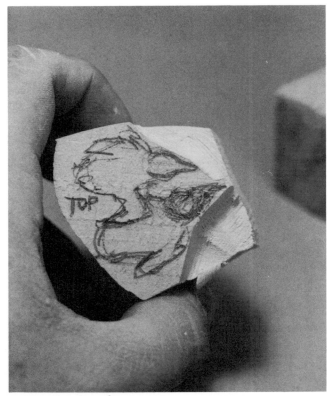

Bob rough-sketches the two baby eagles on the wood, which is tupelo.

Progress up to this point. The birds are brought closer together than Bob had initially drawn them.

Defining the two eaglets with a ruby carver. The excess is removed with a larger Karbide Kutzall bit.

A little farther along.

The birds nearly finished. Bob wants the two eaglets "snuggled up to each other."

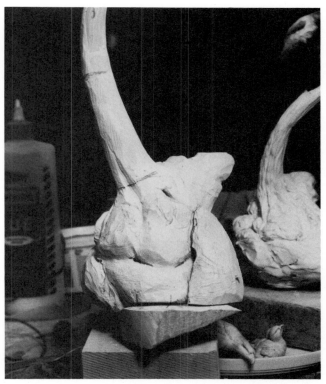

At this point, Bob realizes that for the size of the birds he is carving, the tree and base are too small. He adds pieces of wood to the cliff face on the side and bottom, thereby enlarging the entire piece.

A rough sketch of the adult eagle on a block of tupelo.

The first rough shaping done with a Karbide Kutzall bit. Bob says he is feeling his way through the carving.

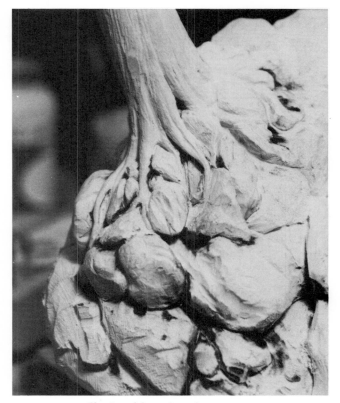

Shaping of the rocks and root system.

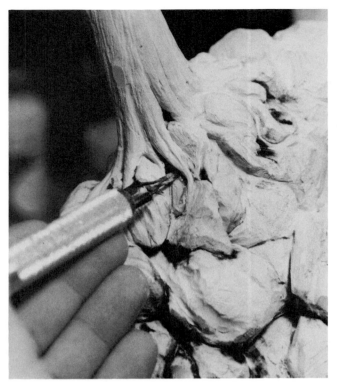

A lot of work is done with a burning tool to cut between the rocks and roots.

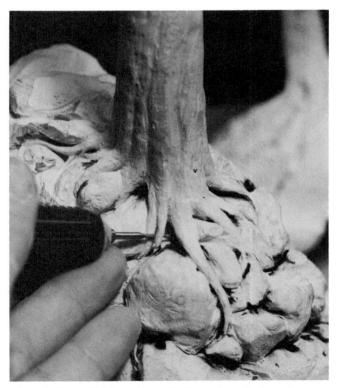

A diamond bit is used to get farther underneath the roots.

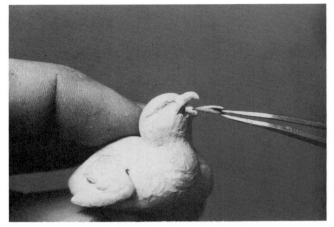

The mouth of this baby is in the open position. The lower mandible is then cut off and carved as a separate unit, with a tongue in the new lower mandible. Here Bob inserts the unit.

The pair of birds, one with its inserted tongue. Their eyes are 1 millimeter in diameter, brown or amber.

Bob has neither burned nor stoned them. Here, he uses a heavy gesso that thickened after air had gotten to it for a day. A heavy brush stipples the paint on the surface.

The head of the adult eagle so far. The eye is yellow, 2 millimeters in diameter.

The eaglets are in place, though they will be removed while the nest is built around them.

Starting the nest. The L-shaped wire will hold the eaglets. An extra wire running horizontally provides added strength.

Before the nest is constructed, Bob will use Tuf-fil on the tree to cover the joints and coat the wire.

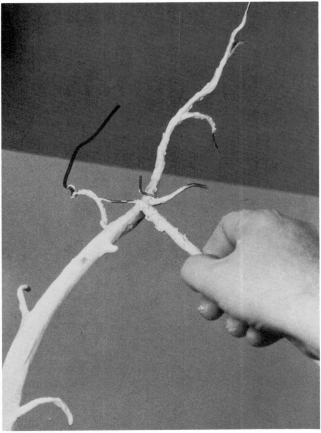

Here he applies the Tuf-fil. Note also that branches have been added along the tree.

The finished bush.

Bob begins to make bushes to be put on the base. Later, however, he decides to remove them. Bob feels they detracted from the overall composition. But to make them he begins with a multiple strand wire. The rubber coating of the wires can be seen in the pliers. Where the wires come out of the rubber, he supplies Super Glue to keep them from unraveling. He then separates and groups the wires.

Blobs of paint are applied to form buds on the branches.

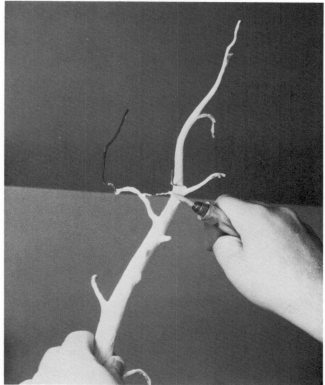

Bob uses a Karbide Kutzall bit to shape the Tuf-fil he applied earlier.

The spoked armature surrounding the post that will hold the eaglets.

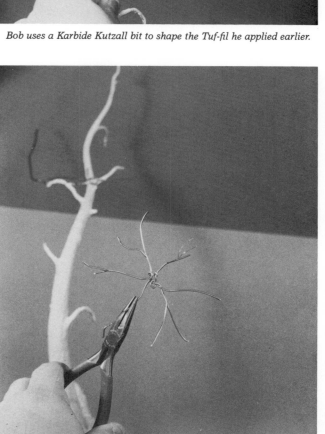

A spoked armature is made that will be the diameter of the nest. This is constructed out of heavier wire for heavier branches.

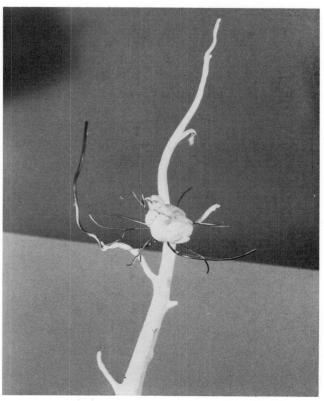

The spoke system with the young on it.

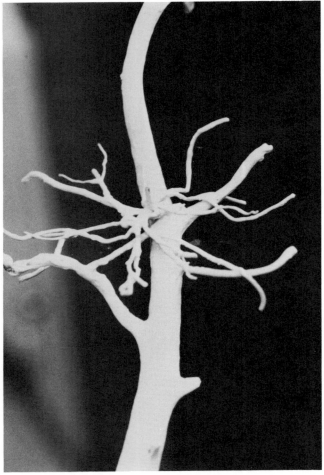

The spoke system is painted with thickened gesso.

Some of the strands twisted together.

The finished branches.

To make some of the branches, he begins with multiple-strand wire.

Bob lets Super Glue run down the wires to build up the branches.

He then dips the branches in lacquer to seal the copper.

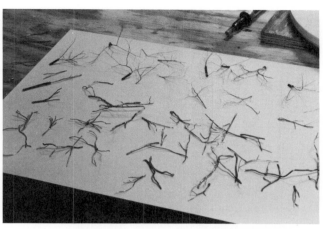

Most of the branches Bob has made—some are soldered together, some glued together, others are formed from twisted strands. Bob says at this point he knows just how a bird feels when it builds a nest.

The next step is to dip the branches into thickened gesso. The excess is shaken off.

Sticks and branches are applied one at a time. A few of the larger ones are soldered. Others are held with Super Glue. Bob says the process is slow, but this way the branches will not come loose later on.

Another branch, this one suggesting a branch from a pine tree.

The nest gets thicker.

The completed nest.

A piece of brass tubing will solve the problem of working on the bird. This is the separate piece of branch loosely joined to the main support.

The bird attached to the separate piece of tubing.

Bob thinks that making the toes for the adult eagle will be a problem. He would not be able to make the feet separately and then attach them because the toes will have to be wrapped around a branch, which is very close to the nest, leaving little room to work on them. He decides to have a removable branch so that he can work on the feet and the bird more easily.

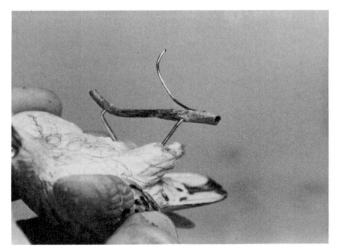

The branch has been shaped and a smaller branch has been added.

Bob forms the armature for the middle toe.

The eagle composition so far. The adult eagle has all its toes, and it has been primed with gesso.

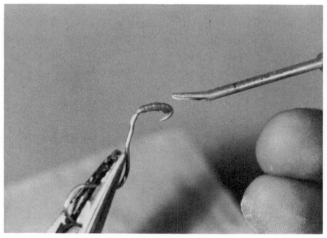

Duro epoxy is added and shaped with a tool Bob designed himself from a piece of brass tubing.

The first blocking in of the colors.

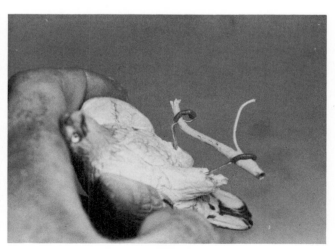

The first toes attached to the foot bones.

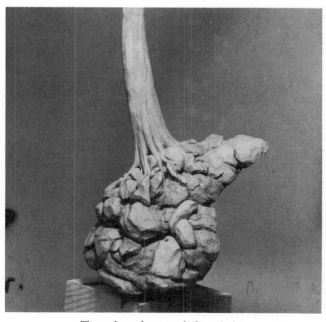

The rocks and tree ready for painting.

A walnut box painted black.

A close-up of the birds and nest.

The finished composition, which stands nearly two feet tall.

Another close-up.

Bob says he likes the horizontal pose of the adult bird, which could be either a male or female.

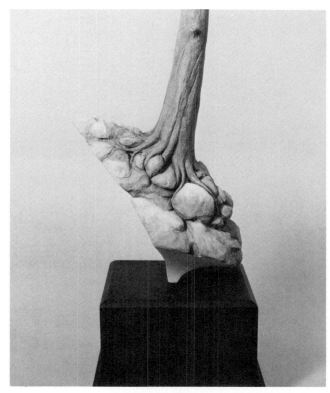

A side profile of the rocks.

A close-up of the back of the sculptured cliff face.

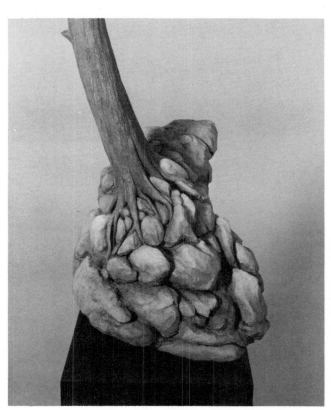

Another view of the rocks. Bob left the rocks with a rough texture, but used a lot of gesso in the paints so that the colors he applied would leave the surfaces with a dull or flat color.

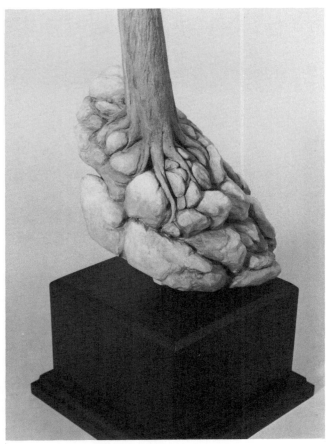

Bob admits to using some unusual acrylic colors for the rocks. Called fantasy colors, they have such names as Gnome Green and Dinosaur Gray. But they have a flat finish to them, Bob explains, which blends the entire piece together.

East to Easton

Larry Barth has climbed a knoll off the Pennsylvania Turnpike. With a small pocketknife, he is going to remove a low-growing branch from a sycamore tree as a model for a future composition. Bob narrates the moves. "He's almost there. He's making his way through some briar. He's at the tree. I see thumbs up. He's got it!"

Bob and Barth are on their way to Easton, Maryland. A small town on Maryland's Eastern Shore with a population of less than seven thousand, Easton is host town to an annual event. In November of each year the community brings in twenty-five thousand visitors for the biggest waterfowl festival in North America. It is an ultimate event in bird consciousness. Store mannequins take on duck heads, shops sell bird art, schools and civic centers house carvers and painters exhibiting and demonstrating, and plates of oysters are sold on the streets. Even the expected cold November rains do not deter visitors who stand in line for up to two hours waiting to see the artists and their works for sale.

At the 1986 festival both carvers will be giving talks and demonstrations to auditorium-size crowds. But neither has much to sell. Bob hopes to finish painting a goldfinch for his display table. The eagle nest and rock need more work, and the primitives he has are shorebirds on sticks and cedar log bases.

It is a few minutes past 8 A.M. They are only an hour from Barth's home in Stahlstown, Pennsylvania. "Tell us where we're at, Larry," Bob says with a broad grin that reveals both rows of teeth.

Barth, driving his van, says without turning to Bob, "Well, Bob, we're currently enjoying the scenic island of western Pennsylvania between the exits of Donegal and Somerset on the Pennsylvania Turnpike, exits nine and ten respectively." Larry elevates his face slightly and droops his eyelids impishly. "Somerset is only two miles. Thirty-seven miles to the next exit. Let's floor it. The power of this machine is awesome."

Bob says he sees an animal in a tree they pass at sixty-five miles an hour. Larry wants to know if it is a saber-toothed tiger. Without waiting for Bob's answer, he offers that there are no woodland bison in the area.

"Tell me about the woodland bison, Larry."

"It's not as big as the Plains buffalo, but it's roughly similar in appearance. It's the closest thing you can get to it. Barnyard chickens aren't going to even get close to it."

Larry says they are being followed by a snowy owl. "Don't look back. He doesn't see us yet."

The van's cassette deck plays songs by Donovan, the folk-rock singer of the 1960s. They talk about memorable lyrics. Larry says he wants to market his own album that would comprise introductions and back-ups "of girls who do she-bop, she-bop. They should be full-length songs with vocals only of doo-wah singers who do ooh, baby, wah-ooh or shu-bop."

Bob sees a log cabin that reminds him of one that sells red cedar knickknacks. Bob says he enjoys seeing red cedar boxes. Barth translates that into bird compositions. "A bird has to have a base," he says. "It has to have basal properties to support the carving. That's probably why we call them bases."

They pass a turnpike restaurant, but Larry convinces Bob that they must pass it by. He says they'll be turning off at the next exit. "Hang in there, Bob. If you go comatose, I could revive you later."

Breakfast is finally eaten in a fast-food restaurant. They comment on the artwork over the tables. Bob points to one painting and says, "That portrait of mourning doves flying through the trees is beautifully done. Reminiscent of blue-wing teal, which we all know is what a dove's head looks like."

"That is indicative of a successful dove portrayal," Larry says.

"The artist has depicted the doves the way I would."

"They certainly say doves to me," Larry adds.

"That turkey is exceptional," says Bob.

"I like the way the artist pulled off the illusion of the turkey looking thirty feet tall."

"That's something not many people can do."

"Maybe I misinterpreted it," Larry offers. "Maybe they were from the Pleistocene and they were really thirty feet tall, ancestors of what we know today as the wild turkey."

They are back in the van with more Donovan music in the tape deck. As Barth continues to drive, Bob starts to talk about his eagle and nest composition. The unfinished piece has been neatly packed in a box in the rear of the van. It is one of the few serious conversations he will have during his four days with Barth. "I decided to use tupelo and promptly used a couple of different pieces for the tree. That I reinforced with copper tubing."

He also made the decision to use tupelo for the birds, feeling that this wood would give more strength to the birds' fragile wingtips and beaks. Another decision was not to texture the birds with a grinding stone or ruby carver.

Barth makes a *sotto voce* imitation of Donovan that is convincing. Bob restrains his giggly laugh and points out the genius of Donovan's lyrics.

"I increased the size of the tree slightly," he says, ejecting the cassette. "Even though I saw an eagle close to a cliff face on a short, black spruce, my tree didn't seem tall enough. I also lengthened and narrowed the cliff face slightly to give the effect of a higher, taller piece."

Retaining his original idea of two immature birds in the nest, Bob carved them both from the same piece of tupelo. He rejected the idea of using a pattern, using a top view he sketched on the wood instead. He says he started carving it, "in an inspirational way. It was letting the wood dictate what you're going to carve. They're real cute looking. I made one a little larger than the other. You could say that's the older of the two."

The nest presented a challenge. "I found a really neat way to make branches," he explains. "I made a frame for the nest, a couple of pieces of wire that acted like big spokes. I soldered those to the tree to give me a solid base and a good solid frame to add the rest of the sticks to."

The "sticks" were made from pieces of copper wire of different gauges. Some of these he joined with solder, some he twisted together. He says he built the nest the way an eagle would make one: a single piece at a time.

"When I finished shaping each piece, I dipped it into gesso and shook off the excess. That seemed to give it enough texture to look like a real branch. But I also highlighted the pieces with colors and shading. For the bigger branches, I took some gesso and left it open to thicken. It became like a putty or spackling paste. That, I brushed on."

He smiles contentedly. "I have a good idea how a bird feels when it has to build a nest. It's tedious."

For the eaglets, he stippled or dabbed the surface with thick gesso, which created a soft, downy look. "I didn't think I could texture the birds finely enough to make the scales look good. I probably won't texture a lot of small birds from now on."

"A big problem was the feet of the adult bird because of the small branch she's standing on. It's a small diameter, so I had to decide how to mount the feet and still be able to work on them, especially since they'd be behind the nest. I decided to cut the branch off and insert a piece of brass tubing on the end. I shaped that to fit the other part of the branch. Then I built the feet on the branch."

Bob explains that little is left to be done with the eagles. What he calls intricate painting has to be done. Some fine branches still have to be made. And moss must be put into the nest.

"I decided the night before I left on this trip that I wouldn't rush it as I did the puffin piece. I would bring it as is and take it home and finish it. That's a big step for me."

Five more hours of driving brings the two carvers to Kent Island, Maryland. Route 301 passes through some one hundred miles of Maryland before it becomes Highway 50, the route to and across the Bay Bridge going toward Annapolis. As signs mark down the miles of the twin-spanned bridge, the Kent Narrows Bridge is hardly noticed. It is more an overpass than a span of steel and girders, for Kent Island is really a peninsula separated from the mainland by a channel of water.

One of the three traffic lights that legally divide up Kent Island's portion of Highway 50 indicates Cox's Neck Road, a four-mile stretch of rolling, buckling blacktop through properties that were once farmland. Near its end, flat, wooden geese painted in grays and blacks are posted notices of Jim Sprankle and his neighbors. A right turn onto a compacted oyster shell road and a half-mile of driving bring Bob and Barth to another sign. It is a readily recognizable, half-in-the-round canvasback duck, part of a larger sign that indicates the Sprankle home.

This will be the second stay with Sprankle for both Bob and Barth. On the previous visit the three taught a five-day seminar on bird carving.

Sprankle has carved ducks almost exclusively since 1970. During that time, he has taken nearly 250 blue ribbons, many from the World Championships. He was one of the first carvers to have an aviary, a place to keep ducks as living references. His style is unique. His birds project a personality that comes with an upturned head and the shape of the eyes. One carver describes his birds as having "a benign interest in the world."

During their stay with Sprankle and his wife, Bob and Barth will visit what may be the largest oak tree in North America. They will mimic bird songs as they walk across fields and imitate flying ducks in their room. They will spend late nights together talking about birds and art. They will even shape costumes out of poster board and dyed underwear to make them look like mallards. The name Barth will give them is "Mallardotrons."

It is nearly midnight of their first night. The Sprankles have gone to bed. Barth has wound his alarm clock. Tomorrow they will drive to Easton, twenty-five miles away. There they will have a table on which to display their work.

"Tomorrow you're going to have to deal with a host of people asking questions," Barth says from his bed.

"Is that the hostess with the mostest?" Bob asks.

"She's going to be there, too," Barth responds. As if speaking to a small child, he says, spacing his words out precisely, "You should be prepared. I'm going to pose as different spectators and I'm going to ask you to respond. Ready?"

"Ready, Larry."

"Gee, mister, these birds are really nice. How much are they?"

"I'm sorry, they're not for sale, but each one is individually priced."

"What do you mean they're not for sale?"

"These birds are already sold," Bob answers pleasantly.

"How much did they go for?"

"They went for five thousand dollars."

Barth gags out, "Oooh, oh, my."

Barth's voice takes on the raspy sound of an elderly woman. "Those are very beautiful pieces. Did you make the leaves?"

"I sure did."

"How did you make them?"

"They're made out of copper sheet."

"Where did you buy it?"

"At a hardware store or hobby center," Bob answers in a bubbly voice.

"Did you really? Well, you might try white bread. That's what we use back home."

"I'll remember that when I get home. Thanks a lot, old lady."

"Hi, my name is George. I like your birds."

"Thanks. I like them, too."

"How long have been doing this?"

"A long time."

"When did you start?"

"I've been doing this since I came here. I've been doing this bird for twelve years."

"When did you start carving?"

"Twelve years ago."

With a young woman's voice, Barth says, "Oh, these are so beautiful. May I touch this one? May I pick it up? May I scratch its eyes? I'd like to bend its tail feathers. May I do that? I'd like to scrape it on my shoe. May I scrape it on my shoe?"

—— ● ——

They are on the way back to Barth's home in Stahlstown. Barth says, "My mouth feels like Sculpey with pencil shavings stuffed through it."

Bob says, "My mouth feels like a barnyard after two months without any rain."

Suddenly, Bob lets out a minute-long scream. He calls it a preprimal scream. Barth initiates his own minute-long scream with Bob joining him. He calls it a postprimal scream.

A Partridge in a Field

It is the end of November. The Easton Show has been over for three weeks, and Thanksgiving with its overabundance of fowl is past. Bob is sitting in his office workshop looking through books. He has taken all of his Audubon and Peterson guides to birds off the shelf.

"Different pictures have variable colors. Some show more umber, some more gray, less brown, a cooler gray with a bluish tint to it. I like the muddy look of the bird, but not all muddied out. That's how it got its name, gray partridge. So I want to make the color stand out bright enough, but not cool looking. A warmer gray, but not too brown."

A native of Europe and parts of Asia, the gray partridge was introduced into North America during the late nineteenth and early twentieth centuries. Here, it has a range from New York State to Oregon. Only 12 to 13 inches long, it can be found in pastures, grasslands, grassy ridges, and agricultural lands, but it seems to be most successful in the farmlands of the Midwestern states. There, conditions may resemble those in Europe and Asia.

He likes the colors of the bird, though he says he is not partial to any particular plumage coloration. He has a mount of the bird, from which he can copy the grays, browns, and complex bands of vermiculation that appear like closely knit dots and dashes of black.

The Max McGraw Wildlife Foundation is a 10-minute drive south of Carpentersville. A wooden sign before the entrance calls the land a game farm. Birds are raised there for sale. Pintail ducks, pheasants, geese, mallards, and other birds are kept in pens and bred. Bob has spent time on the farm banding birds, and did bird counts on the property during past Christmases.

In a long, one-story building, subdivided into wood and chicken-wired enclosures measuring 10 by 20 feet, are gray partridges. Several hundred are kept in the pens, with males being separated from females until the breeding season. In one cage, there are anywhere from seventy-five to one hundred birds. Bob visited McGraw in July to look specifically at the feet of gray partridges. One was taken out of its pen and brought out into the sunlight, where Bob took photos

The partridge composition really begins at the McGraw Wildlife Foundation, where partridges are raised.

A mounted specimen of a gray partridge. Bob calls it "a nicely feathered bird."

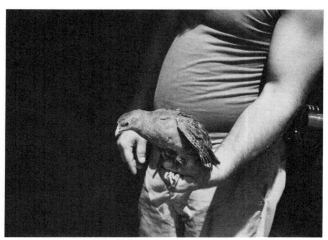

A close-up of a live male partridge.

One of the purposes of the visit is to look at the feet of the bird.

of the feet. But he admits he did make notes on the feather coloring, saying that the adult birds were in mature plumage.

Pointing to the mount that now is on his worktable, Bob says that some areas on the bird stand out as very red. "The mount has a good pattern, but it's real red, a chestnut red. I want to make my bird browner." He adds that the feet of the mount are in bad shape, a major reason for having visited the game farm. "I was curious how long the nails would be. Caged birds don't have to scrape for food. So nails and beaks will grow longer than normal. They have to be clipped. But at least I got an idea from the live birds," he says.

Bob had seen a flock of them not far from Carpentersville. In fact, they can be found in residential areas of the Midwest. He has seen very few carvings of the species and feels it is an interesting gamebird. He thinks his will be less than half size.

The same day he visited the game farm, Bob took his camera to photograph a patch of roadside. The

Gray Partridge

approximately ⅓ scale

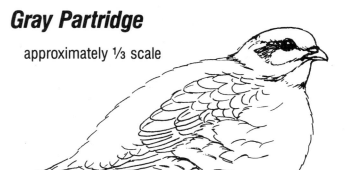

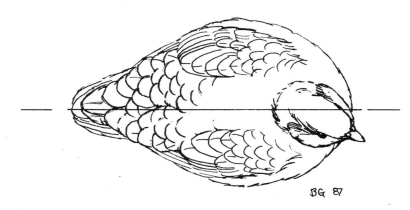

area comprised gravel, dirt, leaves, grasses, and low plants. He plans on having his partridge in a habitat that would suggest a field with a hedgerow. Starting at the mount, he explains that he wants dirt, some grass, and weeds. "I don't want to cover the bird up. I can't have this huge green mass and a bird in it. The grass I photographed was too much. I know I can use some rocks. Those get thrown up along a hedgerow by a farmer. That's typical. But you wouldn't have to have a hedge. I don't know how I could," he says, frowning. He moves the mount a few inches. "It would overpower the bird. Maybe just the edge of a hedgerow. Toward the back I can have some bigger things to give the effect of the edge of a field, a hedgerow, so one side will be more dirt, the other more plants. That's kind of what I have pictured in my mind."

Early thinking about the piece came up with a hedge or bush plus grass. But the grass would take

Some partridge models done in Super Sculpey.

The model Bob ends up with.

The partridge profile in wood.

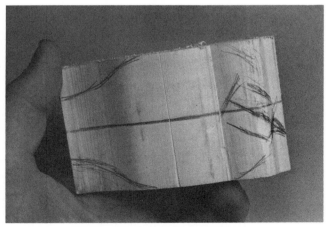

Drawing the turned head on the block.

weeks to make, and might hide the bird. More thinking suggests barbed wire and a post in the habitat. He calculates that the size of the bird will determine the size of the post, which does not have to be very big. He remembers having found a field in which every other post was very thin, some not more than large branches planted in the ground. He thinks a fence post will give some necessary height to the composition.

———•———

Bob has taken a small, cardboard box and taped a thin piece of plywood to the bottom. Through that he has inserted a wood screw that picks up the base of the partridge piece. It is the third week in March 1987, and he is sending it to a writer friend who will enter it in the U.S. National Decoy Show, held in Melville, New York. The box with the partridge and base will be put into a larger box filled with Styrofoam pellets. Bob ships nearly every one of his birds in a box within a box.

The partridge does not stand, but rests on gravel and sand. There are small stones imbedded in the ground habitat. Behind the bird is a small bush with wiry branches and clusters of small red berries. Bob explains how this habitat developed from his original concepts. "Originally, I wanted a field with grass and a fence post, but I wasn't real picky about what I wanted to do. I went back to the preserve in the fall and winter with the kids. I saw there multiflora roses and rose hips. I thought one would be nice on the base. It's twisty, and it's typical of the kind of area where you might find a partridge.

"I decided to use that and grasses. I brought home samples of milkweeds and I experimented with different grasses and put together a rosebush. The ones I saw had little rose hips. I figured their color would bring out the red, fleshy area around the eyes of the bird." He smiles as he works the partridge box into the pellets filling the larger box. "That eye color comes around breeding time, so I took some liberties and made the composition late fall, early winter. But I still left that red color on the bird. The color of the branches has a nice gray patina down to all different browns. Those reflect the colors of the bird. The arch of the branches as they hang down reflects the same shape as the back of the bird. And the partridge nestled under the plant perfectly. So the branches make it a circular piece."

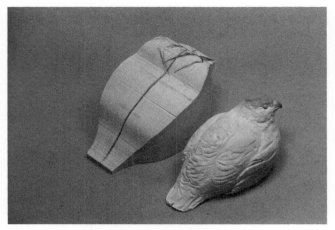

A comparison of the clay model and the cutout.

Getting the roundness of the body.

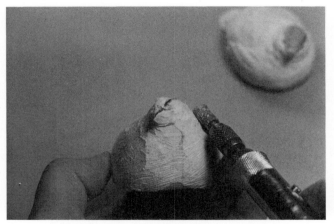

Rough shaping begins with a Karbide Kutzall cutter.

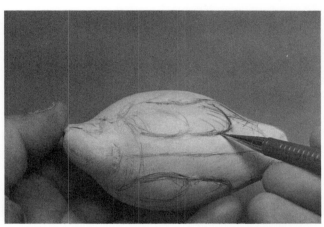

Establishing the larger feather groups: the primaries, secondaries, tertials.

Progress so far.

The rear of the bird. Bob says the partridge has a twist to it, with one foot sticking out from under one side. A slight lopsidedness will indicate that the bird is lifting its body.

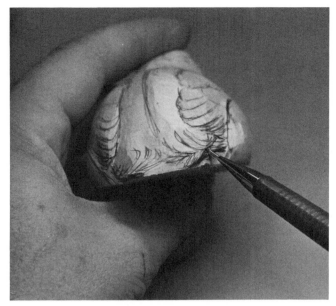

Drawing in the tail feathers.

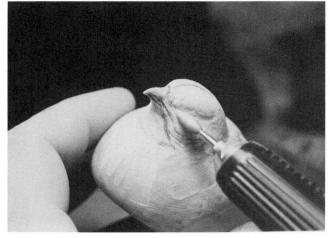

Cutting in the details with a flame-shaped ruby carver.

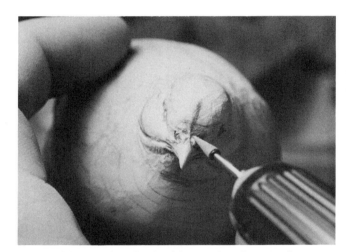

Establishing the finer details of the nostrils with a pointed stone.

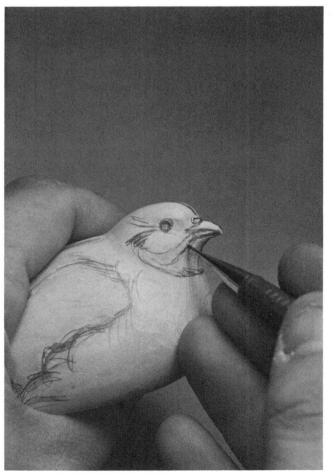

Sketching in some of the facial details.

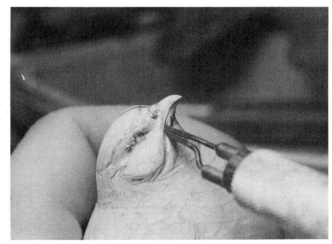

Bob uses a burning pen to divide the upper and lower mandibles.

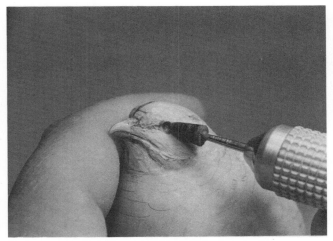

Putting in the eyeholes with a grinding stone.

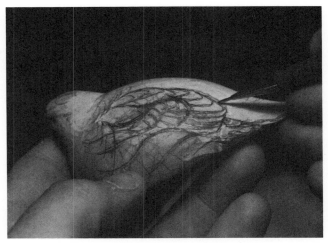

More layout of the wing feathers.

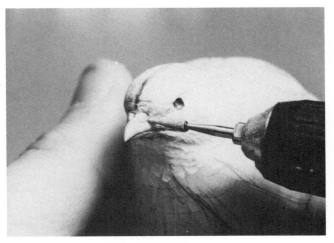

More detailing on the beak.

Landscaping on the breast by cutting in some of the larger feather groups.

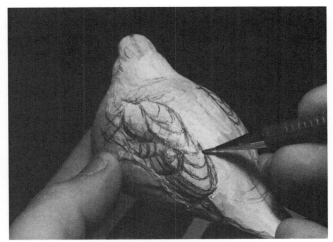

Laying out the individual feathers on the wings.

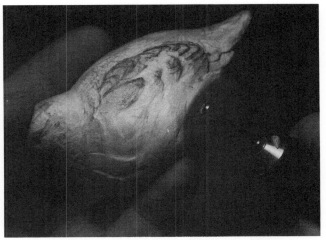

Running a sanding pad over the area previously worked. This softens the look, Bob explains.

Bob next lays out individual feathers on the groups just defined.

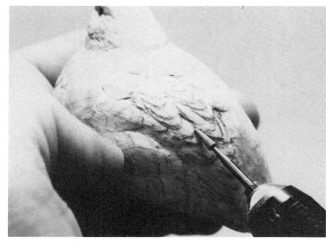

Cutting in the scapular feathers.

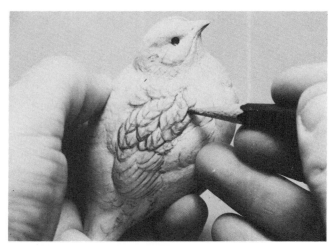

Sketching in the scapular feathers.

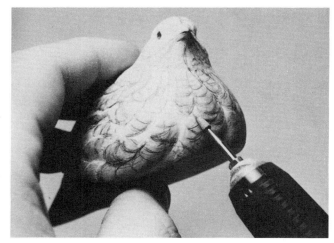

Using a stone with a rounded end, Bob cuts in the breast feathers.

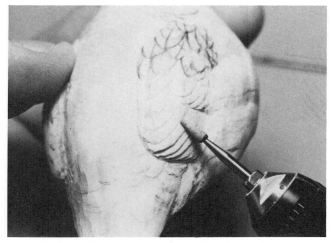

Cutting in the secondaries and tertials with a small stone.

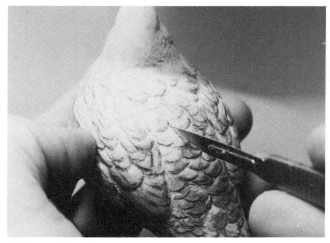

With a scalpel, Bob makes splits and deeper cuts between the feathers.

Defining the cheek feathers.

Redefining the beak.

Using an X-acto knife, Bob goes back and undercuts these feathers to raise them slightly and open them up more.

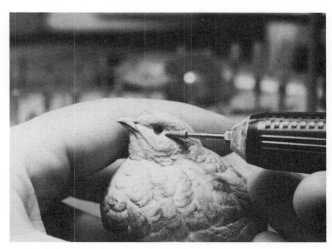

Finished detail work on the face is done with a small stone and a Gesswein.

More feather work on the face with a small pointed stone.

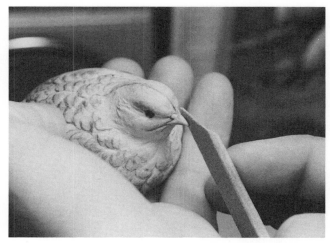

Bob uses a small stick with sandpaper glued to it to smooth the beak.

The head so far.

Bob uses Duro two-part epoxy to make the fleshy part around the eye and shapes it with a dental tool.

Bob says that because of the way the head is pushed down, some of the breast feathers will stick out. Bob uses an X-acto or scalpel to undercut them.

More shaping around the eye. The eyes will be hazel, 3 millimeters in diameter.

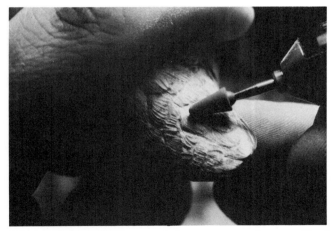

Bob uses a ball-nosed stone to put in large grooves on the upper side of the tail. Then he will go back and texture them. The stoning helps soften the look.

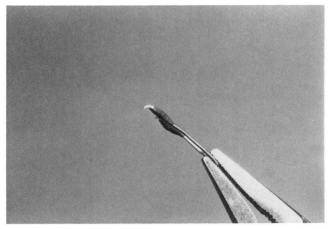

These two toes are made from the same piece of wire bent in half. Bob applies Duro epoxy over them. Note also that the nails are shaped in the copper wire.

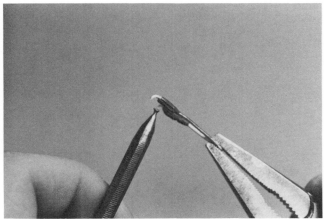

Rolling this tool down the sides of the toes splits the pads.

The completely textured bird, primarily stoned.

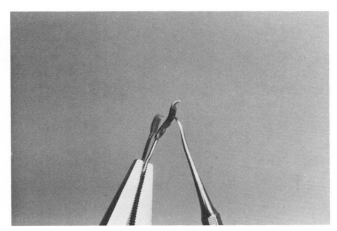

The scales are formed using a small dental instrument.

A side view of the textured partridge.

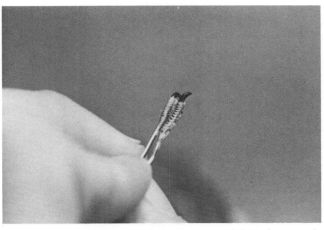

The painted toes. The feet are a silvery blue-gray and the pads are a pale yellow.

Bob employs a holding device when sealing and painting a bird.

Sealing the bird with lacquer.

Bob first blocks in the main colors and patterns. Getting color on the bird helps with blending later on.

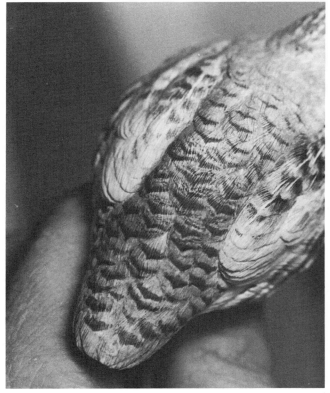

Several thin coats of gesso are then applied.

Working from the back down to the tail.

Vermiculation is done with a fine technical pen. Acrylics are used to make a dark, brown-black vermiculation.

The walnut pedestal to be used with the composition.

He tapes the larger box closed. "Putting other things around the piece seemed to ruin it."

The base for the piece is really two parts. On top of a mushroom-shaped piece of turned walnut is the ground or habitat base with bird and rose bush. "What I was trying to do was get the base off the ground a little bit rather than sticking it on a piece of walnut. You can view a bird carving without a base detracting from the piece. I wanted it to be kind of baseless, almost as if it's hovering. It looks dug out of the ground. You can hardly see the ualnut. It's something different. I like it."

He says that leaves and grasses detracted from the bird. "It's so small, and there's a lot going on. Lots of colors, lots of things to look at. Anything more would draw away from the bird. That's why I left the ground bare."

The primary base is a piece of plywood covered with a material called Durham's Rock Hard Water Putty. Much like plaster of Paris, it comes in powder form and is combined with water to create a paste that hardens after one hour. Sprinkled over that were different gravels and dirt. The rose bush Bob made from pieces of brass tubing bent, shaped, and soldered together.

The berries presented a problem. He had originally made them with an epoxy putty that could be shaped and would harden overnight. But these were not consistent enough. Then he was making L-shaped pieces of wire, putting the berries on the ends of these, and gluing the pieces to the branches in groups. "I couldn't solder them together because I couldn't get close enough with my fingers to form the berries. Rose hip

Attaching the plywood "earth" base to the pedestal with a wood dowel.

Shaping the plywood. Bob chose plywood because he thought there would be less chance of its warping after he had applied Durham's Rock Hard Water Putty to it. It is a good grade of plywood, Bob says.

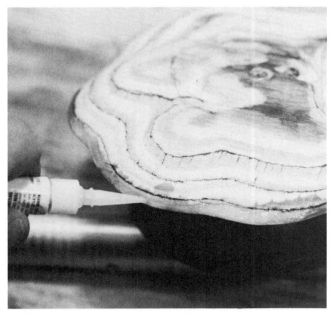

Bob impregnates the wood with Super Glue to harden it and prevent chipping or cracking.

Basic habitat materials: brass tubing, wire, pliers and sheet metal.

berries taper out from the branch side like teardrops. Their L-shaped stems kept coming off because the glue would not hold well enough. If I tried to solder them, the epoxy berries would heat up and melt.

"I had a box I made for shipping that had been glued together with hot-melt glue. Some of the glue had oozed out of one of the seams. With my woodburner I cut off the excess glue. When I touched the burner to the glue, it formed a little drip. So I went ahead with a piece of wire and put some glue on the end of it and then touched my burner to the glue." Bob's speech gets more animated as he explains the discovery. "It instantly formed a kind of teardrop. It was perfect. So I went back and soldered all the stems to the branches and used the glue gun and burner to form the berries."

Bob may use round or square tubing for making large branches. Here, he shows that by telescoping pieces together, he is able to recreate the true shape of branches.

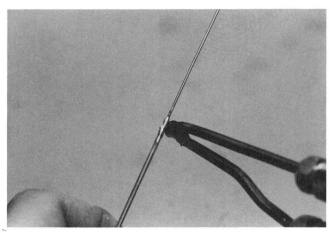

Soldering two round pieces that fit one inside the other. This begins the making of a small rosebush.

A small disc sander is used to grind smooth the stepped-down pieces of tubing.

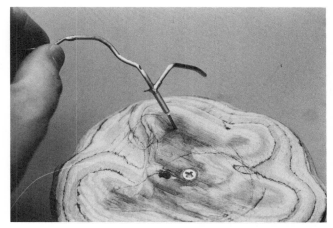

A square brass peg will hold a portion of the bush in place.

Bob wants to add a limb to this main branch. To do this, he must first cut a notch in the tubing with a small disc coated with carbide grit.

The carbide-coated disc will cut tubing to accept two more pieces.

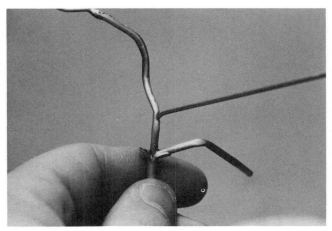

The smaller piece of tubing is put into the notch. This will then be soldered in place.

All three pieces for this forking branch will be soldered together.

Joining the pieces together.

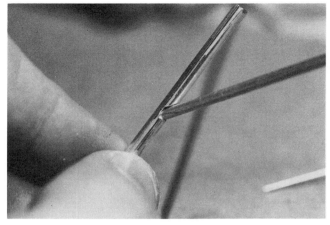

The added branch.

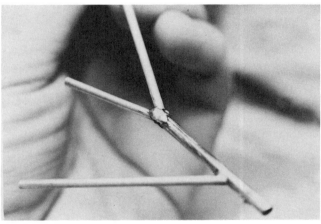

The soldered-together pieces of tubing.

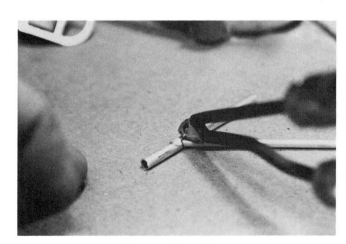

The pieces being soldered.

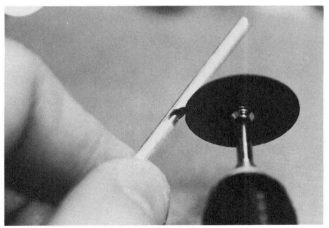

Here Bob makes a slot for another branch insertion.

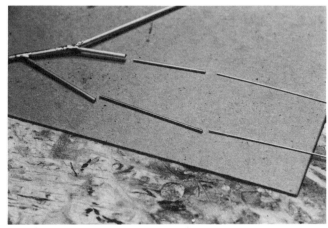

Stepping down the long branches of the rosebush.

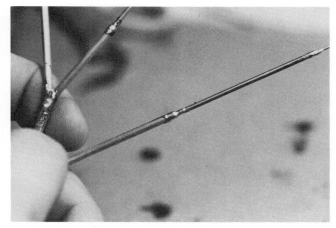

The pieces soldered together.

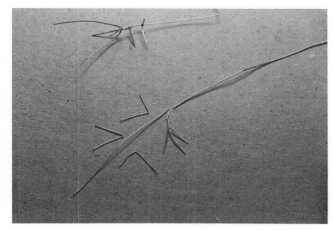

Bob lays out the small branches on which the rose hips will be attached.

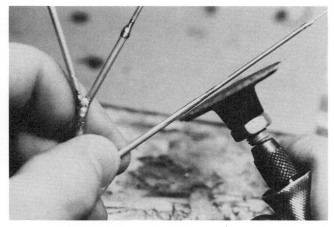

The disc sander blends the pieces together. Bob warns that the tubes have to be far enough inside one another before grinding on them so that the grinding does not create holes.

A very fine notch is cut to make for a better solder joint.

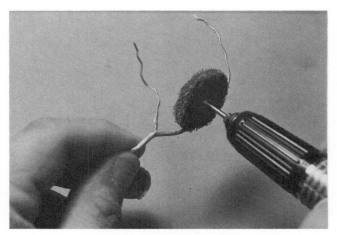

After the tubing is shaped, it is then polished with a defuzzing pad.

Soldering the small pieces onto the main branch.

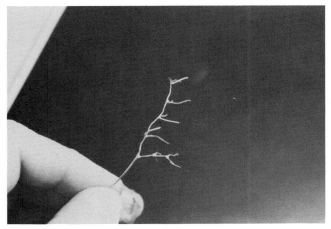

A completed branch.

A close-up of the branches and rose hips.

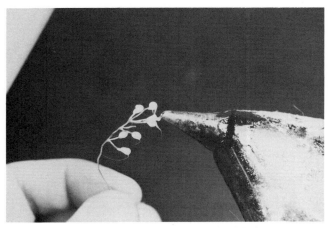

Bob puts globs of hot-melt glue on the ends of the branches.

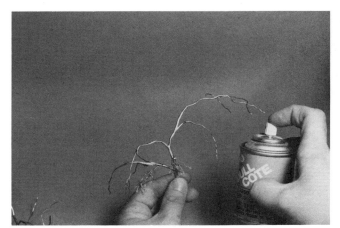

Bob sprays lacquer on the bare metal branches.

With a very hot burning pen tip, Bob touches the glue globs, which then liquify momentarily and form teardrop shapes.

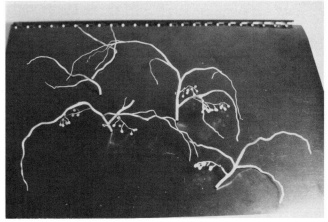

A coat of pale gray gesso is then applied.

Bob makes the rose thorns from equal parts of modeling paste and gesso. He uses a small pointed tool to apply the mixture.

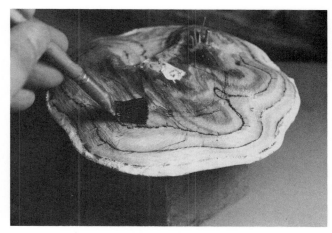

The plywood base is sealed with lacquer.

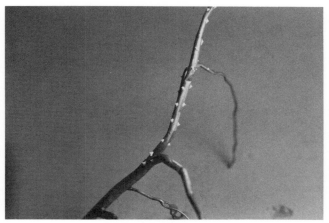

The finished thorns.

The rocks are made from Durham's Rock Hard Water Putty. After mixing it with water, Bob takes the putty and rolls it in his palms to make the rocks.

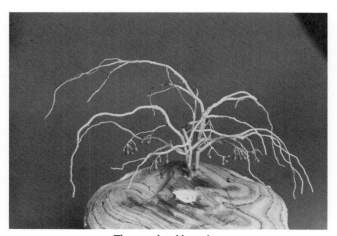

The completed branches.

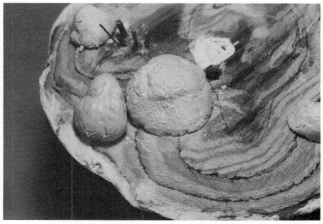

After placing the rocks on the base, Bob pulls a wet but stiff brush across the surfaces. He will later have to glue the rocks in place.

The dirt and gravel are made from different-size pieces of Durham putty. They are colored with acrylic paints—grays and browns primarily—that are put into the mix of water and putty. Bob is careful choosing the colors so that they will not camouflage the partridge.

The completed base.

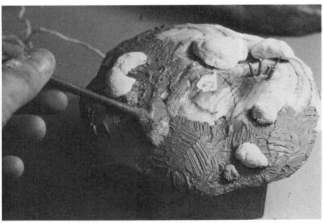

Before applying the dirt and gravel, Bob applies putty that is the same color as the grit put on the surface. The wet mix also will bond the dirt and gravel to it.

The finished composition.

Applying the dirt and gravel.

A close-up of the partridge. Notice the toes that emerge from under the body.

The profile of the bird.

Another close-up of the breast and flank areas.

The head.

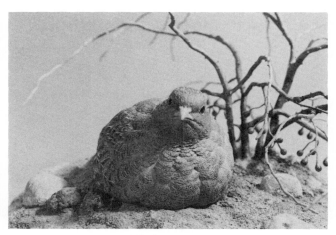

The breast area.

The back of the bird.

The rear of the composition.

Winter Miniatures

Cardinal

½ scale

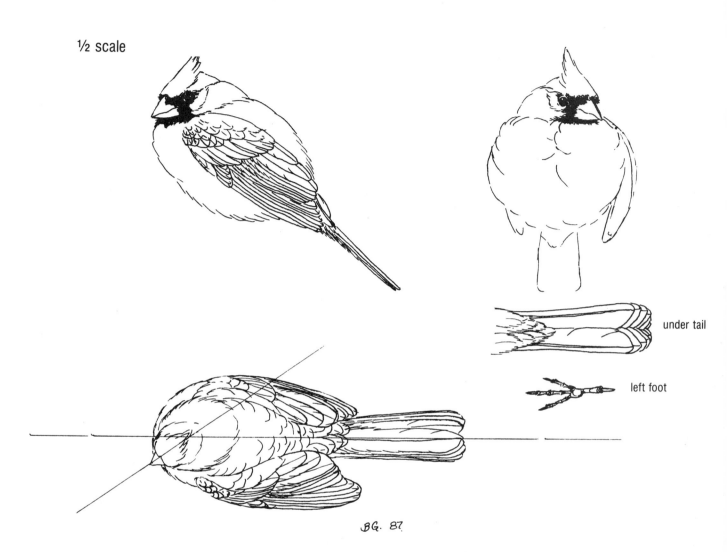

under tail

left foot

BG. 87

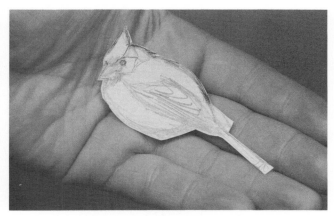

The cardinal pattern.

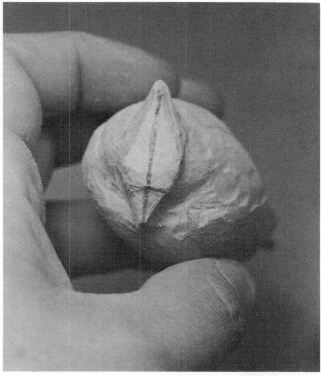

Note the twist of the head and how it relates to the body. The head is also cocked slightly.

The cutout with a centerline.

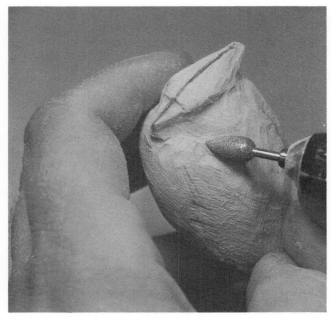

The preliminary roughing begins with a large carbide cutter. A ruby carver does more shaping.

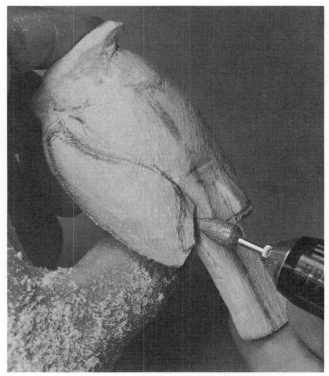

Roughing in the wing. Bob drops and opens the bird's left wing slightly.

The wing is also pulled away from the body slightly.

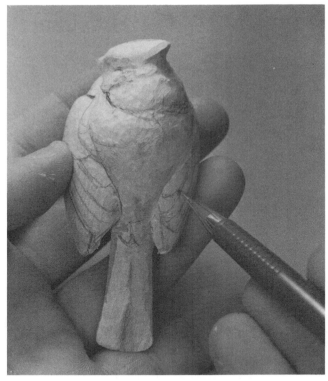

Drawing the wing groupings.

Separating the scapulars and wing.

Cutting the areas around the nape and cape of the bird with a diamond bit.

Progress so far.

Bob mounts the bird. Part of the belly has been hollowed out so that the cardinal fits over the branch.

Notice how the head is cocked to one side and how the wing extends off the body.

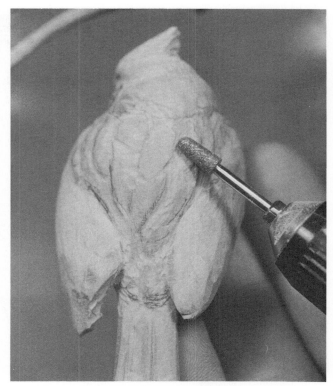

Working on the feather groupings on the back.

Work on the scapular feathers and cheek patch. Bob says he has a feel for putting feathers into groupings, and that this is not something easily taught to students, since he makes it up as he goes along.

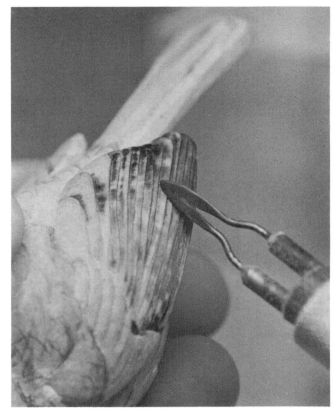

Another view of the separations.

Separating the wing feathers with a thin burning pen tip.

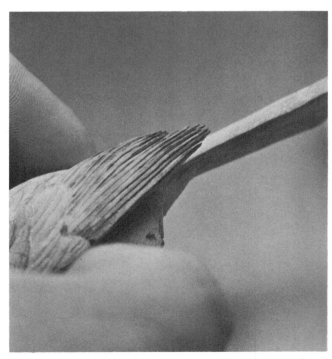

The separations viewed from the side. Note that the feathers twist from a vertical to a horizontal plane from the lower left of the photo to the middle. This twist allows them to follow the shape of the body and tail.

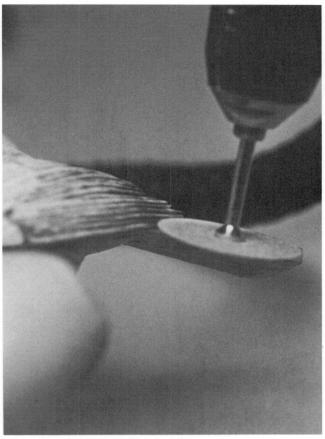

More separating of the flight feathers is done with a sanding disc covered with carbide grit on one side.

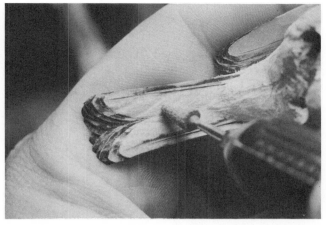

With a stone, Bob makes grooves to give the wavy appearance he has seen in this area.

A fine-pointed stone cuts the shafts in at the base of the tail. Bob says these are stiff and stick out from the flat surface of the feathers.

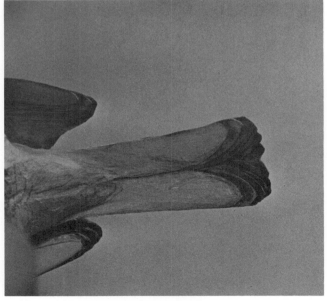

The underside of the tail.

A close-up of the fine-pointed stone.

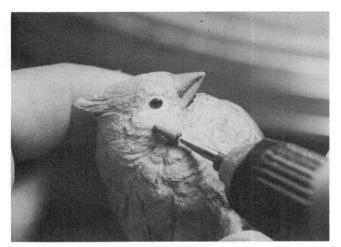

A similar stone but one with a rounded end to cut the face feathers.

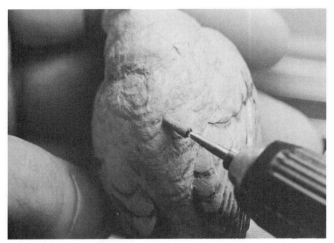

The same stone with a rounded end cuts the back feathers.

Cutting the lower feathers. Notice the groupings and tracts. Also note the notch cut where the bird sits down over the branch.

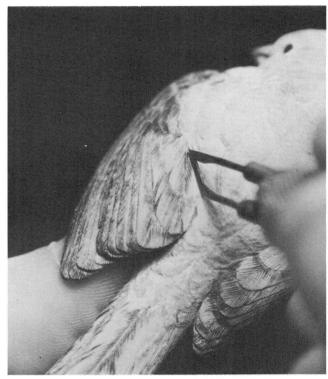

Burning in the flight feathers. The body feathers are textured with a stone.

A view of the burning.

A holding device is used to prepare the bird for painting. A screw at the end of the holder is inserted into the notch cut into the bottom of the bird.

Note the stoning on the breast of the cardinal.

The bird is sealed with lacquer, and gesso is applied with a stiff brush.

A profile view.

Details on the head, with 3-millimeter brown eyes.

Bob makes a groove up the underside of the branch into which he will insert copper wire for support.

Bob wants this bird to sit up high on a spindly branch. Two pieces of wood have been joined to achieve the shape Bob wants.

The small rotary grinder that makes the groove.

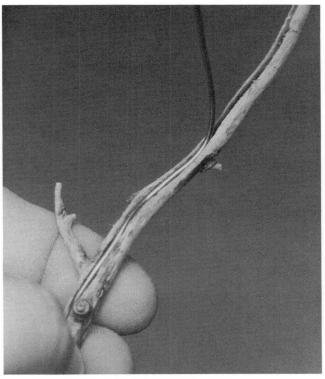

Inserting the copper wire.

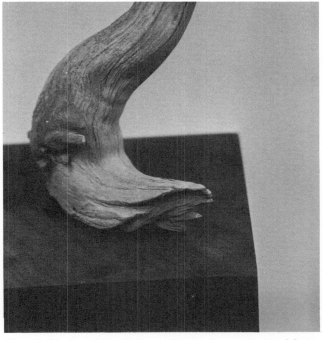

The end of the branch that Bob carved to give it some shape and design.

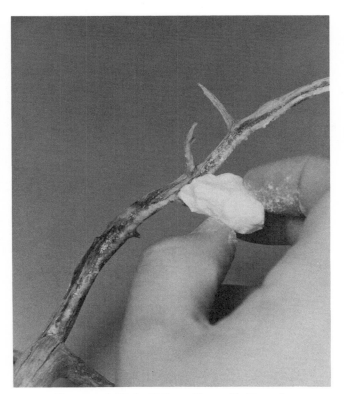

The groove is filled with Super Glue and baking soda.

The completed piece.

The branch stands about 12 inches high.

A close-up of what Bob describes as a winter cardinal.

The pencil indicates just how small the bird really is.

The back of the bird.

Cardinal

Note how the wing comes off the body. Bob says this is one of his favorite pieces.

Sanderling

½ scale

BG. 87

Bob puts tracing paper on his finalized pattern for the sanderling. He does this so he can transfer it to wood.

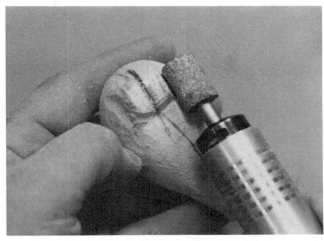

Shaping the body and the head with a Karbide Kutzall cutter. Note the centerline of the body and the head.

Darkening the back of the tracing paper allows him to transfer the pattern to a block of jelutong.

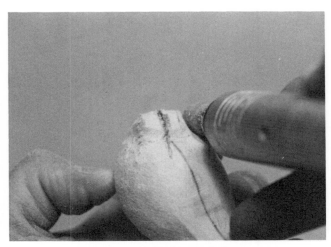

Bob calls this blocking in the head.

The bird on the wood.

Note how the head is twisted around and turned into the body.

A Gesswein and a steel-edged burr. This combination leaves a very smooth surface.

Drawing the scapulars and wing feathers.

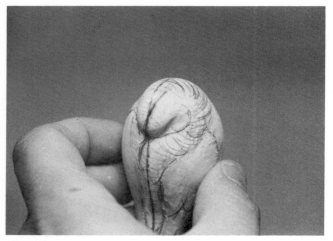

This view shows the twist of the neck and what happens to the feathers when the bird turns its head.

Another view of the feather groupings.

A profile of the sleeping sanderling so far.

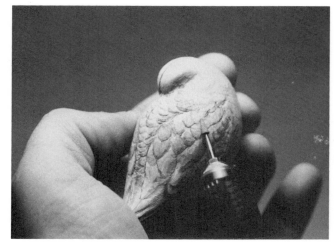

Cutting in the groups with a rounded-end stone.

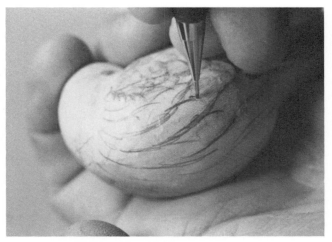

The flow lines of feathers on the flanks and breast.

The finished undertail area.

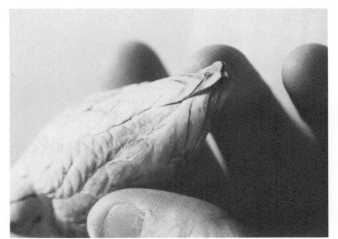

The crossed primaries. The rest of the bird has been stoned.

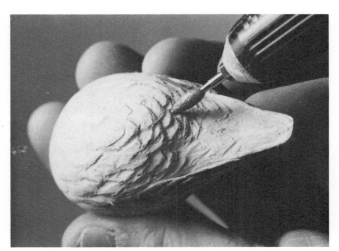

Separating the puffy feathers under the tail with a ruby carver.

The rocks start as three pieces of tupelo.

Bob grinds, shapes, and rounds them. He burns the rocks with a blow torch.

Applying a lacquer sealer.

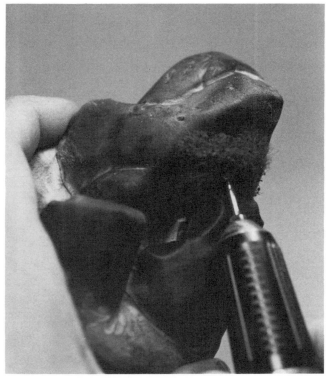

Bob uses a defuzzing pad to smooth the surface and to remove the charred areas. He says that the burning helps give a natural look to the rocks. Sand marks are removed, as are sharp corners.

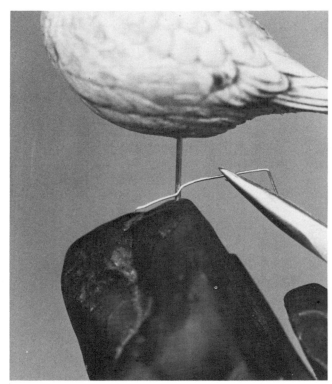

The bird is mounted on a piece of brass that will be the foot bone. Bob is measuring for one of the toes.

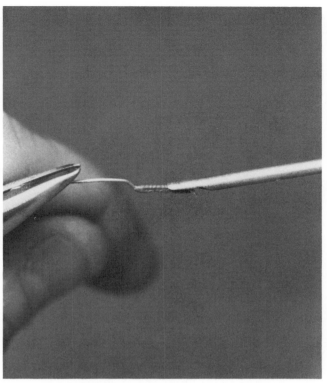

Bob applies Duro two-part epoxy to this toe and makes the scales with a homemade tool.

Positioning the toe and making it stationary with Super Glue.

Comparing the finished toe with the foot bone.

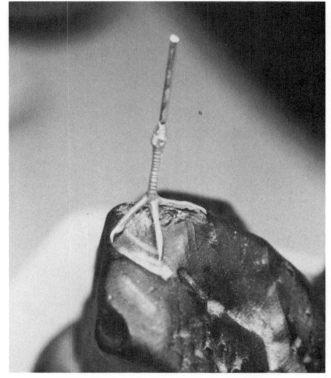

Epoxy fills in the gap between the toes and the foot.

Filling in the eye cavity with spackle.

Closing up the eye, though the spackle is pulled back a bit to create a tiny slit.

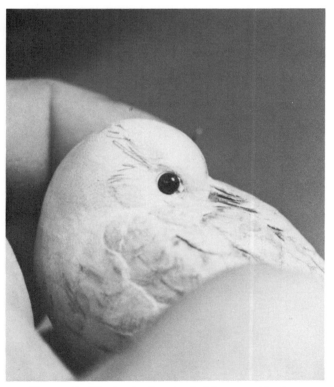

The eye—3 millimeters in diameter, dark brown—set in place.

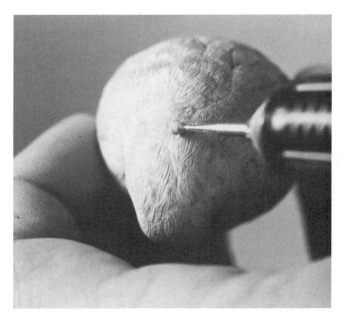

Stoning on the bird.

The gessoed sanderling.

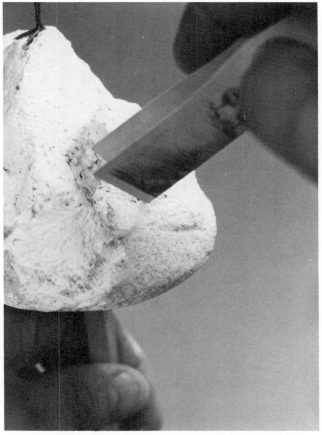

Bob pours real sand between the rocks. (The sand can be seen coming out of the bottom of a folded card.) Bob wants a different texture at the bottom of the composition.

Back to the rocks, Bob applies a mix of gesso and modeling paste, leaving it fairly thick.

An old, stiff brush stipples the mix before it dries.

After the rocks dry, Bob takes a defuzzing pad to knock off the nubs left by the stippling. This leaves a smooth but pitted surface.

The rocks are painted with a mix of ultramarine blue, burnt umber and gesso to produce a pale gray. The rock is then coated with a dark wash of ultramarine blue, burnt umber, and a small amount of white.

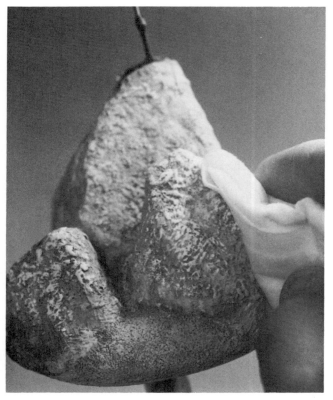

The rocks are then rubbed with a soft pad and denatured alcohol. This removes the dark glaze and leaves the gray underneath.

The miniature carving compared with the study skin.

The finished sanderling composition. The bird is in a resting position, Bob says, fluffed up with one foot tucked up into the belly, typical of birds at rest. He also says that this is the adult plumage, with soft grays. He adds that he wanted to elevate the bird and thought the rocks would be fun to make.

A close-up.

The breast area.

The back of the bird.

Mourning Dove

½ scale

BG. 87

The cutout for the mourning dove, half size. The wood is jelutong.

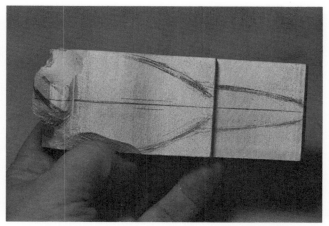

The head is blocked in and lines are drawn on top of the cutout where excess wood is to be removed.

Establishing a centerline with a compass. Bob cut a notch at the bottom of the leg so that it rides along the edge of the wood.

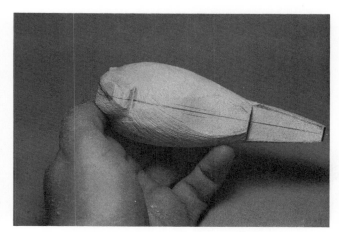

The bird is rounded with a Karbide Kutzall bit.

The blocking in of the head using a Karbide Kutzall bit. Note that Bob begins with parallel sides.

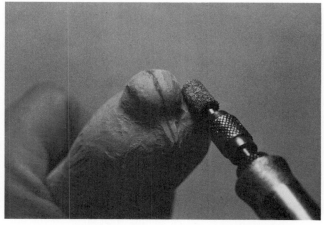

With a smaller Karbide Kutzall bit, detail is put into the head. Note that the beak has been established.

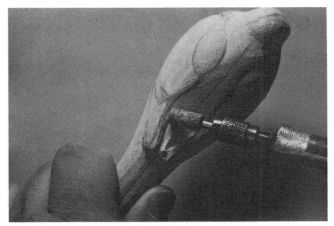

Roughing in the wings with a square-ended Karbide Kutzall bit.

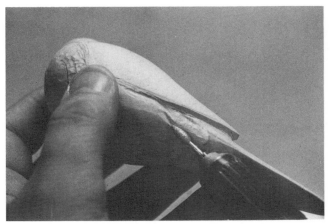

Defining the flank area where it meets the lower coverts.

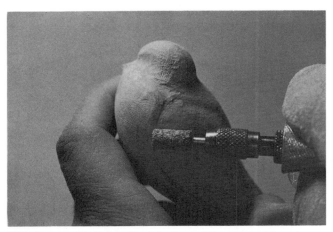

With the same bit, Bob outlines the front of the wing and breast area.

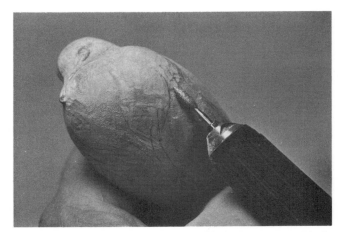

Bob establishes the larger feather groups on the breast area with the ruby carver.

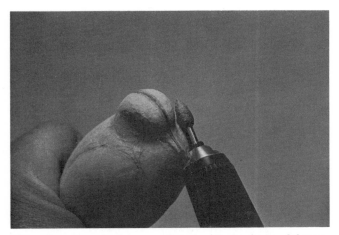

With a flame-shaped ruby carver, Bob gives the head more definition.

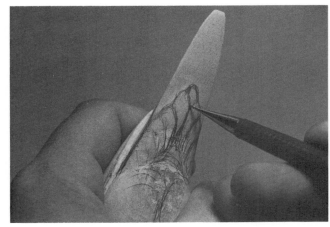

Laying out the undertail coverts, which, he notes, are large feathers.

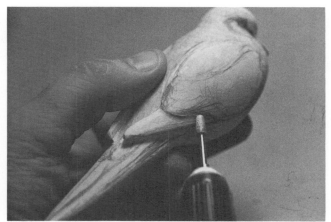

A ball-nosed diamond bit cuts in the main feather groups on the wing.

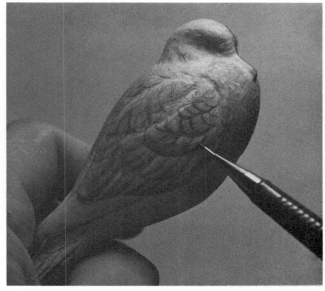

After the initial cuts are made in the last step, feathers removed by the grinding are resketched.

The feathers laid out on the wing.

Cutting the feathers with the diamond bit by defining each row with deep cuts.

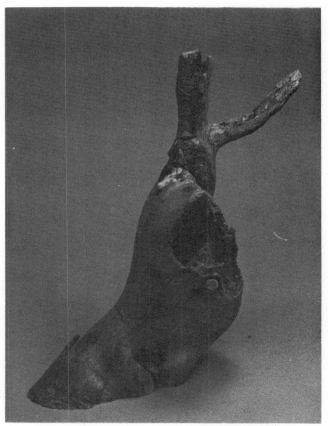

Bob will start work on the branch that the bird will sit on.

Determining how the bird will sit on the branch.

The reworked branch.

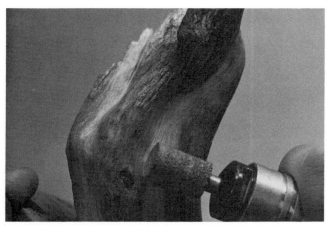

With a Kutzall bit, Bob reshapes the branch to make it look the way he wants.

With a disc-shaped cutter and Gesswein, Bob puts cracks and fissures in the wood.

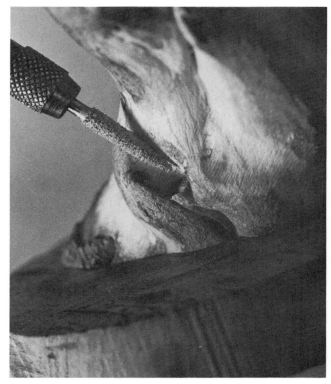

Bob cuts out a notch into which he will insert a smaller branch. On this he will hang leaves.

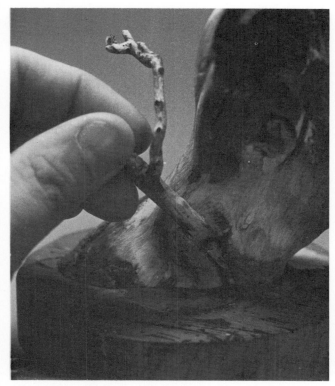

The added branch, which will be joined to the main wood with Super Glue and baking soda.

The first step in fitting the bird to the branch. Bob makes alignment marks on the bird and the branch. When he removes the bird, he will be able to replace it in the same spot.

Before Bob can fit the bird to the branch, he must first mount the dove on a dowel.

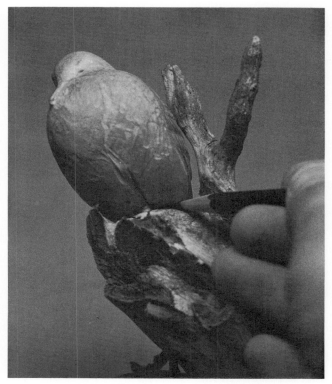

An outline is drawn on the bird where it meets the branch. The area within will be cut out.

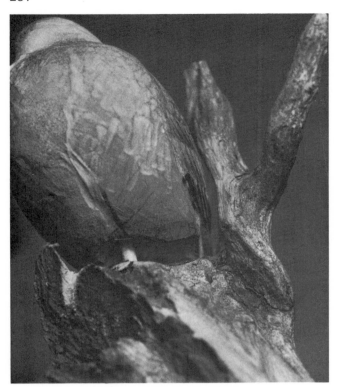

The area ground out up to the pencil line.

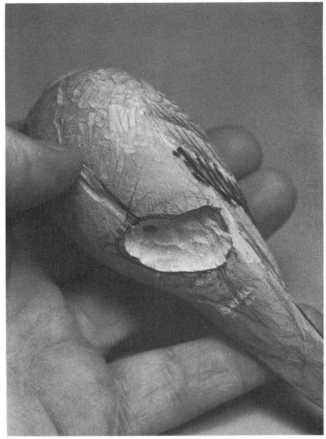

The area cut out in the underside of the bird.

The dove nestled down on the branch.

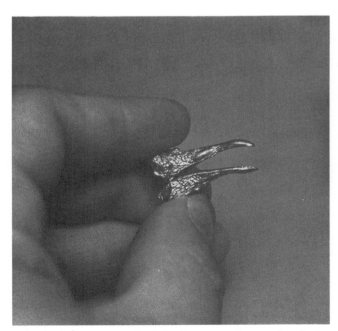

A dove beak cast in pewter that Bob will use as a reference when shaping the wood.

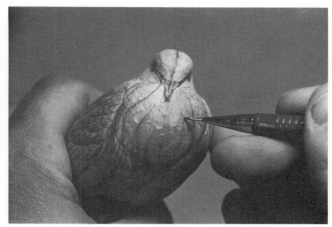

Back to the bird, Bob works on the breast area. This he does only after the dove has been properly mounted.

With a flame-shaped ruby carver, Bob does more defining around the head area. He works to achieve a fluffy look.

More of the same. Note that the breast area is puffed because the head is pressed down.

Using a burning pen, Bob defines and reshapes feathers.

With a small, pointed stone, Bob defines the edges of the beak.

Putting in details on the beak with a burning pen. Here, he separates the mandibles.

A through-cavity is made and filled with spackle.

Putting the eye-ring in place with a spatula.

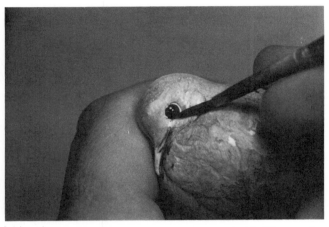

The 4-millimeter brown glass eyes are put into each side. Water and a paintbrush clear away excess spackle.

Penciling in individual feathers on the breast area.

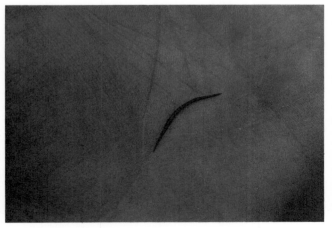

A "worm" of epoxy putty that will be the eye-ring.

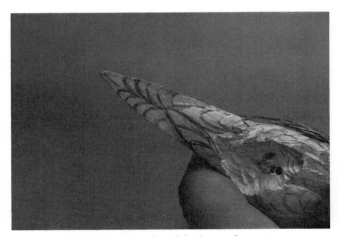

Drawing in the undertail feathers and coverts.

Cutting the soft breast feathers with a ball-nosed stone and Gesswein.

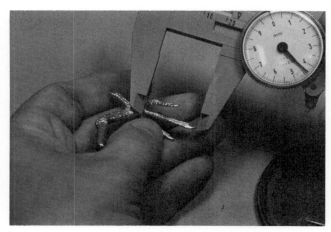

Calibrating half the scale.

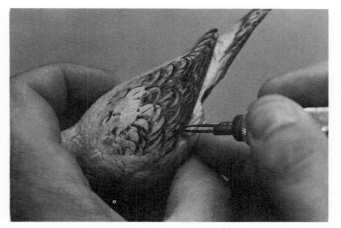

Burning the flank feathers with a skew-tipped burning tip.

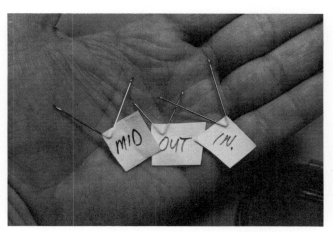

Bob makes the toes in sets, or pairs. The tape indicates which toe each is.

A mourning dove's pewter cast foot that Bob will use as a reference.

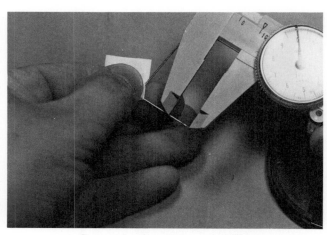

Determining the toe joints or knuckles.

After measuring, Bob applies epoxy to the toes. Bob says that holding the epoxy under a lightbulb heats it up slightly and makes it adhere better.

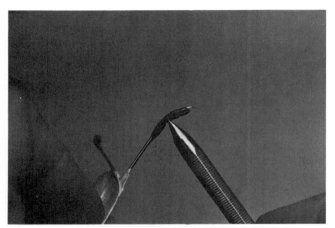

A small, ground-down dental tool splits the pads from the scaly area.

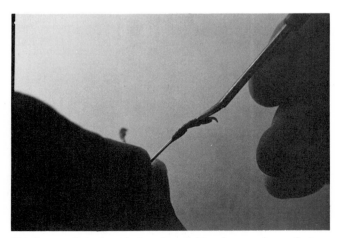

This homemade tool, made from brass tubing, forms scales on the toes. Setting it on top of the epoxy and pushing it back forms perfect scales, Bob says.

The finished feet are in place.

Making the leaves, for which Bob says he used his imagination. He recommends trying different gauges of sheet copper for different types of leaves. Heavier-gauge metal makes for a sturdier leaf, he points out.

A homemade tool burnishes the leaf to form the vein. He uses a tele-phone book underneath, saying it is firm enough to hold the leaf but soft enough to absorb the pressure of the burnishing tool.

A defuzzing pad is run over the leaf to take off excess solder. It smooths the metal and at the same time dulls it, making a better surface for the paint to be applied later.

The finished leaves before the stems are applied.

Attaching two leaves to the tree. Holes are drilled into the branch and the leaves are held in place with Super Glue. The third leaf is attached to the base.

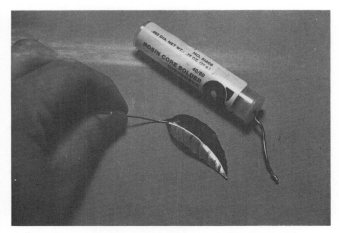

A piece of copper wire, one end of which is ground and tapered, becomes the stem for this leaf. Solder holds it in place.

Stoning the bird with a ⅛-inch-diameter inverted cone, run at full speed on the Gesswein.

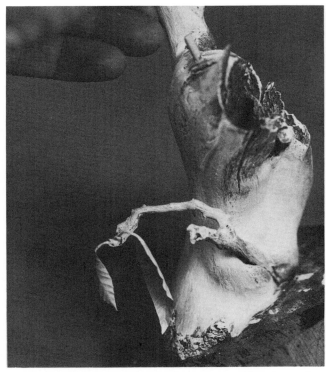

After the bird has been textured, Bob uses a rotary bristle brush at slow speed. This cleans up rough areas. At too high a speed, he says, the dust that fills up the pores of the jelutong would be removed.

The branch and leaves are primed with a gray gesso. Near the top there is a gray patina, but, near the bottom, the branch looks "more alive," Bob says. There, he applies burnt umber, white, and ivory black. The leaves are painted with the same mix and raw sienna. The resulting color will complement the colors on the dove.

Dull Cote lacquer is sprayed on the branch and leaves.

The finished bird.

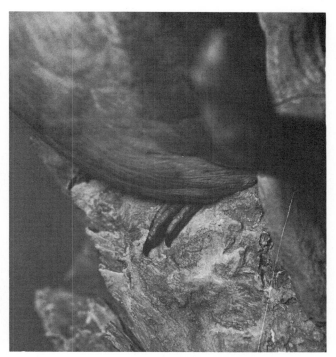

The feet.

Bob chose this pose because he has seen doves sit like this. He points out that the pose is similar to one he did for the World Championships in 1984. That bird and its mate won the Best-in-World title for miniatures.

A close-up of the head and breast.

The back of the mourning dove.

Back to The World
with Bluebirds

Twisted-together strands of wire spiral up from a precisely cut and sanded walnut block like a piece of abstract sculpture. Perched at the top are two tiny birds, their toeless wire feet making contact with the springy wire. One has a wing out for balance, the other keeps a more peaceful pose. Both have little landscaping and neither has paint. It is March 25, and Bob is three weeks into his entry for the 1987 World Championship Wildfowl Carving Competition.

The house is quiet. Three of the children are off with Jody to shop. Joshua and Seth are at a neighbor's house. Removing the birds from the wire, Bob says, "I'm in real good shape. What I have left is not hard work. What's still up in the air is the wire. I've tried different shapes, but I haven't formalized anything yet." The shape he has given the wire suggests a spiral that reverses its direction halfway between the block and the birds. "I may end up with just an arc shape." But whatever his decision, he has decided that the two miniature bluebirds will sit in opposite directions while looking in the same direction. "This barbed wire

is real typical of a bluebird habitat. They just love to sit on it out in a field."

He presses down on the wire strand with two fingers, compresses it slightly, and releases it. "The scale of the wire being half size is a problem. It's pretty springy. I'm using hard brass right now, which was a problem. I couldn't at first get the length I needed plus the strength. It's springier than I want it. This is going to dictate how much spiral can be done. I might even try stainless steel. But once I establish the curve, redoing the barbed wire in a different metal won't be a problem."

Bob indicates that the walnut block has a square base while its height is twice the width of one side. He thinks he might put another piece on its bottom. He calls it a flange.

The habitat will be limited to the barbed wire, Bob explains. "This block idea is being used by a lot of people now. I favor it after seeing it used by Scheeler and Larry [Barth]."

The birds will be finished before he leaves for

Bluebirds on wire are not unfamiliar to Bob. He had done this composition several years before making his pair for the 1987 World Championship Wildfowl Carving Competition. In the collection of Mr. and Mrs. Stephen Keibler.

The back of the bird.

A close-up of the bluebird.

The barbed wire made from coat hanger wire.

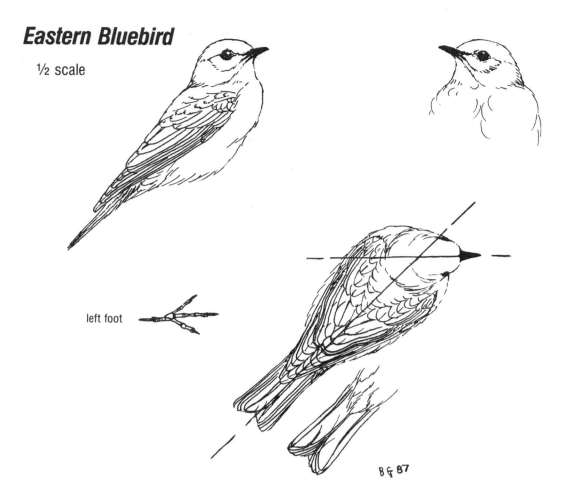

Eastern Bluebird

½ scale

left foot

BG 87

Ocean City, Maryland, he says. "By the end of the first week in April, I hope. There's not much left to do. We're talking tiny little burn lines. That's a lot of work even on little birds. They'll just be painted."

The original composition for the competition was to have been towhees. He says he lost interest in the idea. "I worked it up on paper and I started thinking about the piece, and I wanted to put them in their natural setting on the forest floor with lots of leaves and stuff. I thought that would be a good way to bring in a lot of different colors. But the problem was, I was going to end up with a low piece. I couldn't come up with an idea I felt good about."

He feels he turned himself off to doing the towhees. "I started thinking about some other ideas, something to give a pair of birds height. I thought about a couple of different things, and bluebirds on barbed wire just popped into my mind."

—— • ——

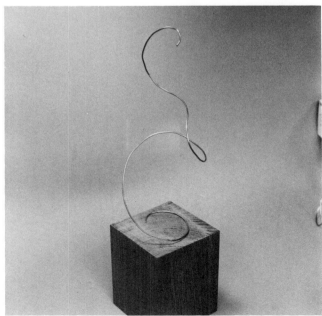

The start of the new bluebird composition for the World Championship. Bob is trying different wires, different twists. But the height varies little between this and the final composition.

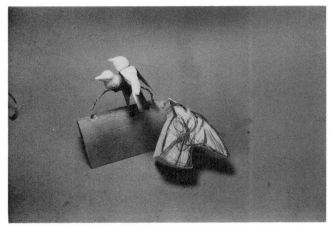

A pair of small, clay models for the placement of the birds. No details were put into the clay. Bob will do three different male bluebirds, all carved in tupelo. This is the first one, posed with its wing under the tail. He will later reject the shape.

The female sketched on the wood, half size, with no previous pattern.

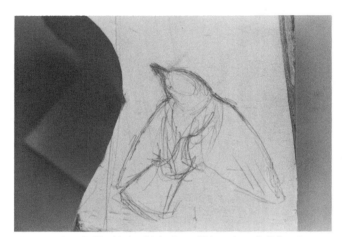

The first male bluebird roughly cut to shape.

The second male bluebird, which also will be rejected. Bob points out that one wing is extended farther than he would like.

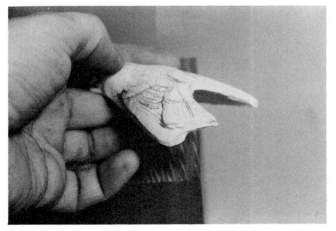

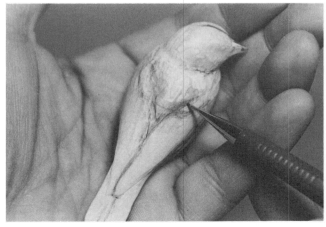

Bob has a photograph of a Swainson's thrush with one wing under the tail. That may have been the inspiration for this unusual position.

Going back to the female, Bob draws in the wings, scapulars, and cape.

The third and final male. Note how the whole body is twisted. The pencil lines indicate to Bob how the angles of twist work with each other.

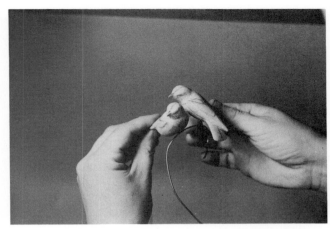

Holding the birds above the wire to see how they will work together.

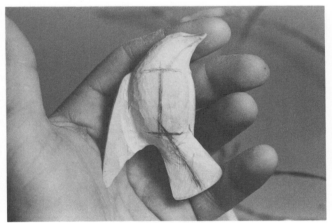

The bottom of the male bird.

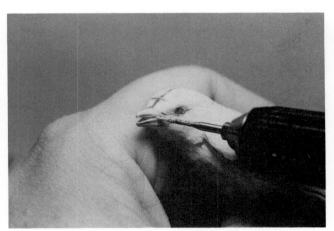

A small diamond bit opens the beak of the male bird.

The profile of the male.

Bob uses a Gesswein with the bit to separate the mandibles.

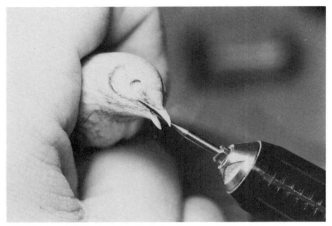

A small steel burr with a small rounded end shapes the throat area.

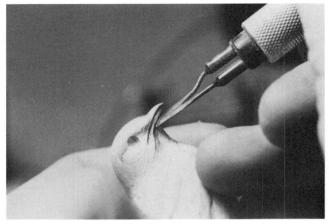

Using a burning pen to cut the sharp lines of the female's beak.

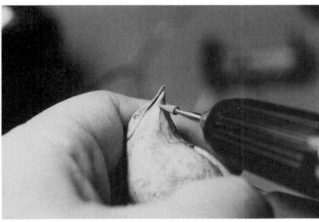

A small stone used for fine details separates the area between the feathers and the lower mandible.

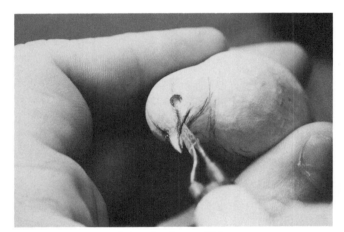

Separating the mandibles.

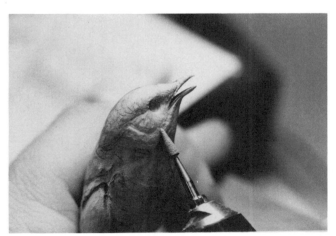

Cutting the cheek patch of the male bluebird.

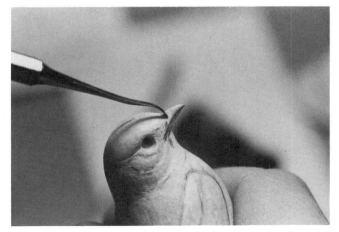

Bob uses a dental instrument for cleaning up the nostril hole. He says he is really burnishing or polishing the wood rather than removing it.

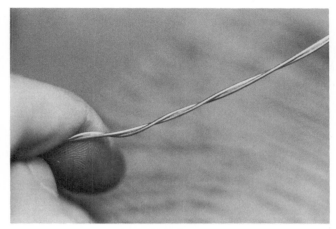

Bob uses brass wire for the composition. The first step is to twist two strands together.

The final shape of the composition. The birds are only wired in place. Bob did two other shapes of wire the same height that were too flexible. This piece differs because there is a contact point at the juncture of one of the loops. Only a short piece is left free standing. There is, then, little spring to the wire.

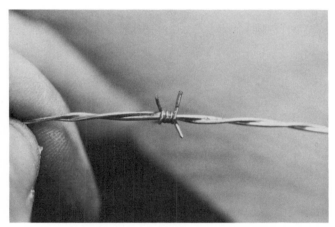

The next step is wrapping the barbs. They are really two pieces of brass wrapped together and tacked in place with solder.

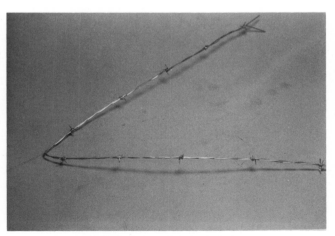

A finished piece of the barbed wire.

After laying a piece of paper on the working block and marking holes where there are points of contact, Bob transfers the points to the finished walnut base.

At the contact points, Bob drills holes and inserts brass tubing. Two barbs and one peg will then be inserted into the tubing.

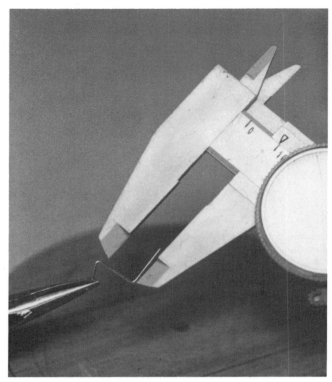

Work begins on the feet.

A contact point of peg and tubing.

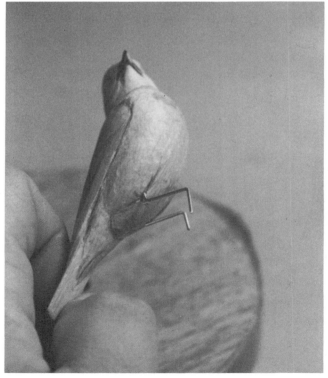

The feet are bent to shape and inserted.

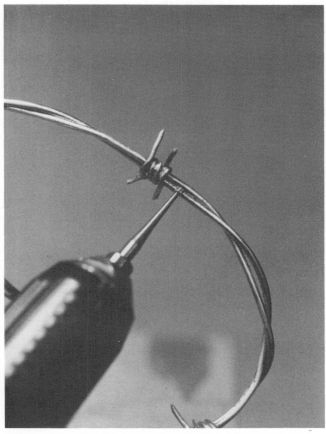

The wires are soldered together where the birds will be standing. Bob grinds off excess solder with a steel burr.

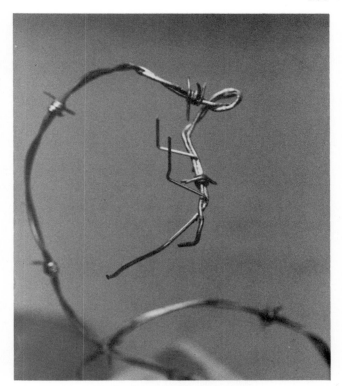

The feet inserted in the barbed wire.

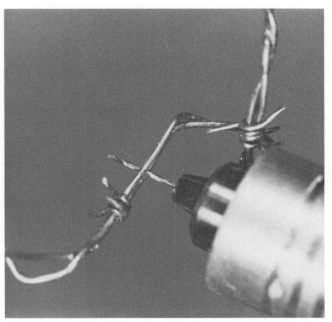

Bob drills an opening the same size as the rod chosen for the feet.

Sketching feathers on the wing of the male bird, while making sure there is room for the various sections of the wing. Bob says it is hard laying out open wings if a good reference isn't available.

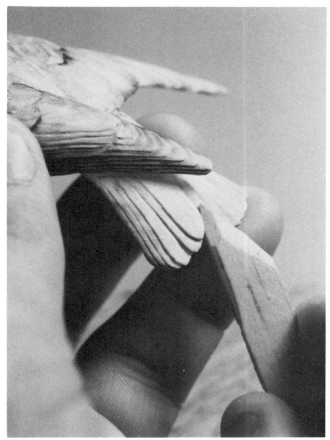

Some of the feathers are split apart and layered. Bob uses a Popsicle stick with sandpaper glued on it to sand up between some of the feathers. With a knife it can be easily shaped.

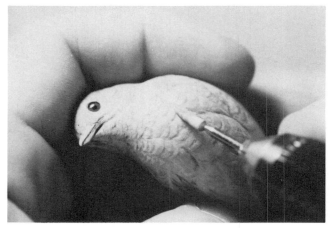

Working on the female breast.

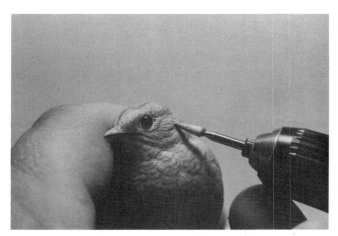

Stoning on the head of the female.

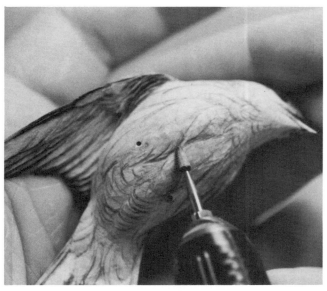

Cutting individual breast feathers.

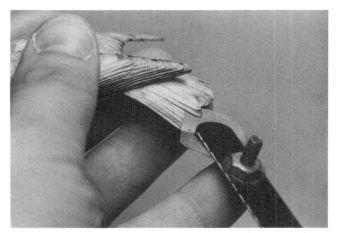

A holding device made from a hacksaw blade holds a metal sanding disc that separates tail feathers.

A close-up of the tool.

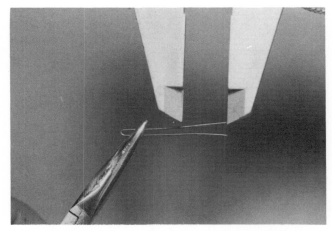

Making the toes in pairs. A caliper takes measurements. Bob now prefers gluing toes together rather than joining them with solder.

Here, feather separations can be seen.

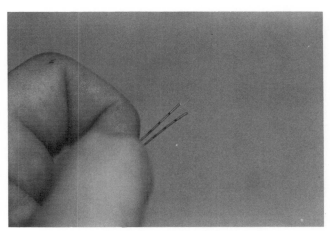

Each dot represents a joint.

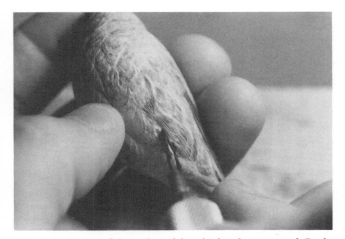

Bob originally wanted the surface of these birds to be untextured. But he decides later that the sharpness of the burning would help with the crispness of the painting. Also, some hard grain lines in the wood will not respond well to stoning. A stone will jump up over the hard areas.

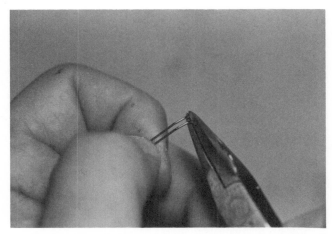

Bending the wires at the joints. This procedure guarantees that the bends will be equal.

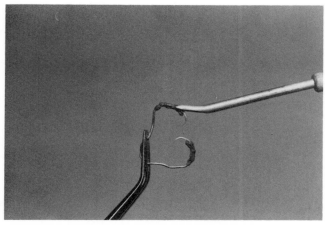

Applying Duro two-part epoxy and forming the scales with a homemade tool.

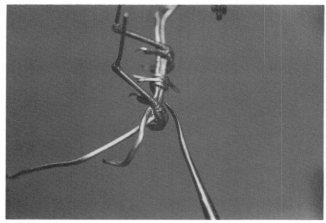

A small amount of epoxy is put in the joint. This is shaped with a dental tool.

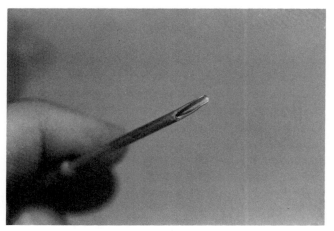

A close-up of the tool.

The burned male, which is then primed with a lacquer sealer and several thin coats of gesso so that the texture is not filled.

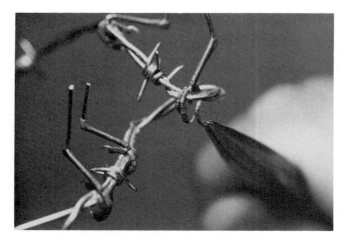

Applying the toes to the foot. The foot bone is shaped with epoxy, and the toes are glued on with a small amount of Super Glue.

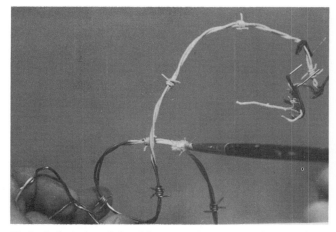

The barbed wire is sealed with lacquer and then a coat of gesso and very fine sawdust is applied. This will give the wire its rusty surface.

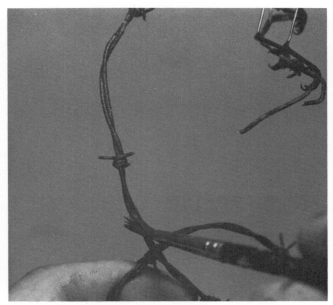

Burnt sienna and burnt umber are the base coat; a wash coat of raw umber follows.

Painting the birds with the help of study skins, magazines, and book references. Their glass eyes are 3 millimeters in diameter, brown.

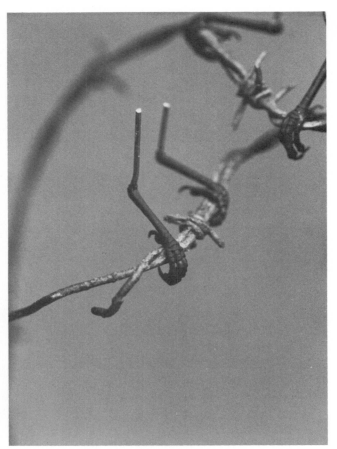

The finished feet, basically black with a pale gray wash over them.

Ocean City has had rain for most of the third week in April. Torrential at times, it has been accompanied by gusty winds and sand blown across the peninsula. Bob left Carpentersville shortly after having the bluebirds photographed. That was Wednesday, April 22. The last washes of paint were applied that morning.

Two weeks before leaving, he decided to texture the birds after all. It was not until the Monday of that week that he completed working on the surfaces of the bluebirds. That gave him only two days to paint the pair.

Jody and the five children drove with Bob to Maryland. The bad weather has kept them all inside, but the children do not seem to mind. They stay close to Jody, often trailing behind her in a line. The order seems based on their heights, with Seth, the oldest, nearest Jody, and Jordan, the second youngest, at the end. Bob and Jody take turns holding Asher.

It is Saturday, the second day of the show, shortly after three-thirty. The waterfowl pairs, scaup for this year's competition, have already been judged. Hens and drakes sit together on long tables, the water collected from the flotation tanks nearly gone from their painted and hollow bodies.

On the previous day all Open, Intermediate, and Novice Class birds for the Decorative Lifesize, Floating, and Miniature divisions have been judged. Ribbons hang from necks or lie under bases.

Also at the front of the Convention Center are round tables, white clothed and separated from the crowds by curtained railings. On them are the birds entered in the World Class Decorative Lifesize category. A pair of yellow-headed blackbirds stand on tall grasses. Two roadrunners confront each other in a desert setting. Blackburnian warblers perch on a hemlock branch that lightly descends from the air and touches a top edge of a tall, black block. It is Larry Barth's entry. Many in the crowd believe he will win for the third year in a row. He will not.

Other entries are just as ingeniously composed. A group of stellar jays rest on a base with a pine branch,

complete with cones and needles. Like Barth's branch, it descends from an unseen tree and touches a corner of a walnut block held above the cloth by a four-legged, diminutive, oriental-style table. A pair of blue jays perch on thick gray branches that have no base but the display table itself. The two branches are not connected and can actually be moved, separating the birds or bringing them closer together.

Also to the front, but to the far right, are the natural sculpture carvings. Unpainted and untextured with burn lines, they are impressionistic birds that might emerge from a block of wood or a stump of a tree. This is a new division for the World Championships.

Several tables butted end to end make up the area for the miniature songbirds. They are positioned nearest the stage and in front of the life-size birds. Bob's bluebirds are at the far end, not far from the stage. Other entries, moving away from them, are roadrunners, barn swallows, more bluebirds, crows, and shrikes.

Three judges have been scrutinizing the life-size

The finished composition.

Another view.

Bob says that these adult birds are in their breeding plumage.

The first idea for this composition had two birds with bodies turned in different directions.

Bob also says, "They're doing a lot of what they like doing, and that's sitting on wire."

Perhaps the two birds see something together, but basically, it is a moment frozen in the birds' lives.

birds, another three, the natural sculpture, and three have been examining the miniatures, all making notes on paper supplied with clipboards. Judging Bob's birds and the others of half size or less are Larry Barth, Ernest Muehlmatt, and Gladys Hopkins. Muehlmatt and Bob have come to be well acquainted. They have attended many of the same competitions for at least ten years. Muehlmatt, though he won the 1985 Best-in-World title with five life-size bobwhite quail, is familiar with miniatures. He won Best-in-World with a pair of woodcocks in 1979 and with two least bitterns in 1981. As he is judging Bob's birds, others are judging his stellar jays on their oriental-style base.

Bob stands with Jody during the judging. The five children have found the edge of the stage a place to sit, with Asher held by Joshua. Bob has positioned himself between the life-size area and the miniature tables.

Someone asks him how he is feeling at the moment.

"It's exciting. This is what the show is all about," he says, glancing over at Larry Barth, who is writing on his clipboard. "It's interesting watching the judges, wondering what's going through their minds. I wish I could hear what they're saying."

Loud-speakered phrases come over the general din of a crowd that may number one thousand or more people. Names of persons asked to report to the information desk are read out, trustees of the Ward Foundation are requested to report to different locations.

"I know Larry is going to be a hundred percent objective." Bob adds that the others will be, too. "They're all totally qualified to be judging." He puckers his mouth for a moment. "This is going to be good, fair judging."

"You can get too close to your own work," he says after talking to a carver from Michigan, who asks Bob how he will do competitively. "It's like having blinders on, but everybody else has the same problem."

He starts to inhale frequently as he sees Barth,

At the 1987 World Championships, the eagle nest and rock composition took third Best in Show in the Birds of Prey category.

The partridge composition got first Best in Show in the Gamebird category.

The three judges for the Miniature division: from left to right, Larry Barth, Ernest Muehlmatt, and Gladys Hopkins.

Muehlmatt, and Hopkins conferring. "This is something you have to get used to if you enter competitions. You have to roll with the punches. And if you don't win, it's because somebody else has something better."

There is an announcement that the judging for the three divisions is nearly complete. A speaker's platform is in front of the stage but right of its middle. More railings and curtains form a semicircle around it, leaving a large area with the floatation tanks and pairs of scaup on its inside. Bob and Jody stand on the outside of this, behind others who have gathered to see the awards given. Bob will stand tiptoe for most of the presentations.

The children have joined Bob and Jody as the judging is over. It is announced that a special presentation will be given to a retiring chairman of the competition. An award is given to a young carver of merit. The crowd applauds.

The first awards are for carved feathers. Made of wood, they must be mounted on bases next to the actual feathers. The first-place purchase award is $400. A carver from Bethel, Pennsylvania, named Jim Sherman is called to receive his check and rosette. There is more applause. Bob's breathing starts to increase. He thinks the miniature winners will be announced next.

The mayor of Ocean City is introduced. He will present the award to the "World-Class Natural Finish Lifesize Wildlife Sculpture." First place is won by a Floridian named Mark Gates for his egrets. His check is for $4,000. The crowd applauds again. "This is the

first year the Ward Foundation has set aside this particular art form and given it due recognition," the announcer says. "I think it's welcome within the entire art society."

Second place goes to an Ohioan named John Sharp with a check for $1,000, for a pair of kingfishers. But Sharp is not in the hall to receive his prize money.

"Third place, Leo E. Osborne from Warren, Maine, a $500 trophy and rosette for—" the announcer pauses because he cannot read what the birds are. He thinks they are pipes, but Osborne, who has gotten to the podium, corrects him with "peeps." He adds that his wife, Lee Osborne, also worked on the piece.

Bob holds his breath as the announcement is made that the miniature winners are next.

The announcer continues, "Division C, with a trophy and rosette and a $250 check," then a long pause. "Does anyone want to tell me what these are? They're not written in here." After another, longer pause, he says, "While Manfred Scheel is walking up here to pick up his award, I'll find out the species." Scheel, from Quakertown, Pennsylvania, is applauded by the spectators. Bob lets out a burst of air that he may have held for several minutes.

"They're magnolia warblers," the announcer says officially. Bob tenses as he rises on tiptoes to look above those who stand in front of him. The children are quiet as if expecting to hear their father's name. Bob hopes his name is not announced next.

"Second place, and a $750 check to Peter Kaune of Gig Harbor, Washington, with loggerhead shrikes." The applause is louder than that received by Scheel.

The Guge children in anticipation of the judging: from left to right, Seth, Jordan, Asher, Joshua, and Caleb.

The awarding of the check and plaque for Bob's Best-in-World miniature bluebirds by Sam Dyke, chairman of the Ward Foundation.

Bob holds his last intake of air. He had offered the opinion that he would be among the three winners. His face goes through subtle changes of expression that suggest doubt, hope, frustration. He may be remembering the painting that was finished only three days before, the wire that was too springy, or the towhees that he almost carved. Jody moves closer to him. People are starting to look in his direction. He stands immobile.

"First place, a five thousand–dollar check, trophy, and rosette to Robert Guge of Carpentersville, Illinois!"

———●———

Nearly two months after the competition, Jody wrote the following poem for her husband:

He takes an ordinary block
    of wood
carving, cutting,
      burning lines
with confidence
until
    tiny wings appear,
      detailed feathers
lifted,
    airborne,
so delicate you expect
      them to bend
      in the wind.
But they remain
      firm and strong,
like his
    hands,
      as he turns
      the head
and shapes the
      puffed-out breast
      of a bluebird
      that watches you,
      intently.
He sits, quietly,
      his hands moving
faster as the wood
    around him
rises higher and higher,
tiny fragments
    of the first creation,
    imitating
    life
    with
    his perfect specimen
of
    wings
      in
        wood.

Jody Woods Guge

Bibliography

Alcorn, Gordon Dee. *Owls.* Prentice-Hall Press. 1986.

Armstrong, Robert H. *Guide to the Birds of Alaska.* Alaska Northwest Publishing Company. 1983.

Audubon, John James. *The Birds of America.* Crown Publishers. 1966.

Austin, Oliver L. *Birds of the World.* Golden Press. 1961.

Aymar, Gordon. *Bird Flight.* Dodd, Mead & Company.

Barber, Joel. *Wild Fowl Decoys.* Dover Publications. 1954.

Beebe, C. William. *The Bird: Its Form and Function.* Dover Publications. 1965.

Bellrose, Frank C. *Ducks, Geese and Swans of North America.* Stackpole Books. 1980.

Boulton, Rudyard. *Traveling with the Birds.* M.A. Donahue & Company. 1960.

Boyer, Trevor, and Burton, Philip. *Vanishing Eagles.* Dodd, Mead & Company. 1981.

Brown, Leslie, and Amadon, Dean. *Eagles, Hawks & Falcons of the World.* Two volumes. Country Life Books. 1968.

Bruun, Bertel, and Zim, H.S. *Birds of North America.* Golden Press. 1966.

Burk, Bruce. *Game Bird Carving.* Winchester Press. 1982.

Burn, Barbara. *The National Audubon Society Collection Nature Series: North American Birds.* Bonanza Books. 1984.

Burton, John A., Editor. *Owls of the World.* E.P. Dutton & Co., Inc. 1973.

Burke, Ken, Editor. *How to Attract Birds.* Ortho Books. 1983.

Campbell, W. D. *Birds of Town and Village.* Country Life Books. 1965.

Campell, Bruce, Editor. *The Pictorial Encyclopedia of Birds.* Paul Hamlyn Ltd. 1967.

Casey, Peter N. *Birds of Canada.* Discovery Books. 1984.

Chinery, Michael, and Pledger, Maurice. *Garden Birds of the World.* Dodd, Mead & Company. 1983.

Clement, Roland C. *The Living World of Audubon.* Grosset & Dunlop. 1974.

Coleman, Bruce. *Birds.* Crescent Books.

Coles, Charles, and Pledger, Maurice. *Game Birds.* Dodd, Mead & Company. 1985.

Cruickshank, Allan D. *Cruickshank's Photographs of Birds of America.* Dover Publications, Inc. 1977.

Cruickshank, Helen G. *The Nesting Season—The Bird Photographs of Frederick Kent Truslow.* The Viking Press. 1979.

Davison, Verne E. *Attracting Birds from the Prairies to the Atlantic.* Thomas Y. Crowell. 1967.

Dennis, John V. *A Complete Guide to Bird Feeding.* Alfred Knopf. 1976.

Derry, Ramsey. *The Art of Robert Bateman.* The Viking Press. 1981.

Dossenbach, Hans D. *The Family Life of Birds.* McGraw-Hill Book Company. 1971.

Dougall, Robert, and Ede, Basil. *Basil Ede's Birds.* Van Nostrand, Reinhold. 1981.

Duval, Paul. *The Art of Glen Loates.* Cerebrus Publishing Company, Ltd. 1977.

Earnest, Adele. *The Art of the Decoy: American Bird Carvings.* Schiffer Publishing Ltd. 1982.

Eckert, Allan W., and Karalus, Karl F. *The Wading Birds of North America.* Doubleday. 1981.

Elman, Robert, and Osborne, Walter. *The Atlantic Flyway.* Winchester Press.

Farrand, John, Jr., Editor. *The Audubon Society Master Guide to Birding.* Three volumes. Alfred A. Knopf. 1983.

Fisher, James, and Peterson, Roger Tory. *World of Birds.* Revised. Crown Publishers. 1969.

Forbush, Edward H., and May, John R. *A Natural History of American Birds of Eastern and Central North America.* Bramhall House. 1955.

Gillette, John, and Mohrhardt, David. *Coat Pocket Bird Book.* Two Peninsula Press. 1984.

Gilley, Wendell H. *The Art of Bird Carving.* Hillcrest Publishers, Inc. 1972.

Gilliard, Thomas E. *Living Birds of the World.* Doubleday & Company. 1958.

Godfrey, W. Earl. *The Birds of Canada.* National Museums of Canada. 1966.

Gooders, John. *Collins British Birds.* William Collins Sons & Co Ltd, 1982.

Grossman, Mary Louise, and Hamlet, John. *Birds of Prey of the World.* Clarkson N. Potter. 1964.

Halliday, Jack. *Vanishing Birds.* Holt, Rinehart and Winston. 1978.

Ham, John, and Mohrhardt, David. *Kitchen Table Bird Book.* Two Peninsula Press. 1984.

Hammond, Nicholas. *Twentieth Century Wildlife Artists.* The Overlook Press. 1986.

Harrison, Colin. *A Field Guide to the Nests, Eggs and Nestlings of North American Birds.* Collins. 1978.

Harrison, George H. *The Backyard Bird Watcher.* Simon and Schuster. 1979.

Harrison, Hal H. *Wood Warblers' World.* Simon and Schuster. 1984.

Hickey, Joseph J. *A Guide to Bird Watching.* Dover Publications. 1975.

Hosking, Eric. *Eric Hosking's Waders.* Pelham Books Ltd. 1983.

James, Ross. *Glen Loates Birds of North America.* Prentice Hall of Canada. 1979.

Jeklin, Isidor, and Waite, Donald E. *The Art of Photographing North American Birds.* Whitecap Books. 1984.

Johnsgard, Paul A. *The Plovers, Sandpipers, and Snipes of the World.* University of Nebraska Press. 1981.

———. *Grouse of the World.* University of Nebraska Press. 1983.

———. *North American Game Birds of Upland and Shoreline.* University of Nebraska Press. 1975.

Kastner, Joseph. *A World of Watchers.* Alfred A. Knopf, Inc. 1986.

Kress, Stephen W. *The Audubon Society Handbook for Birders.* Charles Scribner's Sons. 1981.

Lacey, John L., and McBride, Tom Moore. *The Audubon Book of Bird Carving.* McGraw-Hill Book Company, Inc. 1951.

Lansdowne, J. Fenwick. *Birds of the West Coast.* Houghton Mifflin Company. 1976.

———. *Birds of the West Coast, II.* Houghton Mifflin Company. 1980.

Lansdowne, J. Fenwick, and Livingston, John A. *Birds of the Eastern Forest.* Houghton Mifflin Company. 1968.

———. *Birds of the Eastern Forest, II.* Houghton Mifflin Company. 1970.

———. *Birds of the Northern Forest.* Houghton Mifflin Company. 1966.

Lawson, Glenn. *The Story of Lem Ward.* Schiffer Publishing Ltd. 1984.

Laycock, George. *The Birdwatcher's Bible.* Doubleday & Co., Inc. 1976.

Leopold, Aldo. *A Sand County Almanac.* Oxford University Press. 1968.

Line, Les. *Audubon Society Book of Wild Birds.* Harry N. Abrams. 1976.

Lyttle, Richard B. *Birds of North America.* Gallery Books. 1983.

Mace, Alice E. Editor. *The Birds Around Us.* Ortho Books. 1986.

Mackey, William F., Jr. *American Bird Decoys.* Schiffer Publishing Ltd. 1965.

Marcham, Frederick George, Editor. *Louis Agassiz Fuertes & the Singular Beauty of Birds.* Harper & Row Publishers. 1971.

Matthiessen, Peter. *The Shore Birds of North America.* Viking Press. 1967.

McKenny, Margaret. *Birds in the Garden.* The University of Minnesota Press. 1939.

Mitchell, Alan. *Lambart's Birds of Shore and Estuary.* Charles Scribner's Sons. 1979.

Mohrhardt, David. *Bird Reference Drawings.* Publication of David Mohrhardt, 314 N. Bluff, Berrien Springs, Michigan 49103. 1985.

———. *Bird Studies.* Publication of David Mohrhardt, 314 N. Bluff, Berrien Springs, Michigan 49103. 1986.

———. *Selected Bird Drawings.* Publication of David Mohrhardt, 314 N. Bluff, Berrien Springs, Michigan 49103. 1987.

Nice, Margaret Morse. *Studies in the Life History of the Song Sparrow.* Dover. 1937.

Pearson, T. Gilbert, Editor. *Birds of America.* Garden City Publishing Company, Inc. 1936.

Peck, Robert McCracken. *A Celebration of Birds.* Walker and Company. 1982.

Perrins, Christopher, and Middleton, Alex, Editors. *The Encyclopedia of Birds.* Facts on File Publications. 1985.

Perrins, Christopher. *Bird Life—An Introduction to the World of Birds.* Peerage Books. 1976.

———. *Birds—Their Life, Their Ways, Their World.* Harry N. Abrams. 1976.

Peterson, Roger Tory. *A Field Guide to the Birds.* Houghton Mifflin Company. 1980.

———. *A Field Guide to Western Birds.* Houghton Mifflin. 1961.

Poole, Robert M., Editor. *The Wonder of Birds.* National Geographic Society. 1983.

Porter, Eliot. *Birds of North America: A Personal Selection.* A&W Visual Library.

Pough, Richard H. *Audubon Water Bird Guide.* Doubleday & Company. 1951.

Rayfield, Susan. *Wildlife Painting Techniques of the Modern Masters.* Watson-Guptill Publications. 1985.

Reilly, Edgar M. *The Audubon Illustrated Handbook of American Birds.* McGraw-Hill Book Company. 1968.

Schroeder, Roger. *How to Carve Wildfowl.* Stackpole Books. 1984.

———. *How to Carve Wildfowl, Book Two.* Stackpole Books. 1986.

Schroeder, Roger, and Muehlmatt, Ernest. *Songbird Carving with Ernest Muehlmatt.* Stackpole Books. 1987.

Schroeder, Roger, and Sprankle, James D. *Waterfowl Carving with J. D. Sprankle.* Stackpole Books. 1985.

Scott, Peter. *Key to the Wildfowl of the World.* Wildfowl Trust. 1957.

———. *Observations of Wildfowl.* Cornell University Press. 1980.

Scott, Shirley L., Editor. *Field Guide to Birds of North America.* National Geographic Society. 1983.

———. *Stalking Birds with Color Camera.* National Geographic Society. 1961.

———. *Water, Prey and Game Birds.* National Geographic Society. 1965.

Shetler, Stanwyn G. *Portraits of Nature Paintings by Robert Bateman.* Smithsonian Institution Press. 1987.

Shortt, Michael Terence. *Wild Birds of the Americas.* Pagurian Press Limited. 1977.

Simon, Hilda. *The Splendor of Iridescence.* Dodd, Mead & Company. 1971.

Small, Anne. *Masters of Decorative Bird Carving.* Winchester Press. 1981.

Snow, David, Chisholm, A.H., and Soper, M.F. *Raymond Ching: The Bird Paintings.* William Collins & Company Limited. 1978.

Spaulding, Edward S. *Quails.* Macmillan.

Stefferud, Alfred, Editor. *Birds in Our Lives.* Arco Publishing Company, Inc. 1970.

Stepanek, O. *Birds of Heath and Marshland.* West Book House. 1962.

Stokes, Donald W. *A Guide to the Behavior of Common Birds.* Little, Brown and Co. 1979.

Stokes, Ted, and Shackleton, Keith. *Birds of the Atlantic Ocean.* The Macmillan Company. 1968.

Terres, John K. *The Audubon Society Encyclopedia of North American Birds.* Alfred A. Knopf. 1980.

———. *Songbirds in Your Garden.* Hawthorn Books. 1977.

Tunnicliffe, Charles. *A Sketchbook of Birds.* Holt, Rinehart and Winston. 1979.

Van Wormer, Joe. *The World of the Swan.* J.B. Lippincott Company. 1972.

Waingrow, Jeff, and Palmer, Carleton. *American Wildfowl Decoys.* E.P. Dutton. 1985.

Walsh, Harry M. *The Outlaw Gunner.* Tidewater Publishers. 1971.

Welty, Joel Carl. *The Life of Birds.* W.B. Saunders. 1975.

Wetmore, Alexander, Editor. *Song and Garden Birds of North America.* National Geographic Society. 1964.

———. *Water, Prey, and Game Birds of North America.* National Geographic Society. 1965.

Zeleny, Lawrence. *The Bluebird.* Indiana University Press. 1976.

Zim, Herbert, and Sprunt, Alexander. *Game Birds.* Western. 1961.

Magazines of interest to wildfowl carvers:

American Birds. 950 Third Ave., New York, NY 10022.

Audubon. Membership Data Center, P.O. Box 2667, Boulder, CO 80321.

Birder's World. 720 E. 8th St., Holland, MI 49423.

Birding. American Birding Association, Inc., Box 4335, Austin, TX 78765.

Bird Watcher's Digest. P.O. Box 110, Marietta, OH 45750.

Breakthrough Magazine. P.O. Box 1320, Loganville, GA 30249.

Chip Chats. The National Woodcarver's Association, 7424 Miami Ave., Cincinnati, OH 45243.

Continental Birdlife. P.O. Box 43294, Tucson, AZ 85733.

Wildfowl Art, Journal of the Ward Foundation. 655 S. Salisbury Blvd., Salisbury, MD 21801.

National Wildlife. National Wildlife Federation, 1412 Sixteenth St., N.W., Washington, D.C. 20036-9967.

Natural History. P.O. Box 4200, Bergenfield, NJ 07621.

Sporting Classics. 420 East Genesee St., Syracuse, NY 13202.

Wildfowl Carving and Collecting. Box 1831, Harrisburg, PA 17105.

The Living Bird Quarterly. Laboratory of Ornithology at Cornell University, 159 Sapsucker Woods Rd., Ithaca, NY 14850.

A Sampling of Competitions and Exhibitions

This list was compiled from *Wildfowl Carving and Collecting* Magazine.

The California Open and Wildfowl Arts Festival
4351 Whittle Ave.
Oakland, CA 94602
Held in mid-February, this show attracts 400 carvers and exhibitors and 8,000 visitors.

Canadian National Decoy Carvers Competition
Sportsmans Association
61 Edgehill Rd.
Islington, Ontario M9A 4N1
This show is held in mid-March with some 300 entries of wildfowl carvings.

New England Woodcarvers Festival and Competition
Valley Shore Waterfowlers
43 Ridgeview Circle
Guilford, CT 06437
Held in late October or early November, this show made its debut in 1985.

U.S. National Decoy Show
Five Flint Rd.
Amity Harbor, NY 11701
Held in middle to late March, it is the oldest show of its kind in this country.

Clayton Duck Decoy and Wildlife Art Show
P.O. Box 292
Clayton, NY 13624
Held in July, this show offers auctions, demonstrations, painting, and carving contests.

Loyalhanna Wildlife Art Festival
Loyalhanna Watershed Assoc.
P.O. Box 561
Ligonier, PA 15658
Held in September, the show offers demonstrations, wildlife films, and an auction.

Pennsylvania Wildlife Art Festival
R.D. #1
P.O. Box 128A
Glen Rock, PA 17327
This show is held in York in mid-November and features a wide variety of decorative carvings.

Annapolis Wildfowl Carving and Art Exhibition
1144 Riverboat Court
Annapolis, MD 21401
Carving and art exhibits are featured in this late January show.

World Championship Wildfowl Carving Competition
The Ward Foundation
655 S. Salisbury Blvd.
Salisbury, MD 21801
Held in Ocean City, Maryland, in late April, the show features some 800 carvers and attracts around 16,000 visitors. This three-day show is a must for anyone interested in bird carving.

The Ward Foundation Wildfowl Carving and Art Exhibition
The Ward Foundation
P.O. Box 703
Salisbury, MD 21801
This early October show, held in Salisbury, is not a competition but an exhibition of carvings and flat work art. Some 150 artists attend with some 9,000 visitors.

Louisiana Wildfowl Festival
3112 Octavia St.
New Orleans, LA 70125
Held in New Orleans, this September show features some 300 carvers and exhibitors with some 10,000 visitors.

Leigh Yawkey Woodson Art Museum "Birds in Art"
  Exhibition
Leigh Yawkey Woodson Art Museum
Franklin and Twelfth Sts.
Wausau, WI 54401
This show may come the closest to treating bird sculpture as an art form. It is held mid-September to early November.

Easton Waterfowl Festival
P.O. Box 929
Easton, MD 21654
This is an early November town-wide wildfowl art exhibition, features 450 carvers and exhibitors and attracts some 25,000 visitors. A number of the carvers in this book and *How to Carve Wildfowl* exhibit their work there.

International Decoy Contest
Decoy Contest
P.O. Box 406
Davenport, IA 52805
This is an early August show which attracts over 100 carvers and some 5,000 visitors.

North American Wildfowl Carving Championship
4510 Kircaldy Road
Bloomfield Hills, MI 48013
Point Mouille State Game Area is the site for this key show in late September; it attracts nearly 300 carvers.

Cajun Hunters Festival
Rt. 2
P.O. Box 337
Cut Off, LA 70345
Held in the Bayou Centroplex in Galliano, this show features over 100 carvers and exhibitors with some 5,000 visitors.

Sources for Supplies

Al's Decoy Supplies
27 Connaught Ave.
London, Ontario N5Y 3A4
CANADA
519-451-4729

Albert Constantine & Sons, Inc.
2050 Eastchester Rd.
Bronx, NY 10461
212-792-1600

American Sales Co.
Box 741
Reseda, CA 91335
213-881-2808

Big Sky Carvers
8256 Huffine Ln.
Bozeman, MT 59715
406-586-0008

Buck Run Carvings
Box 151, Gully Rd.
Aurora, NY 13026
315-364-8414

Canadian Woodworker Ltd.
1391 St. James St.
Winnipeg, Manitoba R3H 0Z1
CANADA
204-786-3196

The Carver's Barn
P.O. Box 686
Rte. 28
Hearth & Eagle Shopping Plaza
South Yarmouth, MA 02664

Carvers Corner
153 Passaic St.
Garfield, NJ 07026
201-472-7511

Chez La Rogue
Rt. 3, Box 148
Foley, AL 36535
205-943-1237

Craft Cove, Inc.
2315 W. Glen Ave.
Peoria, IL 61614
309-692-8365

CraftWoods
10921 York Rd.
Cockeysville, MD 21030
301-667-9663

Curt's Waterfowl Corner
123 Le Boeuf St.
Montegut, LA 70377
504-594-3012

Decoy Carving Supplies
8919 151st Ave.
Edmonton, Alberta T5E 2P8
CANADA
403-478-7602

The Duck Butt Boys
P.O. Box 2051
Metairie, LA 70004
504-443-3797

Electric & Tool Service Co.
19442 Conant Ave.
Detroit, MI 48234
313-366-3830

P.C. English Enterprises
P.O. Box 7937
Lafayette Blvd.
Fredericksburg, VA 22404
800-221-9474

Exotic Woods Inc.
2483 Industrial St.
Burlington, Ontario L7P 1A6
CANADA
416-335-8066

Feather Merchants
279 Boston Post Rd.
Madison, CT 06443
203-245-1231

The Fine Tool Shops, Inc.
P.O. Box 1262
20 Backus Ave.
Danbury, CT 06810
800-243-1037

The Foredom Electric Co.
Rt. 6
Bethel, CT 06801
203-792-8622

Forest Products
P.O. Box 12
Avon, OH 44011
216-937-5630

Garrett Wade
161 Avenue of the Americas
New York, NY 10013
800-212-2942

Gerry's Tool Shed
1111 Flint Rd.
Unit 6
Downsview, Ontario M3J 3C7
CANADA
416-665-6677

Gesswein
Woodworking Products Division
255 Hancock Ave.
P.O. Box 3998
Bridgeport, CT 06605
800-243-4466
203-366-5400

J. H. Kline Carving Shop
R.D. 2, Forge Hill Rd.
Manchester, PA 17345
717-266-3501

Ken Jones
P.O. Box 563
Salem, NH 03079

Kent's Woodshed
625 W. Main
Broussard, LA 70518
318-837-9470

Lee Valley Tools Ltd.
2680 Queensview Dr.
Ottawa, Ontario K2B 8J9
CANADA
613-596-0350

Little Mountain Carving Supply
Rt. 2, Box 1329
Front Royal, VA 22630
703-662-6160

L. I. Woodcarvers Supply
60 Glouster Rd.
Massapequa, NY 11758
516-799-7999

McGray Wildlife Sculpture
6553 Panton St.
Kilbride, Ontario L0P 1G0
CANADA
416-335-2512

Master Paint Systems
P.O. Box 1320
Loganville, GA 30249
800-334-8012

Montana Decoy Co.
Rt. 1
Box 251
Wilsall, MT 59086
406-578-2235

Northwest Carving Supply
P.O. Box 5211
216 West Ridge
Bozeman, MT 59715
406-587-8057

Plympton Wildlife Studios
David Coelho
244 Brook St.
Plympton, MA 02367
617-585-9107

Denny Rogers
309 Daisy Ln.
Normal, IL 61761
309-452-8005

Ross Tool Co.
257 Queen St., W.
Toronto, Ontario M5V 1Z4
CANADA
416-598-2498

Sand-Rite Mfg. Co.
1611 N. Sheffield Ave.
Chicago, IL 60614
312-642-7287

Seto Co., Inc.
"Serabian Tool Co."
P.O. Box 148
195 Highway 36
West Keansburg, NJ 07734
201-495-0040

Susquehanna Decoy Shop
Kitchen Kettle Village
Intercourse, PA 17534
717-768-3092

Tool Bin
10575 Clark Rd.
Davisburg, MI 48019
313-625-0390

Troy Woodcraft
301 Scottsdale Dr.
Troy, MI 48084
313-689-1997

Veasey Studios
955 Blue Ball Rd.
Elkton, MD 21921
301-392-3850

Joe Veracke and Assoc.
P.O. Box 48962
Chicago, IL 60648
312-824-9696

The Walnut St. Hand Tool Co.
233 Linden St.
Fort Collins, CO

Warren Tool Co.
Rt. 1 14AS
Rhinebeck, NY 12572
914-876-7817

Welbeck Sawmill Ltd.
R.R. 2
Durham, Ontario N0G 1R0
CANADA
519-369-2144

Wildlife Carvings Supply
317 Holyoke Ave.
Beach Haven, NJ 08008
609-492-1871

Wildlife Woodcarvers
Avian Art, Inc.
4288 Staunton Dr.
Swartz Creek, MI 48473
313-732-6300

Wood Carvers Supply Co.
3056 Excelsior Blvd.
Minneapolis, MN 55416
612-927-7491

Wood Carvers Supply, Inc.
P.O. Box 8928
Norfolk, VA 23503
804-583-8928

Woodcraft Supply
41 Atlantic Ave.
Box 4000
Woburn, MA 01888
800-225-1153

Wood-Regan Instrument Co.
Vermiculation Pen
107 Forest St.
Montclair, NJ 07042

Books
Books Plus
133 St. Joseph's Blvd.
P.O. Box 731
Lodi, NJ 07644
201-777-3033

Highwood Bookshop
P.O. Box 1246
Traverse City, MI 49684
616-271-3898

Burning Tools
Chesterfield Craft Shop
P.O. Box 208
Chesterfield, NJ 08620

Colwood Electronics
715 Westwood Ave.
Long Branch, NJ 07740
201-222-2568

Hot Tools
7 Hawkes St.
P.O. Box 615
Marblehead, MA 01945
617-639-1000

The Detail Master
Leisure Time Products
2650 Davisson St.
River Grove, IL 60171
312-452-5400

Carving Knives
Cheston Knotts
106 S. Ford Ave.
Wilmington, DE 19805
302-652-5046

Lominack Knives
P.O. Box 1189
Abingdon, VA 24210
703-628-6591

Makepeace
1482 Maple Ave.
Paoli, PA 19301
215-644-6318

Cast Feet
Richard Delise
920 Springwood Dr.
West Chester, PA 19380
215-436-4377

Taylormade Bird Feet
78 Grove St.
Braintree, MA 02184
617-848-3135

Wildlife Studios
244 Brook St.
Plympton, MA 02367
617-585-9107

Cast Study Bills
Bob Bolle
26421 Compson
Roseville, MI 48066
313-773-3153

Bob Miller
General Delivery
Evergreen, LA 71333
318-346-4270

Oscar Johnston Wildlife Gallery
Rt. 2, Box 1224
Smith River, CA 95567
707-487-4401

John W. Sebalusky
P.O. Box 1062
Bensalem, PA 19020

Display Cases
Rioux's Wildlife in Wood and Pewter
P.O. Box 3008
Syracuse, NY 13220-3008

Glass Eyes
Carvers Eye
P.O. Box 16692
Portland, OR 97216

Eyes
9630 Dundalk
Spring, TX 77379
713-376-2897

Hutch Decoy Carving Ltd.
7715 Warsaw Ave.
Glen Burnie, MD 21061
301-437-2501

Schoepfer Eyes
138 West 31st St.
New York, NY 10001
212-736-6934

Robert J. Smith
14900 W. 31st Ave.
Golden, CO 80401
303-278-1828

Tohickon Glass Eyes
P.O. Box 15
Erwinna, PA 18920
800-441-5983

Grinding Tool Burrs and Accessories
Pfingst & Company, Inc.
P.O. Box 377
South Plainfield, NJ 07080

Gamzon Bros. Inc.
21 W. 46th St.
New York, NY 10036
212-719-2550
800-223-6464

Molded Birds
Beaver Dam Wildlife
1662 Beaver Dam Rd.
Point Pleasant, NJ 08742
201-892-2546

Greenwing Enterprises
Rt. 2, Box 731-B
Chester, MD 21619
301-643-3717

StudyKast
Godin Art, Inc.
P.O. Box 62
Brantford, Ontario N3T 5N3
CANADA
519-756-1613

Paints and Brushes
Jim and Beebe Hopper
731 Beech Ave.
Chula Vista, CA 92010
619-420-8766

Christian J. Hummul Co.
404 Brooklets Ave.
Easton, MD 21601
301-636-2232

Windsor & Newton Inc.
555 Winsor Dr.
Secaucus, NJ 07094
201-864-9100

Ruby Carvers
Elkay Products Co.
1506 Sylvan Glade
Austin, TX 78745
512-441-1155

Taxidermists
American Wildlife Studio
Box 71, Tuckahoe Rd.
Dorothy, NJ 08317
609-476-2941

Cooper Taxidermy
County Road 50W.
Valparaiso, Indiana
219-462-0643

Frank Newmyer
8872 Matthews Rd.
Gladwin, MI 48624
517-426-2213

Mike's Taxidermy Studio
5019 Lolly Lane
Perry Hall, MD 21128
301-256-0860

Richard Smoker
19 W. Pear St.
Crisfield, MD 21817
301-968-3044

Video Cassettes
"Bird Carving: Art in Detail"
Windsor Promotions, Inc.
127 Bruckner Blvd.
New York, NY 10454

Videotapes by J. D. Sprankle
Greenwing Enterprises
Rte. 2, Box 731-B
Chester, MD 21619
301-643-3717

Waterfowl Video Tapes
The Duck Blind
8721-B Gull Rd.
Richland, MI 49083
616-629-9198

"World Championship Video Series featuring Pat Godin"
Georgetowne, Inc.
P.O. Box 625
Bethel Park, PA 15102

Wildfowl Photos
Cardinal Carvers Supply
P.O. Box 571
Houma, LA 70361

John E. Heintz, Jr.
6609 S. River Rd.
Marine City, MI 48039
313-765-5059

Larry Stevens
3005 Pine Spring Rd.
Falls Church, VA 22042
703-560-5771

Wooden Bases
Birds of a Feather
Box 386
41 Edstrom Rd.
Marlborough, CT 06447
203-295-9469

K. R. Thomas Custom Bases
1909 Woodstream Dr.
York, PA 17402